Rigour and complexity in educational research

Conducting educational research

Series Editor: Harry Torrance, University of Sussex

This series is aimed at research students in education and those under-taking related professional, vocational and social research. It takes current methodological debates seriously and offers well-informed advice to students on how to respond to such debates. Books in the series review and engage with current methodological issues, while relating such issues to the sorts of decisions which research students have to make when designing, conducting and writing up research. Thus the series both contributes to methodological debate and has practical orientation by providing students with advice on how to engage with such debate and use particular methods in their work. Series authors are experienced researcher and supervisors. Each book provides students with insights into a different form of educational research while also providing them with the critical tools and knowledge necessary to make informed judgements about the strengths and weaknesses of different approaches.

Rigour and complexity in educational research
Conceptualizing the bricolage

Joe L. Kincheloe and Kathleen S. Berry

Open University Press

Open University Press
McGraw-Hill Education
McGraw-Hill House
Shoppenhangers Road
Maidenhead
Berkshire
England
SL6 2QL

email: enquiries@openup.co.uk
world wide web: www.openup.co.uk

and Two Penn Plaza, New York, NY 10121–2289, USA

First published 2004

A catalogue record of this book is available from the British Library

ISBN 0335 21400 2 (pb) 0335 21401 0 (hb)

Library of Congress Cataloging-in-Publication Data
CIP data applied for

Typeset by YHT Ltd, London
Printed in Great Britain by MPG Books Ltd, Bodmin, Cornwall

#56965965

To Shirley Steinberg
Commemorating Catorce
Mad Love, Shadow Love, Random Love,
and Abandoned Love
(Thank You, Warren)

To Amber Letourneau
In Loving Memory of Her Mother
Debbie Letourneau

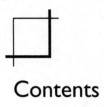

Contents

Preface
Joe L. Kincheloe

My desire to write this book comes from two sources. The first involves my fascination with Norman Denzin and Yvonna Lincoln's (2000) use of the term 'bricolage' in their work on research methods over the last decade. From my perspective no concept better captures the possibility of the future of educational research. When I first encountered the term in their work, I knew that I would have to devote much effort to specifying the notion and pushing it to the next conceptual level. The second, coupled with this recognition of the power of bricolage, was the experience several of my doctoral students brought back from their job interviews. Prepped and ready to answer in detail questions about their methods and research agendas, my students spoke of their theoretical embrace and methodological employment of the bricolage. Much too often for our comfort, search committee members responded quite negatively: 'Bricolage, oh I know what that is,' one professor opined. 'That's when you really don't know anything about research but have a lot to say about it.' Much to our dismay, the use of the concept persuaded such committee members not to employ the students. I had no choice – I had to respond.

I was working on the book in the summer of 2002 when I taught a summer course on the bricolage and research at the University of New Brunswick in Fredericton. Working with a group of brilliant graduate students – 'Maritimers' through and through – I was challenged to clarify my conception of the bricolage. Sitting in on the class was my good friend and colleague, Professor Kathleen Berry, who possesses one of the most brilliant pedagogical minds I've ever encountered. I knew she would have compelling insights to offer about the conceptualization and teaching of the bricolage and I was excited to hear her responses to what I was teaching.

Exceeding even my high expectations, Kathy provided one brilliant insight after another. I listened carefully and learned much. After she offered her sixty-third gem of wisdom, I realized I had no choice but to invite her to be my co-author. Working tirelessly, Kathy wrote the last three chapters of the book – the portion that provides theoretically sophisticated concrete examples of the process of employing the bricolage. We worked hard to make sure that my Chapters 1–4 and her 5–7 conceptually resonated. We decided to keep our individual names on the chapters we wrote to enhance readability and let our distinctive styles come through. Sometimes we will use the pronoun 'I' and at other times 'we'. Since the reader knows who wrote each chapter, I do not think such usage will pose a problem.

In the first four chapters I describe the bricolage. Chapter 1 introduces the concept *vis-à-vis* Denzin and Lincoln's theoretical/methodological grounding. In this context I attempt to link the bricolage with notions of complexity and multilogicality. Making sure everyone understands that I conceive it as a critical discourse, I focus attention on the way the bricolage operates on an understanding of dominant forms of power. Asserting that the bricolage is grounded upon a philosophical form of research, the chapter traces how an awareness of the historical embeddedness of all acts of knowledge production and the social construction of knowledge shape the world of the researcher.

Chapter 2 maintains that the bricolage's understanding of complexity and power, pursued in relation to the ability to deploy multiple research approaches and theoretical constructs, is the path to a new form of rigour in research. Indeed, the best way to pursue complexity and produce thick and useful descriptions of social, psychological and education phenomena while avoiding the reductionism of social science is via the radical pluralism of the bricolage. A central theme of the book emerges in Chapter 2: traditional monological scientific strategies to produce rigorous knowledge have been misguided. Such efforts have sought the faux certainty of reductionistic decontextualization as they ignored the multiple factors profoundly but tacitly shaping both the researcher and the research act. Indeed, rigour itself was defined as the procedure by which these messy components of knowledge production were eliminated from consideration. Thus, the bricolage is offered as a practical way to construct a critical science of complexity.

Chapter 3 asserts that the multilogicality of the bricolage demands not only new forms of research but undermines the very structure of education as it now exists. In this context the bricolage offers a pragmatic escape from the implosion of disciplinarity and the faulty efforts of neoconservatives to reassert the power of the traditional disciplines. In the dialectic of disciplinarity and interdisciplinarity researchers learn both depth and breadth, employing such insights to generate both rich interpretations and useful forms of knowledge that speak to the difficulties of lived experience and the suffering of the exploited. In this synergy of depth and breadth bricoleurs create something new – a deep inter-disciplinarity that helps them understand the occluded processes and relationships that vivify individual and group experiences. In this way bricoleurs move to a new level of analysis, a new expression of scholarly rigour. At this point I bring multiple sources and forms of knowledge to the conversation, including subjugated and indigenous insights that cat-alyse the construction of new multilogical and emancipatory forms of epistemology and ontology. Such manoeuvres move us to a space where we can never again view knowledge production through only Euro-centric, patriarchal, class elitist, and reductionistic lenses.

Chapter 4 focuses the conversation on the ontological realm, as it reconceptualizes the object of study. Bricoleurs account for the influence of 'being in the world' both for themselves, other researchers, and the phenomena they set out to study. Pointing out the inseparability of ontology and epistemology, I explore reductionism's tendency to research things-in-themselves. As reductionists abstract such phenomena from the contexts and processes that give them life and meaning, they destroy them. Thus, in the complex hermeneutics, epistemology, and ontology of the bricolage entities are not simply things-in-themselves. They are embedded in the world, existing in multiple horizons, in mul-tiple, parallel, and intersecting universes. They cannot be reduced to smaller and smaller monads but must be seen in the same way Einstein saw gravity – a part of the process and structure of the universe. Contrary to the reductionistic physics of his day, Einstein figured out that gravity was not a particle or a wave. In a similar way bricoleurs redefine the object of inquiry, embracing a critical, relational ontology. We move from the 'some-thing' of substance to the 'no-thing' of relationship. This ontological concept is no mystical divination but a pragmatic scholarly assertion that holds the power to change the way we research and per-ceive both ourselves and the world around us.

In Chapter 5 Kathleen Berry begins her exploration of how researchers might actually employ the bricolage in real-life, concrete settings. Her concern is with the 'doing' of the bricolage. Because the bricolage refuses to follow a set course and values improvisation, the effort to describe what it might look like in practice becomes a formidable task. Berry works hard to avoid delivering a step-by-step blueprint for how it 'has to be' while providing compelling examples of what it 'could be'. In this spirit Chapter 5 lays out the various structures one could employ in developing one's own research text via the bricolage. Berry guides readers through these structures, employing the theoretical threads of the first four chapters. Using her concept of the point of entry text (POET), Berry shows how bricoleurs can move through various struc-tures that may or may not inform their work.

In Chapter 6 Berry takes the process she develops in Chapter 5 and raises questions and issues that induce the bricoleur to gain new insights into the phenomena being researched. As this process takes shape, new levels of complexity emerge that demand compelling modes of analysis. In this context Berry delineates the process of feedback looping she has developed to engage and consider the multiple structures and discourses she enumerated in the previous chapter. Indeed, in the spirit of the bricolage she plays with the POET, looping it back and forth through the discursive maze. In the process she documents the ideas that emerge in the conceptual shifts such a procedure unleashes. In this way Berry helps the bricoleur create the conditions where autopoiesis (self-production) can take place – interpretations, conceptual development, and new processes of knowledge production emerge in this situation. At this point Berry provides examples of feedback looping that enable bricoleurs to understand diverse levels of complexity operating in relation to all social, cultural, political, psychological, and educational phenomena. This looping of the bricolage initiates reflection about the research texts we create.

In Chapter 7 Berry provides an actual classroom example of teaching the bricolage to help readers better appreciate the actual ways professors and students engaged in the process. In this effort she uses her student Sadie's POET on height discrimination and analyses how it could be informed by looping it through the bricolage. Here Berry documents the ways students collaborated in bringing many different structures of the bricolage to bear on their own and other students' research. What we get is a detailed look at apprentice bricoleurs as they make their way through the intricacies and complications of engaging in the process. In this engagement students begin to get the ideas behind the practice of the bricolage. Indeed, Berry asserts, students moved away from monological and positivistic ways of engaging in research to the more complex, rigorous, and multilogical bricolage. To conclude the chapter, Berry catalogues problems and unexpected consequences of engaging in the bricolage process, including dealing with institutions and researchers unfamiliar and uncomfortable with its assumptions. Such problems are inevitable, she asserts, but the benefits made possible by the process encourage us to confront such difficulties and the resistance that often accompanies them.

We hope that you find the bricolage as exciting as we do. Please be patient, we are in the initial phases of working it out and observing what it looks like in practice. In this spirit we welcome your comments and critiques as we attempt to move research to a new level of complexity, rigour and usefulness.

Acknowledgements

Kathleen: Thank you to the students in ED 6902 (Summer 2002) and ED 6315 (Winter 2002) at the University of New Brunswick, Canada, who willingly attempted to explore the complexity and rigour of an emergent field of study called *bricolage*. They will find themselves threaded throughout the text. Heather Little was willing to go the extra mile for her colleagues and professors. Student assistants Jennifer Haley, Vanessa Moeller and Angie Tonge scanned for questions and clarity. Thank you to colleagues Linda Eyre, Pam Nason, Lissa Paul, Evie Plaice and Pam Whitty who helped make Critical Studies in Education a reality. A special thanks to Shirley Steinberg and Joe Kincheloe who, in the summer of 2002 nourished the intellectual curiosity of many Maritimers. Kathy sends love to Joe and Shirley for years of support and friendship.

Joe: All thanks and love to Kathy and her genius both in general and pedagogically in particular. I love New Brunswick, brilliant New Brunswick students, Critical Studies in Education, and rock 'n' roll.

Excerpts from an article published in Qualitative Inquiry, Vol 7, No 6 (Sage 2001) are included in the first four chapters and are published here with permission.

Introduction: the power of the bricolage: expanding research methods

Joe L. Kincheloe

Kathleen Berry and I are passionate about the power of the bricolage to expand research methods and construct a more rigorous mode of knowledge about education. In an era in Western societies where thick forms of qualitative knowledge production are challenged by neo-positivistic and reductionistic modes of 'evidence-based research', this book lays out a complex and textured notion of scholarly rigour that provides an alternative to such approaches to educational inquiry. Our use of the term and concept 'bricolage' comes from the work of Denzin and Lincoln (2000), who used the term in the spirit of Claude Lévi-Strauss (1966) and his lengthy discussion of it in *The Savage Mind*.

The French word *bricoleur* describes a handyman or handywoman who makes use of the tools available to complete a task. Some connotations of the term involve trickery and cunning and remind me of the chicanery of Hermes, in particular his ambiguity concerning the messages of the gods. If hermeneutics came to connote the ambiguity and slipperiness of textual meaning, then bricolage can also imply the fictive and imaginative elements of the presentation of all formal research. Indeed, as cultural studies of science have indicated, all scientific inquiry is jerryrigged to a degree; science, as we all know by now, is not nearly as clean, simple, and procedural as scientists would have us believe. Maybe this is an admission many in our field would wish to keep in the closet.

In the first decade of the twenty-first century bricolage is typically understood to involve the process of employing these methodological strategies as they are needed in the unfolding context of the research situation. While this interdisciplinary feature is central to any notion of the bricolage, I propose that qualitative researchers go beyond this dynamic. Pushing to a new conceptual terrain, such an eclectic process raises numerous issues that researchers must deal with in order to maintain theoretical coherence and epistemological innovation. Such multidisciplinarity demands a new level of research self-consciousness and awareness of the numerous contexts in which any researcher is operating. As one labours to expose the various structures that covertly shape our own and other scholars' research narratives, the bricolage highlights the relationship between a researcher's ways of seeing and the social location of his or her personal history. Appreciating research as a power-driven act, the researcher-as-bricoleur abandons the quest for some naive concept of realism, focusing instead on the clarification of his or her position in the web of reality and the social locations of other researchers and the ways they shape the production and interpretation of knowledge.

In this context bricoleurs move into the domain of complexity. The bricolage exists out of respect for the complexity of the lived world. Indeed, it is grounded on an epistemology of complexity. One dimension of this complexity can be illustrated by the relationship between research and the domain of social theory. All observations of the world are shaped either consciously or unconsciously by social theory – such theory provides the framework that highlights or erases what might be observed. Theory in a modernist empiricist mode is a way of understanding that operates without variation in every context. Since theory is a cultural and linguistic artefact, its interpretation of the object of its observation is inseparable from the historical dynamics that have shaped it. The task of the bricoleur is to attack this complexity, uncovering the invisible artefacts of power and culture, and documenting the nature of their influence not only on their own scholarship but also on scholarship in general. In this process bricoleurs act upon the concept that theory is not an explanation of the world – it is more an explanation of our relation to the world.

An Active View of Research Methodology

In its hard labours in the domain of complexity the bricolage views research methods actively rather than passively, meaning that we actively construct our research methods from the tools at hand rather than passively receiving the 'correct', universally applicable methodologies. Avoiding modes of reasoning that come from certified processes of logical analysis, bricoleurs also steer clear of pre-existing guidelines and checklists developed outside the specific demands of the inquiry at hand. In its embrace of complexity, the bricolage constructs a far more active role for humans both in shaping reality and in creating the research processes and narratives that represent it. Such an active agency rejects deterministic views of social reality that assume the effects of particular social, political, economic, and educational processes. At the same time and in the same conceptual context this belief in active human agency refuses standardized modes of knowledge production (Dahlbom, 1998; Selfe and Selfe, 1994; McLeod, 2000; Young and Yarbrough, 1993).

In many ways there is a form of instrumental reason, of rational irrationality in the use of passive, external, monological research methods. In the active bricolage we bring our understanding of the research context together with our previous experience with research methods. Using these knowledges, we *tinker* in the Lévi-Straussian sense with our research methods in field-based and interpretative contexts. This tinkering is a high-level cognitive process involving construction and reconstruction, contextual diagnosis, negotiation, and readjustment. Bricoleurs understand that researchers' interaction with the objects of their inquiries is always complicated, mercurial, unpredictable and, of course, complex. Such conditions negate the practice of planning research strategies in advance. In lieu of such rationalization of the process, bricoleurs enter into the research act as methodological negotiators. Always respecting the demands of the task at hand, the bricolage, as conceptualized here, resists its placement in concrete as it promotes its elasticity. Yvonna Lincoln (2001) delineates two types of bricoleurs: those who are committed to research eclecticism, allowing circumstance to shape the methods employed; and those who want to engage in the genealogy/archaeology of the disciplines with some grander purpose in mind. My purpose entails both of Lincoln's articulations of the role of the bricoleur.

Research method in the bricolage is a concept that receives more respect than in more rationalistic articulations of the term. The rationalistic articulation of method subverts the deconstruction of wide varieties of unanalysed assumptions embedded in passive methods. Bricoleurs in their appreciation of the complexity of the research process view research method as involving far more than procedure. In this mode of analysis bricoleurs come to understand research method as also a technology of justification, meaning a way of defending what we assert we know and the process by which we know it. Thus, the education of researchers demands that everyone take a step back from the process of learning research methods. Such a step back allows us a conceptual distance that produces a critical consciousness. Such a consciousness refuses the passive acceptance of externally imposed research methods that tacitly certify modes justifying knowledges that are decontextualized and reductionistic (Denzin and Lincoln, 2000; McLeod, 2000; Foster, 1997).

The Subversive Nature of Bricolage: Avoiding Reductionism

There is an impudent dimension to the bricolage that says, 'Who said research has to be done this way?' Such impudence is based on a cynicism toward the notion that monological, ordered methods get us to the 'right place' in academic research. To say it once more with feeling: we should use the methods that are best suited to answering our questions about a phenomenon. For the bricoleur to use the means at hand, the methods that exist, demands that the researcher be aware of them. Such awareness demands that the bricoleur devote time for rigorous study of what approaches to research are out there and to how they might be applied in relation to other methods. Do not be deceived, this is no easy task that can be accomplished in a doctoral programme or a post-doctoral fellowship (Thomas, 1998). Becoming a bricoleur who is knowledgeable of multiple research methodologies and their use is a lifetime endeavour.

Indeed, the bricoleur is aware of deep social structures and the complex ways they play out in everyday life, the importance of social, cultural, and historical analysis, the ways discursive practices influence both what goes on in the research process and the consciousness of the researcher, the complex dimensions of what we mean when we talk about 'understanding'. In this context the bricoleur becomes a sailor on troubled waters, navigating a course that traces the journey between the scientific and the moral, the relationship between the quantitative and the qualitative, and the nature of social, cultural, psychological, and educational insight. All of these travels help bricoleurs overcome the limitations of monological reductionism while taking into account the new vistas opened by the multilogical. Such victories provide an entrée into the diverse community of inquirers – an inclusive group that comes from academia and beyond. Such individuals critique, support, and inform each other by drawing upon the diversity of their backgrounds and concerns. In this process they expose and discuss each other's assumptions, the contexts that have shaped them, and their strengths and limitations in the exploration(s) at hand. The participants in this community, from a wide range of race, class, gender, sexual, ethnic, and religious groups, enter into their deliberations with humility and solidarity.

As previously mentioned, Norman Denzin and Yvonna Lincoln's work on the bricolage has profoundly influenced numerous researchers from a plethora of disciplines. Concerned with the limitations of monological approaches to knowledge production, we all subscribe to the 'practical reason' of the bricolage that operates in concrete settings to connect theory, technique, and experiential knowledges. Here the theoretical domain is connected to the lived world and new forms of cognition and research are *enacted*. This improvisational enactment of the bricolage, buoyed by the insights of Francisco Varela and Humberto Maturana's Santiago theory of enactivism, moves research to a new level. This is the place where the multiple inputs and forces facing the researcher in the immediacy of her work are acknowledged and embraced. The bricoleur does not allow these complexities to be dismissed by the excluding, reducing impulses of monological methodology (Fischer, 1998; Weinstein, 1995; Maturana and Varela, 1987; Varela, 1999; Geeland and Taylor, 2000). Such a refusal is in itself an act of subversion.

The subversive bricolage accepts that human experience is marked by uncertainties and that order is not always easily established. 'Order in the court' has little authority when the monological judge is resting in *his* quarters. Indeed, the rationalistic and reductionistic quest for order refuses in its arrogance to listen to the cacophony of lived experience, the coexistence of diverse meanings and interpretations. The concept of understanding in the complex world viewed by bricoleurs is unpredictable. Much to the consternation of many, there exists no final, transhistorical, non-ideological meaning that bricoleurs strive to achieve. As bricoleurs create rather than find meaning in enacted reality, they explore alternate meanings offered by others in similar circumstances. As if this were not enough, they work to account for historical and social contingencies that always operate to undermine the universal pronouncement of the meaning of a particular phenomenon. When researchers fail to discern the unique ways that historical and social context make for special circumstances, they often provide a reductionistic form of knowledge that impoverishes our understanding of everything connected to it – the process of research included (Burbules and Beck, 1999; Marijuan, 1994; Cary, 2004).

The monological quest for order so desired by many social, political, psychological, and educational researchers is grounded on the Cartesian belief that all phenomena should be broken down into their constitute parts to facilitate inquiry. The analysis of the world in this context becomes fragmented and disconnected. Everything is studied separately for the purposes of rigour. The goal of integrating knowledges from diverse domains and understanding the interconnections shaping, for example, the biological and the cognitive, is irrelevant in the paradigm of order and fragmentation. The meaning that comes from interrelationship is lost and questions concerning the purpose of research and its insight into the human condition are put aside in an orgy of correlation and triangulated description. Information is sterilized and insight into what may be worth exploring is abandoned (Simpson and Jackson, 2001). Ways of making use of particular knowledge are viewed as irrelevant and creative engagement with conceptual insights is characterized as frivolous. Empirical knowledge in the quest for order is an end in itself. Once it has been validated it needs no further investigation or interpretation. While empirical research is obviously necessary, its process of production constitutes only one step of a larger and more rigorous process of inquiry. The bricolage subverts the finality of the empirical act.

Bricoleurs make the point that empirical research, all research for that matter, is inscribed at every level by human beings. The assumptions and purposes of the researcher always find their way into a research act, and they always make a difference in what knowledge is produced. Even in the most prescribed forms of empirical quantitative inquiry the researcher's preferences and assumptions shape the outcome of the research. Do I choose factor analysis or regression analysis to study the relationship of a student's SAT score to college success? The path I choose profoundly affects what I find. What about the skills and knowledges included on the SAT? Are they simply neutral phenomena free from inscriptions of culture and power? How I answer such a question shapes how my research proceeds.

Such inscriptions and the complexity they produce remind bricoleurs of the multiple processes in play when knowledge is produced and validation is considered. They understand that the research process is subjective and that instead of repressing this subjectivity they attempt to understand its role in shaping inquiry. All of these elements come together to help bricoleurs think about their principles of selection of one or another research perspective. Such decisions can be made more thoughtfully when a researcher understands the preferences and assumptions inscribed on all modes of inquiry and all individuals who engage in research. Thus, an important aspect of the work of the bricoleur involves coming to understand the social construction of self, the influence of selfhood on perception, and the influence of perception on the nature of inquiry (Richardson and Woolfolk, 1994; Pickering, 1999; Allen, 2000).

Forging the Tools of Subversion: Context, Discourse, and Power in the Bricolage

When it comes to the analysis of the construction of self or the nature of texts, bricoleurs are aware of the discursive practices in which self or text is embedded and the context in which self or text operates. Whether one is attempting to make sense of a novelist, an interviewee, or a historical manuscript, discourse and context are central dimensions of the interpretative act. Contrary to the pronouncements of some analysts, the contingent orientation to research created by the bricoleur's attention to discursive and contextual dimensions of knowledge production does not make one anti-empiricist or anti-quantitative. Instead, such concerns make the bricoleur more attentive to the various dynamics that shape what is called empirical knowledge. In this context such a researcher is less willing to make a final statement of truth or meaning based on the empirical investigations in which she has engaged. The bricoleur knows that empirical data viewed from another perspective or questioned by one from a different background can elicit fundamentally different interpretations.

Discourse cannot be removed from power relations and the struggle to create particular meanings and legitimate specific voices. Dominant discourses shape the research process emerging as technologies of power that regulate which knowledges are validated and which ones are relegated to the junk heap of history. Bricoleurs watch carefully as power operates to privilege the data coming from particular academic or political economic locales. The insidious way this process operates is testimony to the axiom that power works best when it is not recognized as power. Power creeps in on little cats' feet to accomplish its regulation and discipline of various individuals and groups. Perceiving the world as we do through a shared culture and language, we tend to see phenomena as those with the most power to shape our consciousnesses want us to. Of course, we resist such a process, but often we are not even aware that it is operating. Indeed, it works best when everything seems normal and comfortable.

Power's construction of subjectivity and validation of particular forms of data takes advantage of the comfort of the everyday. The production of meaning contrary to traditional rationalistic notions is more tied to affective and emotional investments than previously realized. I want to see myself as a 'man of science', some researchers assert. As such a man I will produce hard, objective data that are becoming of such a respectable man. In such cases what forces are at work in shaping the perspective this researcher takes toward social phenomena – rational deliberations or affective impulses? Bricoleurs maintain that such insights are important aspects of the research process and help us understand why particular interpretative and analytic perspectives are chosen both by themselves and by other researchers. With these ideas in mind, bricoleurs ask, 'What is a fact?' Such a question takes on new layers of complexity and nuance when we think about the numerous contextual, discursive, and power dynamics at work at every level of the processes that produce facts.

What exactly is it that is produced as a product of this often bizarre and multidimensional process? Bricoleurs understand the multiple ways that a fact may be defined. They understand that it can be viewed from many perspectives that grant it not only diverse meanings but also different ontological statuses. From an ontological perspective, what is the nature of a fact? How does a fact operate in the world? And importantly, in this context the bricoleur recognizes that given different contexts, discourses, and power relations, what a researcher labels a fact could have been something fundamentally different. In this context a bricoleur can project what alternative facts could have been produced given the reality of different contexts, discourses, and power relationships in the knowledge-production process (Bruner, 1996; Giroux, 1997; Hoban and Erickson, 1998; Capra, 1996). Such an intellectual ability, I believe, is a characteristic of rigorous scholarship.

Specifying the Importance of Philosophical Research in the Bricolage

Researchers concerned with rigour appreciate the importance of 'philosophical research' to the bricolage. I use the phrase philosophical research to denote the use of various philosophical tools to help clarify the process of inquiry and provide insight into the assumptions on which it conceptually rests. In this section I want to focus on this dimension, in the process specifying a few of the benefits such a form of inquiry might bring to this project. Informed by philosophical research, bricoleurs become smarter, more self-reflective about their own role and the role of researchers in general in the knowledge- and reality-creating process. An appreciation of complexity, of course, demands such insights, as it insists on an understanding that conceptual categories are human constructions and posits that such categorization exerts a profound impact on modes of perception and human action itself. Little work has been undertaken on philosophy as research, not to mention its role in a research bricolage. The following offers a few ideas about how bricoleurs might begin to think about these dynamics in light of our previous contentions about the complexity of the bricolage.

The mode of philosophical consciousness advocated here helps bricoleurs bracket their own subjectivity as researchers in ways that force the intersection of notions such as researcher 'invention' and researcher 'discovery'. The bricolage makes use of philosophical research into the boundary between the social world and the narrative representation of it. Such explorations provide profound and often unrecognized knowledge about what exactly is produced when researchers describe the social world. Rigour, I assert, is impossible without such knowledge and discernment. Exploring this complex, ever shifting boundary between the social world and the narrative representation of it, philosophically informed bricoleurs begin to document the specific influences of life history, lived context, race, class, gender and sexuality on researchers and the knowledge they produce (Zammito, 1996; McLeod, 2000; Denzin and Lincoln, 2000).

These aspects of philosophical research help the bricoleur to highlight the ethical, epistemological, ontological, and political features of the research process and the knowledge it produces. Such tasks might be described as a form of research concerned with conceptual clarification. For example, what does it mean to exist in history? To live and operate as a social and historical subject? How do researchers begin the process of exploring such dynamics? How do the ways researchers conceptualize these features shape the research process and the knowledge it produces? How do social-theoretical choices and assumptions affect these issues? All of these questions point to the role of science as first and foremost a cultural activity. Abstract and objective procedural and methodological protocols come to be viewed as the socially constructed entities that they are. Thus, bricoleurs are freed from reductionistic conventions in ways that facilitate their moves not to an anything-goes model of research but to a genuinely rigorous, informed multiperspectival way of exploring the lived world (Bridges, 1997; Foster, 1997; Morawski, 1997).

What bricoleurs are exploring in this philosophical mode of inquiry is the nature and effects of the social construction of knowledge, understanding, and human subjectivity. Realizing the dramatic limitations of so-called objectivist assumptions about the knowledge-production process, bricoleurs struggle to specify the ways perspectives are shaped by social, cultural, political, ideological, discursive, and disciplinary forces. Understanding the specifics of this construction process helps multiperspectival researchers choose and develop the methodological, theoretical and interpretative tools they need to address the depictions of the world that emerge from it. In the context of the philosophical inquiry as conceptual clarification, the bricoleur understands that the objectivist view of knowledge assumes that meaning in the world exists separately from an individual's experience. In such an objectivist context the research act simply involves identifying external objective reality and reflecting it in the research narrative. Such reductionism and its concurrent distortion is exactly what the bricolage seeks to avoid (Varenne, 1996; McLeod, 2000; Cronin, 1997).

The philosophical dimension of the bricolage helps researchers understand the ways that meanings in the research process are often imposed by a monologic that undermines recognition of the multiple forces at work in the meaning-making process. In the multi-methodological dimension of the bricolage, embracing philosophical research allows bricoleurs to gain insights into the assumptions that shape the inquiry process – assumptions often neglected in more monological forms of research. Indeed, these philosophical insights should be an important aspect of any curriculum designed to educate rigorous researchers. What are the assumptions behind the organization of research data into meaningful knowledge? What narrative strategies are used in this process? Are they employed consciously? Philosophical forms of research systematically ask such questions of the research process. Research reports delivered without such narrative understandings are naive and unworthy of being labelled rigorous. In reductionistic, monological forms of research and curricula for preparing researchers such philosophical issues are rarely addressed.

Bricoleurs aware of these philosophical dimensions of the research act maintain that there is no dividing line between the empirical and the philosophical. In the bricolage the two domains blend into one another in a way that enhances the insights of the researcher. When this happens the bricoleur is able to differentiate between a philosophic argument and an empirical assertion based on controlled observation. Such differentiation is necessary in the effort to produce and critique knowledge. Much too often empirical scientific proof is offered for what is a hermeneutic argument. Such empirical proof in such a case is superfluous to the hermeneutic process involved. In addition, it illustrates an epistemological confusion where one form of knowledge production and validation is confused for another, leading to misunderstandings and illogical argumentation.

Many scholars of biology and cognition, for example, make a powerful argument for a philosophically grounded form of interdisciplinary research in order to address previously neglected levels of complexity. In this context the tendency of Cartesian–Newtonian biology to isolate its object of study from the larger cosmological context in which it operated, undermined the researcher's ability to study relationships essential to a more textured understanding of the phenomenon in question. Cosmological questions such as how this part helps us understand the functioning of the whole were deemed irrelevant in such monological, decontextualized modes of research. Monological research has no need to integrate diverse knowledges or to ask larger cosmological questions about how they all fit together. So much of the world cannot be explained in terms of its constituent parts. Bricoleurs are interested in the nature of the relationships between parts. Such studies are out of necessity interdisciplinary as they uncover diverse perspectives on the whole (Bridges, 1997; O'Sullivan, 1999; Kincheloe, et al., 1999b).

Philosophical Inquiry in the Bricolage: Constructivism and Historicity

As bricoleurs gain insight into the social construction of knowledge, understanding, and human subjectivity, they gain a consciousness of their own and others' historicity. What many researchers have referred to as the crisis of historicity is really nothing more than the development of this consciousness, this understanding of the historical, social, cultural, ideological, and discursive construction of science and the research it produces. In this context bricoleurs understand that the effort to distinguish between different social realities and different interpretations of researchers is more difficult than originally assumed. With such an understanding in mind, bricoleurs always have to deal with levels of complexity ignored by less informed researchers. As bricoleurs negotiate their way between the constructed and discovered dimensions of knowledge work, they come to appreciate the blurred line between the historical and historiographical.

Naivety is the result of dismissing these issues of constructivism and historicity. Philosophical inquiry in the bricolage moves us away from this lack of sophistication and rigour, as researchers gain insight into the existential grounds on which diverse approaches to research evolve. Such inquiry helps bricoleurs appreciate the principles and sources that fuel the production of knowledge by both self and others – a facility necessary for good research and good scholarship in general. Indeed, bricoleurs employ philosophical inquiry to explore the logic and psychology of the development of research strategies and their use in the larger effort to produce knowledge. Such logics and psychologies can only be appreciated in historical context, in terms of their historicity. The historicization of research allows bricoleurs to ask questions of knowledge production that have previously gone unasked and, thus, to gain insight into previously invisible processes shaping the ways we come to describe and act in the world. In this way the work of the bricoleur becomes thicker, more insightful, more savvy, and more rigorous (Zammito, 1996; McCarthy, 1997; Bridges, 1997).

The understanding of constructivism and historicity in relation to research cannot be separated from the interpretative dimension of the bricolage and its grounding in hermeneutics. In this context a notion of critical hermeneutics is employed by the bricoleur to understand the historical and social ways that power operates to shape meaning and its lived consequences. Critical hermeneutics alerts us to the ways power helps construct the social, cultural, and economic conditions under which meaning is made and research processes are constructed. Not all parties or all advocates of particular marginalized lived experiences are allowed to sit at the table of official meaning-making. The bricoleur's awareness of constructivism and historicity helps her point out these omissions and their effects on the knowledge-production processes.

In this context critical hermeneutics facilitates bricoleurs' attempts to identify socially oppressive forms of meaning-making and research processes. Bricoleurs understand that constructivism and historicity can be relatively unhelpful concepts without a recognition of this critical dimension of power and its effects. As Peter McLaren (2001) points out in his response to my conception of the bricolage, merely focusing on the production of meanings may not lead to 'resisting and transforming the existing conditions of exploitation' (p. 702). I take his admonition seriously and assert that in the critical hermeneutical dimension of the bricolage the act of understanding power and its effects is merely one part – albeit an inseparable part – of counter-hegemonic *action*. Critical hermeneutics understands that meaning does not 'just happen' – we don't see bumper stickers proclaiming 'meaning happens'. Instead, meaning is imposed on the world and if researchers are not aware of such dynamics they will unconsciously join in this imposition. Joining in the imposition is disguised by the assertion that meaning exists in the world independently of and unconnected to the subjectivities of researchers and other 'knowers'. All objectivist researchers do, they innocently and reductionistically maintain, is discover this independent meaning and report it to their audience.

Power in this construction of knowledge, it is argued, plays no role in the process. Bricoleurs employing critical notions of historicity and constructivism know better. The objective knowledge and the validated research processes used by reductionists are always socially negotiated in a power-saturated context. Assertions that knowledge is permanent and universal are undermined and the stability of meaning is subverted. Forces of domination will often reject such historically conscious and power-literate insights, as such awarenesses undermine the unchallenged knowledge assertions of power wielders. Critical hermeneutics, bricoleurs come to understand, can be quite dangerous when deployed in the sacred temples of knowledge production. It is no surprise that this form of philosophical inquiry is typically excluded from the canon of official research (Cronin, 1997; Lutz *et al.*, 1997). Again in reference to McLaren's (2001) concerns, the criticality of the bricolage is dedicated to engaging political action in a variety of social, political, economic, and academic venues.

Epistemological Analysis in the Bricolage: Extending Philosophical Research

If epistemology involves the exploration of how researchers come to know about the phenomena they study, how this knowledge is structured, and the grounds on which these knowledge claims are tendered, then epistemological understandings are central to the rigour of the bricolage. In multiple-method/interdisciplinary research these epistemological understandings become even more important, as different orientations assume different views of knowledge. In this context researchers learn from comparative epistemological insights, developing a profound understanding of knowledge theory and production in the process. The development of such epistemological insight is yet another dimension of the philosophical inquiry of the bricolage.

Aided by these epistemological understandings, bricoleurs are better equipped to perform subtle forms of knowledge work. As philosophical inquirers working in the epistemological domain, bricoleurs ask informed questions, develop complex concepts, construct alternate modes of reasoning, and provide unprecedented interpretations of the data they generate. All of these dimensions of research involve making sophisticated epistemological decisions and are inseparable from the larger task of producing high-quality research. With these epistemological insights in mind, bricoleurs are empowered to draw upon their conceptual and methodological toolkits depending on the nature of the research context and the phenomenon in question. They are emancipated from the tyranny of pre-specified, intractable research procedures (Foster, 1997; Selfe and Selfe, 1994; Willinsky, 2001).

Mainstream research traditions have been reluctant to admit philosophical inquiry and its associated epistemological analysis into the pantheon of acceptable research methods. Bricoleurs embrace philosophical research for a number of reasons, one of the most fundamental involving its notion that at its most basic articulation research involves asking and answering an unanswered question. Obviously, philosophical inquiry meets this criterion, as it seeks out answers to the most compelling questions of human life and the purposes of research:

- What is the nature of being? In this ontological domain bricoleurs examine the nature of human being (subjectivity) and its relation to knowledge production, but also the nature of the object of study. In the case of the latter, bricoleurs ask whether we study the object as a thing-in-itself or as a part of larger processes and relationships.
- What is the nature of living a good life? In this ethical domain bricoleurs question the ways their research contribute to the social good. How does this work influence the lives of the researcher, the community, the world?
- What knowledge is of most worth? Epistemological questions are profoundly important to the bricoleur. This question demands modes of judgement that move bricoleurs to think about the value of their research projects. What researchers are producing knowledge of worth? What researchers are not producing knowledge of worth? How do we make such a distinction?
- What is knowledge? This epistemological question demands that researchers clearly understand the different ways that different paradigms define knowledge and its production. The awareness that comes from understanding these competing versions provides

bricoleurs with a more profound understanding of the forces that tacitly shape all knowledge claims.

- What does it mean to know something? This question forces bricoleurs to seek out the insights of cognitive theory in relation to their epistemological questions. The cognitive insights gained from, for example, the Santiago school of enactivism and its notions of knowledge-in-action and the power of relationships inform epistemology in compelling ways. Such a synergy is yet another example of the benefits of the multiperspectivalism of the bricolage.
- How do we distinguish between worthy and unworthy knowledge? This question moves bricoleurs into the complex domain of validity. Here they can engage in the contemporary conversation about making judgements about research quality. Are the terms external and internal validity helpful in this context? What does knowledge produced about one context have to tell us about another context? Our philosophical grounding helps us formulate questions about the worth of research that might have never occurred to those without such insights. In this context bricoleurs, with their philosophical grounding, engage seriously with the purposes of research. In this process they invent concepts such as catalytic validity, ironic validity, paralogical validity, rhizomatic validity, voluptuous validity (Lather, 1991, 1993), hermeneutic validity, cognitive validity, and pragmatic validity (Kincheloe, 2004).
- What is rigour in the research process? Here bricoleurs take the opportunity to move beyond traditional definitions of rigour as the degree of fidelity to the unquestioned steps in the research process and the degree to which the research accurately reflects 'true reality'. In this context they study the socially constructed nature of what passes as rigour in research. In doing so, they move a step closer to the complexity of the act of knowledge production. Such proximity helps them redefine rigour in a way that involves developing numerous ways of recognizing and working with this complexity.

If answering such questions is not an act of research, then bricoleurs are not sure what research involves.

In examining these issues, I have encountered several situations in schools of education where excellent scholars who perform philosophical inquiry have been told by administrators and tenure committees that their work does not constitute 'real research'. Such scholars have been punished and traumatized by these narrow and uninformed viewpoints. Exploring the dynamics at work in these academic assaults on philosophical researchers, the issue that emerges at the root of the attack is epistemological in nature. The guardians of 'research purity' proclaim a clear distinction between empirical (scientific knowledge production) and philosophical inquiry (unscientific knowledge production). In this context the epistemological and ontological analysis of philosophical inquiry questions this empirical and philosophical bifurcation.

The deep interdisciplinarity of the bricolage transgresses the boundary between the two domains, illustrating in the process their interaction and inseparability. Bricoleurs are not aware of where the empirical ends and the philosophical begins, because such epistemological features are always embedded in one another. Avoiding reductionistic and uninformed notions of research that are monological and exclusive, the bricolage works to embrace and learn from various modes of knowledge production, including philosophical inquiry as well as historical and literary modes of scholarship. Employing the unconscious epistemological criteria of the elitist excluders, historical and literary inquiry would not meet the criteria of real research (Bridges, 1997). Such exclusion masquerades as a form of rigour, confusing narrow-mindedness with high standards.

Moving to the Margins: Alternative Modes of Meaning-making in the Bricolage

In its critical concern for just social change the bricolage seeks insight from the margins of Western societies and the knowledge and ways of knowing of non-Western peoples. Such insight helps bricoleurs reshape and sophisticate social theory, research methods, interpretative strategies, as they discern new topics to be researched. This confrontation with difference so basic to the concept of the bricolage enables researchers to produce new forms of knowledge that inform policy decisions and political action in general. In gaining this insight from the margins bricoleurs display once again the blurred boundary between the hermeneutical search for understanding and the critical concern with social change for social justice. Responding yet again to Peter McLaren's (2001) important concern: not only are the two orientations not in conflict, they are synergistic (McLaren et al., 1995; DeVault, 1996; Lutz et al., 1997; Soto, 2000; Steinberg, 2001).

To contribute to social transformation, bricoleurs seek to better understand both the forces of domination that affect the lives of individuals from race, class, gender, sexual, ethnic, and religious backgrounds outside dominant culture(s) and the worldviews of such diverse peoples. In this context bricoleurs attempt to remove knowledge production and its benefits from the control of elite groups. Such control consistently operates to reinforce elite privilege while pushing marginalized groups farther away from the centre of dominant power. Rejecting this normalized state of affairs, bricoleurs commit their knowledge work to helping address the ideological and informational needs of marginalized groups and individuals. As detectives of subjugated insight, bricoleurs eagerly learn from labour struggles, women's marginalization, the 'double consciousness' of the racially oppressed, and insurrections against colonialism (Young and Yarbrough, 1993; Kincheloe and Steinberg, 1993; Kincheloe *et al.*, 1999a).

Thus, the bricolage is dedicated to a form of rigour that is conversant with numerous modes of meaning-making and knowledge production – modes that originate in diverse social locations. These alternative modes of reasoning and researching always consider the relationships, the resonances, and the disjunctions between formal and rationalistic modes of Western epistemology and ontology and different cultural, philosophical, paradigmatic, and subjugated expressions. In these latter expressions bricoleurs often uncover ways of accessing a concept without resorting to a conventional validated set of pre-specified procedures that provide the distance of objectivity. This notion of distance fails to take into account the rigour of the hermeneutical understanding of the way meaning is pre-inscribed in the act of being in the world, the research process, and objects of research. This absence of hermeneutical awareness undermines the researcher's quest for a thick description and contributes to the production of reduced understandings of the complexity of social life (Selfe and Selfe, 1994; Paulson, 1995).

The multiple perspectives delivered by the concept of difference provide bricoleurs with many benefits as they weave their way through different research orientations and theoretical dimensions. Confrontation with difference helps us to see anew, to move toward the light of epiphany. A basic dimension of criticality involves a comfort with the existence of alternative ways of analysing and producing knowledge. This is why it is so important for a historian, for example, to develop an understanding of phenomenology and hermeneutics. It is why it is so important for a social researcher from New York City to understand forms of indigenous African knowledge production. The incongruities between such cultural modes of inquiry are quite valuable, for within the tensions of difference rest insights into multiple dimensions of the research act – insights that move us to new levels of understanding of the subjects, purposes, and nature of inquiry (Semali and Kincheloe, 1999; Burbules and Beck, 1999).

Difference in the bricolage pushes us into the hermeneutic circle as we are induced to deal with parts in their diversity in relation to the whole. Difference may involve culture, class, language, discipline, epistemology, cosmology, and so on *ad infinitum*. Bricoleurs, as Kathleen Berry points out in the last three chapters of this book, use one dimension of these multiple diversities to explore others, to generate questions previously unimagined. As we examine these multiple perspectives we attend to which ones are validated and which ones have been dismissed. Studying such differences, we begin to understand how dominant power operates to exclude and certify particular forms of knowledge production and why. In the criticality of the bricolage this focus on power and difference always leads us to an awareness of the multiple dimensions of the social. Paulo Freire (1970) referred to this as the need for perceiving social structures and social systems that undermine equal access to resources and power. As bricoleurs answer such questions, we gain new appreciations of the way power tacitly shapes what we know and how we come to know it.

Examples of Researchers Approaching the Bricolage: Difference in the Pursuit of a New Rigour

Again, one of the best examples of the use of the bricolage in innovative contemporary scholarship involves Maturana and Varela's work in the development of enactivist cognitive theory. As it combines the disciplinary perspectives of biology, psychology, theology, philosophy, and socio-cultural insights, enactivism works to address the fragmentation of modernist psychology. Drawing upon the Western philosophical scholarship of Merleau-Ponty and Heidegger and the Eastern Buddhist philosophy of Nagarjuna, enactivism integrates ways of knowing profoundly separated temporally and spatially to create a new synthesis. In the case of enactivism cognitive studies are viewed from the perspectives of other traditions to create new approaches to theorizing and researching the topic as well as a new understanding of the complexity and multi-dimensionality of the cognitive act (Carter, 2004; Pickering, 1999; Thayer-Bacon, 2000). Tara Fenwick (2000) takes this enactivist insight to a higher level of interdisciplinarity as she integrates it with constructivist epistemological, critical theoretical, and psychological discourses. I have attempted a similar strategy in my work in critical thinking (Kincheloe, 2004; Weil and Kincheloe, 2004). Such interdisciplinary work, Fenwick contends, can not only provide new insights but also confront each perspective with new questions. Such questions can lead to dramatic advances at the frontiers where the diverse perspectives intersect.

Another example of the use of bricolage involves James Lovelock and Lynn Margulis's Gaia theory. Lovelock and Margulis study life in a systemic manner, drawing upon geology, microbiology, atmospheric chemistry, philosophy, sociology and other disciplines of inquiry that operate typically in isolation. Gaia theory questions the dominant Cartesian viewpoint that the aforementioned disciplines are discrete and separate and that geological dynamics alone created the context for the evolution of life on our planet. Valuing the input of diverse disciplines, Lovelock and Margulis challenged geology's long-standing claim that plants and animals were secondary entities who serendipitously found geological conditions congenial to their development and evolution. Instead, Lovelock and Margulis's research indicated that life produces the conditions to enable its own existence. In this context the researchers contended that the surface of the planet, long viewed as the environment in which life developed, is actually a dimension of life. Instead of life merely adapting to an inert physical environment, living things in fact construct the environment with which they interact. Life and its environment feed back on one another, modifying one another in the complexity of the living process. Without the tensions produced by a bricolage of perspectives, such a new view of the nature of life could not have been conceived (Capra, 1996).

One final example of the employment of the bricolage, and one that directly influences our articulation of its meaning here, is, of course, cultural studies. Advocates of cultural studies believe that the study of culture is fragmented among a variety of disciplines – sociology, anthropology, history, literary studies, communications, etc. – to the point that communication between scholars is undermined. This is a fragmentary dynamic that has always adversely affected the work of cultural scholars. Cultural studies as a trans-discipline attempts to overcome this fragmentation by highlighting culture as a living process that shapes the ways we live, view ourselves, and understand the world around us. Scholars of cultural studies argue that by adopting cultural studies' overtly multidisciplinary approach, researchers can study larger social issues, such as race, class, gender, sexuality, ethnicity, immigration, and pedagogy from unique perspectives and theoretical positions. As students of cultural studies question the dominant ways of seeing that evolve around the normal science of disciplinary thinking, they free themselves from the self-validating redundancies that limit insight and chain them to familiar explanations (Kincheloe, 2001a). Obviously, Kathleen Berry's and my construction of the bricolage has been influenced by cultural studies' critique of disciplinarity.

The subversive element of the bricolage takes these examples and uses them in the larger struggle for social justice and the democratization of everyday life. There is no reason, bricoleurs maintain, why scholars should be the only individuals with access to the power of the bricolage. Kathleen Berry and I argue that practitioners such as teachers, social workers, journalists, nurses, business people, and other individuals should become bricoleurs. To make the bricolage the exclusive province of professionals and scholars, however, is to perpetuate the same forms of elitism that have marred and scarred everyday life in Western societies for centuries. Humans are meaning-making life forms and need to be involved in experiences that help us sophisticate our ability to do so. The bricolage provides a beginning framework for helping all people in all walks of life construct systems of meaning-making. Such systems grant us ways of producing knowledge that help us make sense of our species' past as well as our own personal past. Such knowledge empowers us to construct a more equitable, exciting, just, and intelligent future.

Facing the diversity of knowledges of multiple pasts and possible futures, bricoleurs transcend reductionistic modes of fragmented knowledge production that deny the socially constructed nature of all research. The way we conduct research is not a given, an immutable process that contains no creative dimension. Bricoleurs take seriously our creative responsibility to break the lenses of present ways of viewing the world. Such lenses need to be broken, bricoleurs contend, not because of some Oedipal impulse to kill the father, but because such frames have caused such heartbreak and suffering on the part of those who fall outside the favoured race, class, gender, sexual, religious, and ability-related demographic. The blurred genres of the bricolage highlight the mode of difference that creates new respect for the subjugated and the knowledges they produce. One dimension of the respect for difference promoted here involves forming new relationships – often learning relationships – with these previously dismissed and degraded forms of information and their producers. The new perspectives we gain from our deployment of difference demand new criteria for assessing the value of knowledge and knowledge production. Such criteria reflect the bricoleur's meta-awareness of the notion of value itself – a concept that demands reconceptualization in the new world of complexity encountered in the process of constructing and enacting the bricolage (Geeland and Taylor, 2000; Bruner, 1996).

Indeed, what bricoleurs are concerned with here is nothing less than the quality of the knowledge we produce about the world. In this context they address both the reductionism of uninformed research methods and the quest for new ways of seeing. In the intersection of these concerns they uncover new insights into research and knowledge production, new forms of reason that are directly connected to specific contexts, practical forms of analysis that are informed by social theory and the concreteness of lived situations (Fischer, 1998). Understanding non-Western ways of knowing and the epistemologies of marginalized groups within Western societies, bricoleurs transcend regressive forms of reductionism. They see past reductionistic notions that researchers simply produce facts that correspond to external reality, information that is devoid of specific cultural values. With these understandings as valuable parts of their toolkits, bricoleurs expand the envelope of social research, of what we can understand about the world. They are empowered to produce knowledge that can change the world.

She's Not There: Rigour in the Absence

In their move to the margins and transcendence of reductionism, bri-coleurs seek to identify what is absent in particular situations – a task ignored by monological, objectivist modes of research. In this context bricoleurs seek to cultivate a higher form of researcher creativity that leads them, like poets, to produce concepts and insights about the social world that previously did not exist. This rigour in the absence can be expressed in numerous ways, including the bricoleur's ability:

- to imagine things that never were;
- to see the world as it could be;
- to develop alternatives to oppressive existing conditions;
- to discern what is lacking in a way that promotes the will to act;
- to understand that there is far more to the world than what we can see.

As always, bricoleurs are struggling to transcend the traditional observational constraint on social researchers, as they develop new ways and methods of exposing social, cultural, political, psychological, and educational forces not discernible at first glance. Pursuing rigour in the absence, bricoleurs document venues of meaning that transcend the words of interviewees or observations of particular behaviours (Dahlbom, 1998; Dicks and Mason, 1998).

Of course, a central feature of this rigorous effort to identify what is absent involves excavating what has been lost in the naivety of monological disciplinarity. As bricoleurs engaging in the boundary work of deep interdisciplinarity explore what has been dismissed, deleted, and covered up, they bring to the surface the ideological devices that have erased the lived worlds and perspectives of those living at the margins of power. In response to Yvonna Lincoln's (2001) question about the use value of knowledge produced by the bricolage, I maintain that as researchers employ the methodological, theoretical, interpretative, political, and narrative dimensions of the bricolage, they make a variety of previously repressed features of the social world visible. Because they are describing dimensions of the socio-cultural, political, economic, psychological, and pedagogical cosmos that have never previously existed, bricoleurs are engaging in what might be termed the fictive element of research.

The use of the term 'fictive' as previously discussed should not be conflated with 'unreal' in this context. Scientific inventors engaged in a similar process when they created design documents for the electric light, the rocket, the computer, or virtual reality. In these examples individuals used a fictive imagination to produce something that did not yet exist. The bricoleur does the same thing in a different ontological and epistemological domain. Both the inventor and the bricoleur are future-oriented, as they explore the realm of possibility, a kinetic epistemology of the possible. In the process the sophistication of knowledge work moves to a new cognitive level; the notion of rigour transmigrates to a new dimension. As in a 1950s sci-fi movie, bricoleurs enter the 4D – the fourth dimension of research.

In this way bricoleurs create a space for reassessing the nature of the knowledge that has been created about the social cosmos and the modes of research that have created it. In an era of information saturation and hegemony, this space for reassessing knowledge production and research methods becomes a necessity for democratic survival, the foundation of a pro-democracy movement, and as William Pinar (2001) correctly maintains, the 'labor of educational scholarship in general' (p. 698). Overwhelmed by corporate-produced data and befuddled by the complexity of the social issues that face us, individuals without access to the lenses of the bricolage often do not know how to deal with these debilitating conditions (DeVault, 1996; Denzin and Lincoln, 2000; Dahlbom, 1998). As the bricolage provides new insights into the chaos of the contemporary, researchers become better equipped to imagine where we might go and what path we might take to get there through the jungle of information surrounding us. The bricolage is no panacea, but it does allow us new vantage points to survey the epistemological wilderness and the possibilities hidden in its underbrush.

Conclusion: The Bricolage and Human Possibility

Obviously, my concern with the bricolage in social research involves not only improving the quality of research but also enhancing the possibility of being human or human being. Thus, the bricolage not only is a dynamic of research but also operates in the connected domains of cognition and pedagogy. In the epistemological and ontological deliberations of the bricolage we gain insight into new modes of thinking, teaching, and learning. In all of these domains, research included, bricoleurs move from convergent to divergent forms of meaning-making, abandoning the short-sightedness of pre-specified, correct patterns of analysis in favour of more holistic, inclusive, and eclectic models. In this context the 'present awareness' of numerous cultural, historical, and philosophical traditions is explored for insights into new ways of thinking, seeing, being, and researching.

Laurel Richardson (2000) picks up on and expands these ideas with her metaphor of the crystal. The bricolage, like a crystal, expands, mutates, and alters while at the same time reflecting and refracting the 'light' of the social world. New patterns emerge and new shapes dance on the pages of the texts produced by the bricoleur – images unanticipated before the process took place. In this new textual domain we trace the emergence of not only creative narratives but also new notions of humanness. Bricoleurs maintain that there is a profound human drama playing out in this context. In their understanding of social complexity they gain a larger perspective on post-Enlightenment Western history. Viewing the last three and a half centuries from a new multidimensional vantage point, bricoleurs understand that Westerners built not only a system of knowledge production but also a world that could have been very different from what came to be. The questions they now ask of that system and that world are dramatic in their implications for the future.

The system of knowledge production, with its epistemological blinders, that developed and expanded across the centuries shackled human agency to the gospel of so-called natural law and scientific procedures. In the name of an ethnocentric notion of scientific progress it attempted to keep individuals ignorant of their potentials and confused cultural difference with deficiency. This procedure-bound science did not do a very good job of addressing questions involving what it means to be human, what it might mean to live in a good and just society, and the worthiness of those who live in cultures and locales different from the West. This is why bricoleurs ascribe such importance to the critical and hermeneutic traditions and their concern with such human questions. Drawing upon these traditions, combining them with forms of paradigmatic and textual analyses, bricoleurs struggle to connect the research act to the emotion and heart of lived human experience (Pryse, 1998; Lutz *et al.*, 1997; Wexler, 2000). Understanding that research which fails to address the ontology of the human existential situation, with all of its pain, suffering, joy and desire, is limited in its worth, bricoleurs search for better ways to connect with and illuminate this domain. In this context much is possible.

2

Redefining rigour and complexity in research

Joe L. Kincheloe

Avoiding the reductionistic knowledge of externally imposed methods, the bricolage continues its pursuit of complexity by sidestepping monological forms of knowledge. Monological knowledge is produced in the rationalistic quest for order and certainty. In such a trek a solitary individual, abstracted from the cultural, discursive, ideological, and epistemological contexts that have shaped him or her and the research methods and interpretative strategies he or she employs, seeks an objective knowledge of unconnected things-in-themselves. Not only does monological knowledge reduce human life to its objectifiable dimensions, that is, what can be expressed numerically, but it is also incapable of moving beyond one individual's unilateral experience of the world. At its core the bricolage struggles to find and develop numerous strategies for getting beyond this one dimensionality. In this monological context thick descriptions are lost to the forces of order and certainty which are satisfied with right and wrong answers that preclude the need for other perspectives. Thus, monological knowledge is a smug knowledge that is content with quick resolutions to the problems that confront researchers (Thomas, 1998; Madison, 1988).

Chasing Complexity: Avoiding Monological Knowledge in the Bricolage

Bricoleurs understand a basic flaw within the nature and production of monological knowledge: unilateral perspectives on the world fail to account for the complex relationship between material reality and human perception. When this relationship is ignored, knowledge producers have hell to pay. Such a high expenditure includes the costs of not taking into account that what we perceive is shaped by a panoply of factors. Mistaking perception for truth not only reduces our ability to make sense of the world around us but also harms those with the least power to pronounce what is true (Karunaratne, 1997). In his initial speculations on the nature of the bricolage, Lévi-Strauss (1966) emphasized this point. A knowledge producer, he argued, never carries on a simple dialogue with the world but, instead, interacts 'with a particular relationship between nature and culture definable in terms of his particular period and civilization and the material means at his disposal' (p. 19).

Lévi-Strauss, of course, was delineating the bricolage's concern with and understanding of the dialectical relationship between knowledge and reality. In the decades since his pronouncements social analysts have argued that in the complexity of this relationship, knowledge and reality change both continuously and interdependently. In the recognition of this complexity many researchers have come to the conclusion that the description of what really exists may be far more difficult than originally thought. In this context bricoleurs seek multiple perspectives not to provide the *truth* about reality but to avoid the monological knowledge that emerges from unquestioned frames of reference and the dismissal of the numerous relationships and connections that link various forms of knowledge together.

Here rests a central epistemological and ontological assumption of the bricolage: the domains of the physical, the social, the cultural, the psychological, and the educational consist of the interplay of a wide variety of entities – thus, the complexity and the need for multiple ways of seeing advocated by bricoleurs. As part of a larger process that is ever changing, the reality that bricoleurs engage is not a fixed entity. In its impermanence the lived world presents special problems for researchers that demand attention to the nature of its changes and the processes of its movements. In this dynamic context bricoleurs work to avoid pronouncements of final truth. Because of the changing and impermanent nature of the world, bricoleurs propose compelling insights into their engagement with reality and the unresolved contradictions that characterize such interactions (Lomax and Parker, 1996; Young and Yarbrough, 1993; Karunaratne, 1997).

Complexity Demands the Rigour of the Bricolage

As bricoleurs plan their escape from the limitations of monological knowledge, they envision forms of research that transcend reductionism. In this context they understand that complexity sets the stage for the need for the bricolage, the necessity of new ways to understand the complications of social, cultural, psychological, and educational life. Once again, the complexity principle gets in our face: knowledge production is a far more complex process than we originally thought; there are more obstacles to the act of making sense of the world than researchers had anticipated. It was with these understandings in mind that Denzin and Lincoln (2000) issued their rigorous conception of the bricoleur as intellectually informed, widely read, and cognizant of diverse paradigms of interpretation. Realizing that the world is too complex to be revealed as an objective reality, Denzin and Lincoln sought multiple methods to provide richness and depth to a study.

Lévi-Strauss (1966), in his delineation of the bricolage, maintained that the concept originated in an understanding of the complexity and unpredictability of the cultural domain. Complexity in the context of cultural inquiry demands that the researcher develop a thick description that avoids the reductionism of describing the 'functional role' of an individual. Such a 'literacy of complexity' understands the intersecting roles and social locations of all human beings and the multiple layers of interpretations of self, contexts, and social actors involved in rigorous research (Dicks and Mason, 1998). Bricoleurs act on these understandings in the effort to address the complexity of everyday life. Such complexity is embedded in notions of

- *explicate and implicate orders of reality*. The explicate order consists of simple patterns and invariants in time. These characteristics of the world, as theorized by the physicist David Bohm, seem to repeat themselves in similar ways and possess recognizable locations in time and space. The implicate order is a much deeper structure of the world. It is the level at which ostensible separateness disappears and all things seem to become a part of a larger unified process. Implicate orders are marked by the simultaneous presence of a sequence of many levels of enfoldment with similar dissimilarities existing among them (Bohm and Peat, 1987). Bricoleurs who recognize complexity search for this implicate order as a process often hidden from social, cultural, psychological, and pedagogical researchers.
- *the questioning of universalism*. Contextual specificities may interfere with a researcher's ability to generalize findings to a level of universal application. With the recognition of complexity universal theories of intelligence, for example, might have to respect and thus account for the way individuals and groups in diverse social settings conceptualize the concept (Kincheloe et al., 1999c).
- *polysemy*. Interpretation is always a complex process, and different words and phrases, depending on the context in which they are used, can mean different things to different individuals. Thus, the research process is always more complex than initially perceived.

- *the living process in which cultural entities are situated.* In the zone of complexity processes may be more fundamental to understanding the socio-cultural world than isolated entities. Knowledge in this process-oriented context has a past and a future; researchers have traditionally viewed a phenomenon in a particular stage of its development. Bricoleurs operating on a terrain of complexity understand that they must transcend this tendency and struggle to comprehend the process of which an object of study is a part.

- *the ontology of relationships and connections.* In complexity theory the concept of relatedness is deemed to possess properties and influences that are just beginning to be understood. For example, complexity theorists argue that the self is less stable and essentialized than was previously thought. In this context the relationship between self and culture becomes a central focus in particular forms of social, cognitive, and psychological research. Culture is not merely the context in which the self operates, but it is 'in the self' – an inseparable portion of what we call the self. Who we are as human beings is dependent on the nature of such relationships and connections.

- *intersecting contexts.* Bricoleurs operating in the complexity zone understand that knowledge can never stand alone or be complete in and of itself. When researchers abstract, they take something away from its context. Of course we all abstract, but researchers as bricoleurs refuse to lose sight of the contextual field – indeed, the intersecting contextual fields – that provide separate entities diverse meanings. Contextualization is always a complex act as it exposes connections between what were assumed to be separate entities. In this activity researchers come to see dimensions of an object of study never before noticed. When researchers realize that there are always multiple contexts in which to view phenomena, they come to understand that some reductionistic notion of a definitive or final comprehension of an object of study is a reductionistic concept. There is always another context in which a phenomenon can be studied.

- *the existence and utility of feedback loops.* Many phenomena, living things in particular, are composed of a multitude of feedback loops – a central dimension of chaos theory. A home furnace is one of the most familiar forms of a simple feedback loop. We all know that when a room cools down below the temperature set on the thermostat, it responds by switching on the furnace. As the furnace hearts up the room to a point above the second temperature set on the thermostat, the furnace automatically shuts off. The ear-splitting screeches produced when a microphone is placed close to a speaker are another example of a feedback loop. Output from the amplifier is detected by the microphone and looped back into the amplifier. The chaotic sounds that result are the consequence of a feedback loop where the output of one stage turns into the input of another. Because human beings are composed of so many feedback loops – for example, the transformation of food into energy, and the increase in heart-rate in the presence of danger – the attempt to study them takes on far more complexity than traditional conceptions of cause–effect linearity could imagine. The bricolage utilizes the concept of feedback loops as bricoleurs view their knowledge production in light of numerous types and forms of discourses. This process – which Kathy Berry explains in detail in Chapters 5–7 – is central to the enactment of the bricolage. Feedback loops allow for new insights and ideas to emerge as concepts are viewed in light of new perspectives and different ways of making meaning. In this context an autopoietic process is constructed as new modes of knowledge emerge in the interaction of these multidimensional perspectives. The adept bricoleur sets up the bricolage in a manner that produces powerful feedback loops – constructs that in turn synergize the research process.

- *multiple epistemologies.* Depending on where observers stand in the multidimensional web of reality, they will come to see different phenomena in different ways. Bricoleurs understand that in this complex context diverse epistemologies will develop in different historical and cultural locales. As opposed to European modes of knowledge production, diverse peoples of the planet have produced ways of knowing that often have come directly into conflict. In their appreciation of epistemological complexity, bricoleurs seek out diverse epistemologies for their unique insights and sophisticated modes of making meaning. In this search they gain provocative insights into epistemological diversity around issues of the relationships between mind and body, self and other, spirit and matter, knower and known, things-in-themselves and relationships, logic and emotion, etc. These insights allow them to ask new questions of epistemology and the research act.

- *intertextuality.* Adding to the complexity of the bricoleur's understanding of the research act is the notion of intertextuality defined simply as the complicated interrelationship connecting a text to other texts in the act of textual creation or interpretation. Central to the importance of intertextuality in the context of the bricolage and the effort to understand complexity is the notion that all narratives obtain meaning not merely by their relationship to material reality but from their connection to other narratives. A research account in this context cannot be understood without situating it historically in relation to other research narratives. With this understanding of intertextuality bricoleurs are always aware that the researcher, the consumer/reader of the research, and exterior research narratives always occupy points on intersecting intertextual axes. In this way they are always influencing one another and any effort to make meaning of any research act.

* *discursive construction.* All knowledge production is shaped tacitly or consciously by discursive rules and practices. Bricoleurs exploring the complexity of the research act are always exploring the discursive construction of research narratives. They work to uncover the hidden rules that define what a researcher can and cannot say, who possesses the power to speak/write about particular topics and who must listen/read, and whose constructions of reality are valid and whose are unlearned and unimportant. Bricoleurs understand Michel Foucault's assertion that fields of knowledge take their forms as a result of the power relations of discursive practices.

* *the interpretative aspect of all knowledge.* As argued throughout this description of the bricolage, interpretation is always at work in the act of knowledge production – the 'facts' never speak for themselves. As inhabitants of the world, researchers are oriented to it in a manner that prevents them from grounding their findings outside of it. Thus, whether we like it or not, all researchers are destined to be interpreters who analyse the cosmos from within its boundaries and blinders. To research we must interpret; indeed, to live we must interpret.

* *the fictive dimension of research findings.* Since in the zone of complexity no fact is self-evident and no representation is 'pure', any knowledge worker who believes research narratives are simple truths is operating in a naive domain. Thus, bricoleurs assert that there are fictive elements to all representations and narratives. Such fictive dimensions may be influenced by a variety of forces, including linguistic factors, narrative emplotment strategies, and cultural prejudices.

* *the cultural assumptions within all research methods.* Western science as well as any form of knowledge production is constructed at a particular historical time and in a specific cultural place. These temporal and spatial dimensions always leave their mark on the nature of the research methods employed and the knowledges produced. As bricolage pursues complexity, it induces researchers to seek the specific ways these cultural assumptions shape knowledge production, their own research processes in particular. Researchers operating with a consciousness of these dynamics use the insights gleaned from it to seek more complex ways of producing knowledge that are conscious of the many tacit ways cultural assumptions wander unnoticed within the act of researching.

* *the relationship between power and knowledge.* Power, like the research act itself, is more complex than we originally posited. Drawing on

Foucault, power can be a censor that excludes, blocks, and represses like a great superego. On the other hand, however, power is a great producer, creating knowledge and legitimate ways of seeing. As a censor in research, power serves to limit what constitutes a legitimate focus of research, excluding 'dangerous' investigations. As a producer in the research context, power serves to reward particular ways of seeing and specific activities. For example, in higher education researchers who desire success in their fields learn to follow particular research norms allowing them the rewards of funded grants and promotions based on scholarly productivity. The way different research orientations draw boundaries between what is acceptable and what is not constitutes the ideological dimension of the act of inquiry. Here, bricoleurs understand, complexity abounds, as power is at work promoting particular views of research rigour and validity and notions of 'unscientific' or soft research unworthy of certification at any level. The ability to trace the footprints of power in the research domain is a central dimension in the bricoleur's efforts to understand complexity and knowledge production.

Bricoleurs acting on the complexity principle understand that the identification of social structures is always problematic, always open to questions of contextual contingency. This recognition does not mean that we dismiss the notion of structures but that we view them in a different way. For example, the structure of patriarchy is not some universal, fixed, unchanging reality. Patriarchy might better be described as an interpretative concept that varies in relation to time and place, that is constantly mutating in relation to its connections to a plethora of historical, social, cultural, economic, political, psychological, and pedagogical forces. The effects of patriarchy on specific groups and individuals are real but always idiosyncratic and undetermined. Bricoleurs understand in this context that they cannot use a theory of patriarchy to tell them what has happened in a particular situation but must dig, scratch, analyse from different angles and employ multiple research methods and interpretative strategies to examine different aspects of the situation.

Structural analysis is too messy, contradictory, and complex to offer a universally valid and essentialized description of any social structure. As the complexity-sensitive bricolage theorizes structure as an untidy process, it views it like a model in a 'fashion shoot' – from a variety of angles, in numerous contexts and backdrops, and in relation to different moods and affects. Chaos theory has provided bricoleurs with a compelling means of dealing with structures in its concept of fractals. Like social structures viewed through the lenses of the complexity principle, fractals are involved in the analysis of loosely structured entities. These irregular shapes, whose parts reflect the whole of the entity, are similar to social structures such as patriarchy that are non-linear, contextually specific, and irregular in their manifestation (Young and Yarbrough, 1993). The similarities between fractals in physical reality and these social dynamics are compelling. These fractal dynamics deserve more study later in this chapter.

Constructing the Bricolage: Developing a Social, Cultural, Psychological, and Educational Science of Complexity

Some of the best work in the study of social complexity is now taking place in the qualitative inquiry of numerous fields from sociology, cultural studies, anthropology, literary studies, marketing, geography, media studies, nursing, informatics, library studies, women's studies, various ethnic studies, education, to nursing. Denzin and Lincoln (2000) are acutely aware of these dynamics and refer to them in the context of their delineation of the bricolage. Yvonna Lincoln (2001), in her response to my development of the bricolage (Kincheloe, 2001b), maintains that the most important border work between disciplines is taking place in feminism and race-ethnic studies. In his response to this work, William Pinar (2001) correctly points out that the discipline of curriculum theory provides numerous examples of radical forms of interdisciplinarity similar to what I am describing as the bricolage. It is unfortunate that researchers in sociology, cultural studies, psychology, history, and other disciplines are not more familiar with curriculum theory.

In the move to transcend the objective certainty of positivism and the effort to avoid the nihilism of more radical modes of postmodernism, social and cultural analysis has migrated to a more undefined space where no particular paradigmatic view dominates. In this domain an awareness of the complexity of knowledge production undermines efforts to fix the field of social research in a well-defined locale. The development of particular universal ways of operating as researchers is not so easy in a situation where more and more professional practitioners grasp the complexity of their task.

The bricolage does not enter into this paradigmatic situation as a knight on a white horse ready to 'save' the field. Such bravado is not the point of constructing the bricolage. In light of the vicissitudes of the contemporary state of social, cultural, psychological, and educational research the bricolage serves as a way of naming and organizing existing impulses. In this context it serves to promote understanding and communication and create structures that allow for a better-informed, more rigorous mode of knowledge production. Do not misread this humility: I strongly believe in the power of the bricolage to move the field in a positive direction; it is concurrently important, however, to understand its construction and limitations in the context of contemporary social research. The appreciation of the complexity of everyday life and the difficulty of understanding it demands humility on the part of researchers. Bricoleurs understand that certainty and interpretive finality are simply not possible given such complications.

Indeed, a complex social, cultural, and educational analysis is aware that a specific set of variables does not lead to the same outcomes in some linear cause-and-effect manner. Scholars in such analysis transcend reductionistic assumptions such as that only one entity can inhabit the same locale at the same time. In a complex ontology patriarchy can coexist in the same time and space with religion, socio-economic class, gender, sexuality, geographic place, and a plethora of other social dynamics. In such a context the notion of causality and the nature of social interconnections become far more complex concepts and processes to research. With this complexity in mind, Young and Yarbrough (1993) argue that the way researchers discursively define a social phenomenon produces the form the notion takes.

Using class as an example, they argue that it is possible to define it as a lifestyle, a function of formal education, a manifestation of one's father's occupation, or one's relationship to the means of production. Class as a social structure looks very different depending on what definition we choose. A complex sociology or a complex cultural studies understands that there is no final source of authority to which researchers can appeal for a validated definition. Such uncertainty, bricoleurs recognize, is a key aspect of the human condition of being in the world – a complex ontology. Operating in this situation bricoleurs employ 'any means necessary', as many methods as possible to make their way through a world of diverse meanings – not to mention becoming researchers of such a world. These diverse meanings continuously circulate through language, common sense, worldviews, ideologies, and discourses, always operating to tacitly shape the act of meaning-making.

Any social, cultural, psychological, or educational science of complexity takes these dynamics into account. No research act or interpretative task begins on virgin territory. Countless acts of meaning-making have already shaped the terrain that researchers explore. In this context bricoleurs need as much help as they can get to negotiate their way through such overwhelming complexity. This is why we develop the bricolage in the first place: complexity demands a wider definition of research that would include modes of philosophical inquiry that account for these epistemological and ontological dynamics.

On the landscape of complexity I am lost as a researcher if I do not possess an epistemological and ontological map to help me understand the nature of the territory I am exploring. To produce research that provides thick description and a glimpse of what could be I need epistemological and ontological insights that alert me to the multidimensional, socially constructed, polyvocal, ever-changing, fractal-based nature of the social world. Such insights hold profound implications for research methods (Lutz *et al.*, 1997; Bridges, 1997; McLeod, 2000). In this complex context it becomes even more obvious that learning the bricolage is a lifelong process.

Knowledge Production is More Complex than we Thought: Reconsidering 'The Facts'

As we look back from the perspective of the first decade of the twenty-first century to the innovative scholarly work on epistemology and research of the last several decades, one understanding becomes increasingly clear: producing knowledge about the world is more complex than we originally thought. What we designate as facts is not as straightforward a process as it was presented to us. Bricoleurs know that what most people consider the natural social world is a conceptual landmine wired with assumptions and inherited meanings. Critical researchers have learned that what is unproblematically deemed 'a fact' has been shaped by a community of inquirers. All of these researchers accept, often unconsciously, a particular set of theoretical assumptions. Engaging in knowledge work without a deep understanding of the tacit rules of the game is not a manifestation of rigour. Indeed, such a lack of knowledge profoundly undermines the effort to produce compelling and useful data about the world around us (Horn, 2004; Fischer, 1998). Great scholars in diverse historical and cultural settings have admonished individuals not to take fixed viewpoints and concepts as reality (Varela, 1999). Bricoleurs heed such a warning.

Roymeico Carter (2004) extends this concept into the world of the visual. The complexity of researching the visual domain is often squashed by the formal methods of Cartesian aesthetics. Carter reminds us that the intricate layers of visual meaning must be studied from numerous perspectives as well as diverse cultural and epistemological traditions (Rose and Kincheloe, 2003). But such diversity of perception lets the cat out of the bag; it relinquishes control of how we are to see the world. According to Ilya Prigogine, complexity demands that researchers give up the attempt to dominate and control the world. The social and physical worlds are so complex that they can only be understood like human beings themselves: not machine-like, unpredictable, dependent upon context, and influenced by minute fluctuations (Capra, 1996). Thus, bricoleurs focus their attention on addressing the complexity of the lived world, in the process understanding that the knowledge they produce should not be viewed as a transhistorical body of truth. In this framework knowledge produced by bricoleurs is provisional and 'in process'. Bricoleurs know that tensions will develop in social knowledge as the understandings and insights of individuals change and evolve (Blackler, 1995).

A researcher, for example, who returns to an ethnographic study after only a few years may find profound differences in what is reported by subjects. The categories and coding that worked three years ago may no longer be relevant. The most important social, psychological, and educational problems that confront us are untidy and complicated. As we wade through the swamp of everyday life, research methods that fail to provide multiple perspectives at macro, meso, and micro levels do not provide the insights that we need. It is one thing to find out that schools, for example, do not provide many poor students a path to social mobility. It is quite another to take this macro-finding and combine it with the meso-dynamics of the ways particular schools and school leaders conceptualize the relationship between schooling and class mobility. It is also important that these findings be viewed in a context informed by everyday classroom and out-of-classroom interactions between teachers and students and between students and their peers. Obviously, different research methodologies will be used to explore the differing questions emerging at the different levels. Once data from these diverse layers are combined, we begin to discern a picture of the multiple dynamics of the relationship between socio-economic class and education. Only a multidimensional, complex picture such as this can help us formulate informed and just strategies to address such issues.

If researchers refuse to move into the multilevelled swamp of complexity or to integrate the diverse forms of data found at its different levels, they may find themselves asking pedestrian questions of profoundly complicated issues. Simple, unproblematic questions about the domain of schooling and socio-economic class, for example, tend to be the least significant to the society at large. Positivistic standards of rigour as presently employed by many social, psychological, and educational researchers actually preclude the complex, multidimensional, multi-methodological work necessary to producing meaningful and usable research data (Schon, 1995). Francisco Varela (1999) writes about 'the situated embodiments of simple acts' (p. 8), maintaining that such complexity in everyday life undermines total reliance on computational methods where 'knowledge is a manipulation of symbols by logic-like rules, an idea that finds it fullest expression in modern digital computers' (p. 7). In the domain of cognitive science, Varela concludes, even the simplest acts – even those performed by insects – rest outside the understanding of the computational strategy. Varela's pronouncements tell bricoleurs not to throw out computational strategies but to understand what they can and cannot tell us and to carefully consider how we might use them in the bricolage's pursuit of complexity in the social, psychological, and educational spheres.

Even simple acts of cognition, social interaction, learning, and textual analysis are more complex than researchers first suspected. 'Just give me the facts' is not as simple a command as it seemed to appear to Cartesian sensibilities. The situated nature of knowledge questions a variety of Cartesian assumptions. When we pick particular attributions of meaning about specific phenomena, we must consider a variety of factors. Such choices are inevitably political and ideological and have nothing to do with efforts to be objective. Even the decisions researchers make about what to study reflect these same political and ideological dynamics. In the highly ideologically charged first decade of the twenty-first century do educational researchers study how to improve student test scores in the suburbs or the impact of racism on lower socio-economic class African American students in urban schools? The problems and issues that are chosen by researchers are marked by subjective judgements about whose problems are deemed most important.

These interpretative decisions are always complex and influenced by a plethora of social, cultural, political, economic, psychological, discursive, and pedagogical dynamics. As a critical discourse, the bricolage always considers the normative dimension of what should be as well as what is. When immanence (what should be) is added to the complex dynamics surrounding decision-making and interpretation in the realm of research, bricoleurs move to yet a higher domain of complexity. Reflecting on the research process from a perspective shaped by these concerns, bricoleurs gain new insights into the consequences of reductionism. For example, when rational inquiry is positioned in opposition to the emotional, affective, and value-laden dimensions of human activity then it has removed itself as a means of gaining insight into the social, psychological, and educational domains. Life in these domains simply cannot be understood without careful attention to the emotional, affective, and value-laden aspects of human behaviour (Williams, 1999; Reason and Bradbury, 2000). Indeed, a rational inquiry that devalues the role of irrationality will sink under the weight of its own gravitas.

The Bricolage, Complexity, and Enactivism: The Nature of Empiricism

When bricoleurs bring the social, cultural, political, economic, psychological, discursive, and pedagogical together with the emotional, affective, value-laden, and normative, they know that they will be faced with the tension of dissimilar narratives and interpretations. Central to more

Cartesian-oriented empirical models of research is the resolution of conflict and difference. Such complexity and contradiction does not lead bricoleurs into a nihilistic funk, but instead pushes them to a new level of hermeneutic creativity that values the generative interplay of dissimilar perspectives. An awareness of diverse ways of understanding and constructing the social world is necessary knowledge for bricoleurs in their pursuit of rigour. Such insight is invaluable in their challenge to monolithic forms of 'common knowledge' and their detection of alternative knowledges within any canonical construction or research finding. In this aspect of the bricolage the arrogance of the empirical expert is abandoned for the humility of diverse perspectives. The conflicts and differences valued by the bricoleur continuously generate a sense of curious uncertainty. Such a critical uncertainty insists that nothing is beyond questioning and that even what we just found in our research remains perpetually open to reconsideration in the light of what else could it be, what was, and what should be.

So many times in my career as a researcher, as I have explained this element of the bricolage, I have been faced with charges of being anti-empiricist. Nothing delineated in this description of complexity and its relation to the bricolage should elicit such a charge. The purpose of the bricolage is not to subvert the production of empirical knowledge but rather to encourage the production of a richer, thicker, and more rigorous form of it. Richer, thicker, and more rigorous empirical knowledge is aware of what it both can and cannot claim. It is aware of its own assumptions about knowledge production and the nature of knowledge. Thus, bricoleurs are simultaneously calling for a more rigorous form of empirical knowledge and a more humble claim for what it represents. The two characteristics are not contradictory; instead they are synergistic. Empirical findings, contrary to the pronouncements of many, make sense only within particular social, cultural, paradigmatic, discursive and historical contexts. If social science fails to address the contextual contingency of empirical findings, it ends up concretizing a particular perspective on the world.

For example, if we do not understand that IQ tests – positivistic research instruments on the nature of intelligence – reinforce a particular cultural, class, racial, and paradigmatic view of the concept of intelligence, then our research constructs reality more than it describes it. Profoundly talented and creative students, especially from non-white and lower socio-economic backgrounds and with first language other than English, become unintelligent as a result of the research. In this case empirical research is not rigorous; it is unreflective, culturally biased, unaware of alternative knowledges, dismissive of multiple ways of seeing and *dangerous* to the well-being of particular individuals and society in general. In the name of a faux rigour such research operates in the interests of dominant power to maintain the political status quo. Again this does not mean that we discard empiricism. The lesson bricoleurs learn here is that the research community can do better, that the time has come to redefine rigour in the process of producing knowledge. The better we understand the complex socially and politically constructed nature of the research act, the more rigorous and well informed our research can become (Geeland and Taylor, 2000; Roberts, 1998; Fischer, 1998).

Operating with a basic epistemological and ontological grounding, bricoleurs appreciate that empirical knowledge is not just 'out there' in the world floating around, waiting to be discovered. Such a naive realist Cartesian perspective has long outlived its usefulness. While leading to some remarkable scientific and technological achievements, the insidious ways it harms particular individuals, groups, and the physical environment must be contained in the first decade of the twenty-first century. The artificial simplicity promoted by the Cartesian empirical tradition is challenged by bricoleurs. They simply do not believe that the social, psychological, and educational domains can be reduced to a set of laws of causality and that there is a specific method researchers can use to produce such laws. Cause–effect relationships, of course, are notoriously hard to discern. In the Cartesian–Newtonian–Baconian clockwork universe the world was seen as absolutely causal and determinate.

By faithful adherence to the scientific method, researchers in any domain could determine what caused what. Thus, in such a strictly unilinear cosmos the future of a phenomenon could be determined with certainty if its present manifestation was understood. In the social domain rigorous research could allow experts to control workers, mental patients, and school children. Since the political/ideological dimensions of this control were often unexplored and sometimes covertly manipulated, empiricism could be put to some nefarious uses. In the reductionism of the paradigm these ideological dimensions of the research act were deemed outside the purview of the scientist. Thus, some researchers involved in particularly odious projects were not aware of the consequences of the application of their research. Other researchers, of course, knew but chose to ignore the moral, ethical, and political implications of such deployment. This is not a manifestation of rigorous scholarship.

Cartesian causality has never bequeathed the world an adequate perspective on the workings of social, psychological, and educational systems. Because of their complexity and their idiosyncratic interacting parts, such systems do not lend themselves to reductionistic explanation. In complexity theory it is posited that no part controls the behaviour of the system as a whole and that the relationship between the parts produces systemic qualities that are difficult to anticipate. Complexity theorists describe such systems, both physical and social, as emergent and self-organizing. Blinded by their faith in a naive causality, many researchers are unequipped to move into the realm of emergence and autopoiesis (Lemke, 1999).

One way that Humberto Maturana and Francisco Varela (1987) learned about the emergent, self-organizing properties of both the social order and the mind was by monitoring work on the 'superorganic' nature of ant and bee behaviour. The researchers noted that in studies of ant colonies where the most efficient nurses were removed to form a new sub-colony, these specialists changed their behaviour. Instead of performing an exclusive nursing function they became foragers for food and needed materials. In the original colony formerly low-level nurses became more active and increased their nursing activities. In Varela's (1999) words, 'the whole colony ... showed evidence of both configurational identity and memory'. In this example the ants' relationship to the colony shaped individual behaviour. Even though the ants were 'individuals', the colony behaved as a cohesive whole. It operated as if there was a coordinating consciousness directing group behaviour. Such a group consciousness was autopoietic – self-produced. It emerged as a macro-pattern from the actions and relationships of simple individual components. This concept of autopoiesis emerging from relationships between ostensibly simple parts holds compelling possibilities for bricoleurs. It is virtual because it is *not a thing*. It does not exist as a substance, only as a set of relationships. We will discuss the ontological dimensions of relationship in relation to the bricolage in Chapter 4.

Pushing the Boundaries of Scholarship: The Bricolage and the Complexity of Emergence

Maturana and Varela's research holds profound and unexplored implications for constructing the bricolage. Such explorations hold out the hope that when diverse insights from a variety of domains are brought together in new relationships, dramatic intellectual breakthroughs can occur. The notions of autopoiesis and emergence remind us that we are constructing a complex, rigorous mode of research based on what we can become both in an individual and a social sense. In this context the bricolage works to bring together multiple knowledges to form new epistemological and ontological interactions. Something profound happens when we take knowledges, thought systems, and social and epistemological theories from diverse contexts and bring them together in search of new relationships, new patterns of interaction, and new imperatives for intellectual and ethical action in the social, psychological, and educational arena. In this activity we bring the bricolage together with autopoiesis – our research sets the stage for the emergence of ways of seeing, thinking, and being never before imagined. Using different discourses in different domains, bricoleurs familiar with enactivism are better equipped to construct previously discussed feedback loops. Such a complex process, as Kathy Berry illustrates in Chapters 5–7, results in the *emergence* of new ways of seeing the world.

As we construct the bricolage and connect it to enactivist principles of systemic self-organization, our research moves into a new zone of emergent complexity. In this context, when advocates of a critical form of inquiry use the term 'transformative action', they gain a deeper sense of what this might mean using the enactivist concept of readiness-for-action. Knowledge must be enacted – understood at the level of human beings' affect and intellect. In a critical context the knowledge we produce must be enacted in light of our individual and collective struggles. Without this dimension the research act becomes a rather shallow enterprise. Nothing new *emerges* as knowledges and concepts are merely produced rather than related to one another and enacted in the world.

Employing an understanding of complexity theory, Maturana and Varela's Santiago enactivism as the process of life, critical theoretical foundations, the critique of Cartesianism, and discourses such as poststructuralist feminist analysis, we can lay the conceptual foundations for a new mode of complex research and new conceptions of selfhood itself. Such configurations cannot be comprehensively delineated here, but we can begin to build theoretical pathways to get around the Cartesian limitations on the epistemological and ontological imagination. With Humberto Maturana and Francisco Varela's concept that living things constantly remake themselves in interaction with their environments, our notions of a new self (a critical ontology) and new modes of exploring the world are grounded on the human ability to use new social contexts and experiences to reformulate both subjectivity and knowledge. In this context the concept of personal ability becomes a de-essentialized cognition of possibility. No essentialized bounded self can access the intellectual potential offered by epiphanies of difference or triggered by an ostensibly 'insignificant' insight.

As we begin to identify previously unperceived patterns in which the self is implicated, the possibility of cognitive change and personal growth is enhanced. As the barriers between mind and multiple contexts are erased, the chance that more expanded forms of 'cognitive/scholarly autopoiesis' – self-constructed modes of higher-order thinking and intellectual work – will emerge is increased. A more textured, a thicker sense of self-production, the nature of self and other, self and knowledge, and all of these dynamics in relation to larger social, political, cultural, psychological, and pedagogical structures is constructed in this process. As we examine the self and its relationship to others in these contexts, we gain a clearer sense of our purpose in the world especially in relation to justice, interconnectedness, and meaning-making. In these activities we move closer to the macro-processes of the social domain and their micro-expressions in everyday life.

A key aspect of such processes is the understanding of difference that comes from recognition of patterns of interconnectedness. Knowing that an individual from an upper-middle-class European background living in a Virginia suburb will be considered culturally bizarre by a group of tribespeople from the Amazon rainforest is a potentially profound learning experience in the domain of the personal. How is the suburbanite viewed as bizarre? What cultural practices are seen as so unusual? What mannerisms are humorous to the tribespeople? What worldviews are baffling to them? The answers to such questions may shock the suburbanite into reorienting her view of her own 'normality'. The interaction may induce her to ask questions of the way she is perceived by and the way she perceives others. Such a phenomenological bracketing of the personal may be quite liberating. This interaction with difference could be another example of Maturana and Varela's structural coupling that creates a new relationship with other and with self. In Maturana and Varela's conceptualization a new inner world is created as a result of such coupling (Maturana and Varela, 1987; Varela, 1999; Sumara and Davis, 1997). In the bricolage new knowledge is created in the collision of the diverse perspectives.

Such explorations on the ontological frontier hold profound implications for our construction of the bricolage. As students pursue rigorous study of diverse global knowledges, they come to understand that the identities of their peer groups and families constitute only a few of countless historical and cultural ways to be human. As they study their self-production and the construction of their ways of perceiving in wider biological, sociological, cultural studies, historical, theological, psychological and counter-canonical contexts, they gain insights into their ways of being human. As bricoleurs they begin to see the ways such dynamics shape and have shaped, most often tacitly, the production of knowledge throughout the ages. As they engage the conflicts that induce diverse knowledge producers to operate in conflicting ways, researchers become more attuned to the ideological, discursive, and regulatory forces operating in the production all knowledges.

The processual and relational notions of self in the language of enactivism structurally couple with the socio-cultural context and can only be understood by studying them with these dynamics in mind. These characteristics of self hold profound implications politically, psychologically, pedagogically, and epistemologically. If our notion of the self emerges in its relationship with multiple dimensions of the world, it is by its nature a participatory entity. Such an interactive dynamic is always in process and thus demands a reconceptualization of the concepts of individualism and self-interest and their role in shaping the subjectivity of the researcher (Pickering, 1999). The needs of self and others in this context begin to merge, as the concept of self-reliance takes on new meanings. Notions of the purpose of knowledge production are transformed when these new conceptions of the personal domain come into the picture. In the first decade of the twenty-first century we stand merely on the threshold of the possibilities this notion of selfhood harbours. The bricolage is dedicated to exploring these possibilities.

The bricoleur's critical ontological and epistemological consciousness empowers such researchers to explain why decontextualized and reductionistic study of complex cognitive, biological, social, or pedagogical events does not work. The Cartesian study of isolated and fragmented phenomena will not move us to new levels of understanding or set the stage for new, unexplored modes of rethinking subjectivity and social action. The social, cognitive, political, economic and pedagogical domains are not assortments of discrete objects that can be understood in isolation from one another (Pickering, 1999). The fragmented pieces put forth in such reductionistic studies do not constitute reality – even if common sense tells Cartesian researchers they do. The deeper structures, the tacit forces, the processes that shape the physical world and the social world will be lost to such observers. As I argue in the introduction to *The Stigma of Genius: Einstein, Consciousness, and Education* (Kincheloe *et al.*, 1999b), Einstein's general theory of relativity could not have been produced without this understanding of connectedness, process, and the limitations of studying only isolated things-in-themselves. Bricoleurs pay close attention to the lessons for all research found in these notions.

Obviously, Varela and Maturana's enactivism moves our understanding of complexity and the bricolage to a new plateau. An enactivist-informed critique of Cartesian research maintains that perception should not be equated only with sense perception and questions the belief that causality is a simple dynamic of cause and effect between contiguous phenomena (Griffin, 1997). As previously referenced, causality is a much more elusive animal and must be reconsidered in light of enactivist insights. In a complex set of relationships and interactions within multiple contexts and diverse processes, what are the causative and 'effected' agents? Cartesian cause and effect slips from the screen of relevance in the bricoleur's study of complex systems. When bricoleurs engage in the research act or study the research activities of others, they begin to understand the siren call of cause–effect modes of inquiry. Westerners can be lulled into intellectual sleep by the 'common sense' of apparent causality. In such scholarly unconsciousness they abandon the quest for multiple perspectives and tension-producing incommensurable knowledges (Shapin, 1995). The critical enactivist understandings that facilitate our understanding of complexity serve as an epistemological and ontological alarm clock refusing to allow bricoleurs to retreat into the comfort of reductionism.

Subversions of Complexity: The Haunted House of Rationalist and Formalist Reductionism

The confrontation with complexity undermines monodisciplinary approaches to research as well as subverting disciplinarity in general. We will explore questions of bricolage and disciplinarity in depth in Chapter 3. In a cosmos of complexity the categorization of knowledge and knowledge-production strategies constructs an epistemological arrogance. Researchers and scholars come to believe that they and their colleagues have effectively divided the world into neat and efficient compartments. 'Here is the truth about ——— ', they tell us. 'If you want to know the whole story, learn the knowledge base of the discipline.' As many have argued, however, the borders that separate the disciplines are capricious and arbitrary. Like colonial borders in Africa that refused to acknowledge tribal lands and cultural interests, disciplinary boundaries have caused problems for decades. Simply put, no problem is only an educational, a psychological, or a social concern. We encounter everyday life as a seamless whole – only our research strategies and disciplinary approaches fragment and isolate portions of the world. In such rationalistic fragmentation relationships are destroyed and contexts are ignored. Such analytical irrationality has undermined the work of many a graduate student when their dissertation advisor demanded: 'remove this psychological portion of the chapter, this is a sociology dissertation'.

Such rationalistic fragmentation of the research act limits our inquiry, undermines our ability to derive the benefits of multiple perspectives. There is no compensation for the absence of diverse perspectives and alternate viewpoints. As previously maintained, the value of difference is a concept that is central to the construction of the bricolage and, unfortunately, under attack in the academy of the twenty-first century. Any discipline that refuses to move outside its borders privileges its own narratives and regimes of truth. Research emerging from such a disciplinary context produces one-dimensional knowledge about multi-dimensional phenomena (Gee et al., 1996; Thayer-Bacon, 2000; Hinchey, 2004). In cartographic terms such monological research becomes the Mercator projection of knowledge production. Taking a cue from second-order cybernetics, the bricolage rejects the positivist notion of the unity of method. Such a notion insists that the same research methods employed by the physical sciences can be used unproblematically in biology, the social sciences, psychology, and education. Indeed, such methods cannot be used in these areas because the subjects of study are autopoietic, self-referential, and embedded in relationships leading to ever-changing, emergent modes of being (Geyer, 1994).

Social, psychological, and educational researchers are often misled by the proposition that rationalism and positivism are behind us. In the twenty-first century, the argument goes, we are in a post-positivist era and researchers have the freedom to engage in qualitative, narrative-based, and interpretative forms of inquiry that abandon the rationalism and positivism of the ancient regime. As many scholars have argued, many of the newer modes of research that have emerged in the social sciences, psychology, and education over the last few decades retain elements of the positivist and rationalist credo. In this context research that follows particular linear, prescribed, cause-and-effect-oriented strategies of knowledge production can produce universal theories that will help predict and guide work in the social, psychological, and educational domains. As some researchers renounce the reductionism of positivism and rationalism, they enter into their research unaware of the ways such notions insidiously shape their rejection of particular subjugated and indigenous ways of seeing (Kincheloe and Steinberg, 1997; Semali and Kincheloe, 1999). The bricolage attempts to expose these hidden reductionistic assumptions for the purpose of unleashing a renaissance of complexity-driven creative, imaginative, innovative, and rigorous research.

Blinded by the ethos of rationalism, with its correct procedures and methods, researchers find it difficult to pass through the wormhole to complexity. The ghosts of rationalism and positivism haunt us in an era that claims epistemological liberation. The problems of sociology, cultural studies, anthropology, political science, communications, psychology, and education cannot be understood in the rationalism of disciplinary isolation. "Splendid isolation" does not work in the effort to understand systems that are interconnected and interdependent:

- Performance in school cannot be separated from socio-economic forces.
- The health of the ecosystem cannot be viewed in isolation from the poverty of Latin American, African, and Asian nations in the Southern Hemisphere.
- Political apathy in the USA cannot be separated from the new informational climate characteristic of what many observers refer to as hyperreality.

Research orientations haunted by the ghosts of rationalism and positivism are simply not capable of coping with the complexity that faces human beings. The bricolage, with its multiperspectival orientation, maintains that only a rigorous, diverse, discursively informed mode of research can deal with the messy dynamics of the *Lebenswelt*, human experience, and the interrelationship of phenomena. Formalism is another zombie of Cartesianism that haunts the house of research with its narrow assertion that words possess unambiguous and easily discernible meanings. Such clear meanings can be grasped via reason by researchers who employ rationality. Rationality in the formalist sense is an abstract system that operates in a transcultural and transhistorical manner unaffected by the discourses and the contexts that created it in the first place. The purpose of textual analysis and research in the formalist regime of truth is to determine what a text or an interviewee *really* means so it can be passed along to those residing outside the gated communities of the experts. Bricoleurs point out such reductionism and elitism when they see it and devise modes of analysis and inquiry that are more attuned to contingency and multiple possibilities in the Everglades of meaning-making (Thomas, 1998; Capra, 1996; Lomax and Parker, 1996).

All formalist claims to research validity rely on this unproblematized view of language and the process of representation. Bricoleurs are too conversant with the crisis of representation and the existence of language games to buy into claims of language as a neutral mechanism for reflecting reality. Positivist and rationalist data are as ideologically inscribed and contextually grounded as any other modes of knowledge. For all the effort we put into teaching crypto-formalist and positivist research methods, it is ironic that we live in a social cosmos understood through the filter of narrative devices and strategies. In all of the educational preparation for becoming researchers in these formalist and positivist contexts, students of inquiry are rarely exposed to meta-analytical orientations that facilitate the exposure of the effects of such narrative constructions. Such meta-analysis is an epistemological activity that is found in diverse locations. In the study of history bricoleurs find it in historiography; in literature they view it in literary theory; in poetry they uncover it in poetics; in other domains they find it in the study of discursive practices (Ward, 1995; Bruner, 1996).

Formalism in the midst of the anarchy of lived experience is a dead-end street. Essences cannot be finally determined when the phenomenon in question is constantly evolving, is a part of an ever-changing process, and is influenced by multiple contexts. Inquiry in such a domain is the job of the bricoleur – a researcher blessed with multiple perspectives, diverse tools, and flexible assumptions. The social world is not consistent, and if the formalists, rationalists, and positivists cannot accept such complication then serious problems emerge in academic domains dominated by such operatives. Recognizing their situatedness in the *Lebenswelt* of conflicting representations and the phenomenological specificity of micro-experiences, bricoleurs break the stranglehold of hyperrationality. The study of the social, cultural, psychological, and educational domains in particular is characterized by a degree of complexity that is dismissed by researchers operating in the hyperrational domain. Human beings do not act in automatic response to physical forces such as atmospheric pressure. Rather, humans are moved by intentional frames of mind that move them to act in unexpected and sometimes irrational ways. Researchers in this context are never quite sure why people do the things they do.

Thus, the complexity and indeterminacy of the situation forces them to turn to hermeneutics in the effort to interpret these actions and make sense of their motivations. Even those who have witnessed events and seek to describe them must employ their interpretative abilities for they possess no privileged view of the action (Bruner, 1996). Bricoleurs in this context, with their awareness of complexity, understand that there are always other views of the action that differ from their own. A central question facing them involves what to do about those other points of view. Moreover, when the bricoleur engages these other viewpoints they are never provided in a straightforward, transparent manner. Indeed, they are relayed via particular intonations, in the frames of the subjectivity of the speaker, customs, conventions, and cultures of conduct. Bricoleurs know that what they hear from the speaker is interpreted in light of the knowledges, histories, cultures, and understanding they share with them (Thomas, 1998). Their reporting of such conversations must always account for such complex filters. Such analysis allows them to escape from the haunted house of rationalism and formalist reductionism.

Rigour in Research as the Pursuit of Complexity: The Omnipresence of Power

The bricolage is grounded on the multidimensionality of the research act directed at better understanding and acting upon the complexity of the social, psychological, and educational world. The better research accomplishes this complicated task, we argue, the more it deserves to be described as rigorous. Our explorations of complexity touch upon foundational philosophical concerns such as the relationship between chaos and order, determinacy and randomness, and synthesis and analysis. When we add the phenomenon of emergence – the ways complex phenomena arise from the interaction of simple parts – the concept of complexity becomes an exciting new domain of study. Indeed, as maintained throughout this chapter and Chapter 1, it becomes a key aspect of any quest for rigour in knowledge production. Developing the theme that the world is more complex than we thought, bricoleurs familiar with complexity can no longer accept a unidimensional view of the world.

Understanding any knowledge in the context of complexity, we question the multitude of assumptions upon which it rests. In such a context we begin to ask questions of the world previously neglected. Thus, drawing on complexity and a multiplicity of discourses, the bricolage becomes a new way of thinking about all forms of research. Bricoleurs leave behind the normal science of the last 300 years, as they move into a new world of insight. Monological notions of centralized causes in the social, psychological, and educational worlds are deemed inadequate. In the emerging cosmos of the bricolage multiple perspectives reveal multiple causes. In such a universe knowledges previously relegated to the shadows by advocates of centralized causation re-emerge. Bricoleurs constantly seek to bring these shadow knowledges to the surface in order to examine their relationships to traditionally validated knowledges (Resnick and Wilensky, 1999; Fischer, 1998).

Such scholarly acts insert the academic back into the lived world, as bricoleurs seek diverse ways to cope with uncertainty. We gain the ability to reflect on our own and other knowledge producers' assumptions about the research act. In this reflection bricoleurs discern the ways such assumptions have shaped across history what humans think they know. Uncertainty thus becomes a historical reality as Cartesian certainty becomes a historical force that has shaped and continues to shape how human beings act in the world. If we act on the basis of what we think we know, then the epistemological system that provides certainty exerts a profound impact on what we do. Cartesian certainty becomes a power dynamic tacitly shaping the politics of everyday life. Thus, in a socio-political sense bricoleurs are alerted to the multidimensionality of power itself. And thus, the critical dimension of the bricolage re-emerges as attention is turned to the dynamics of power operating at every level of the research process. Understanding that power permeates every dimension of their work and that there are many forms of it, bricoleurs become students of power. Rigour in the study of the social, psychological, and educational domains demands a literacy of power and the ways power insidiously shapes all aspects of the research process (Roberts, 1998; Geyer, 1994; May, 1993).

There is nothing new about announcing that there is an important relationship between knowledge and power. Michel Foucault, of course, had a few things to say about this dynamic. The relationship between knowledge and power is nothing if not multilogical. Indeed, the connection between knowledge and power is constantly shifting in different historical eras. It manifests itself in different modes in different places and times, as well as in multiple forms in the same place and time. A central point in this context is that in many delineations of complexity circulating in the first decade of the twenty-first century recognition of this power dynamic is sorely missing. Bricoleurs understand that any act of research that claims the mantle of rigour must add an examination of the way power is implicated in knowledge production – one's own included. The effort to develop meta-analytical understanding of the way knowledge is constructed becomes a frivolous exercise outside this understanding of power.

Operating with a literacy of power as it shapes knowledge production, bricoleurs see through all one-dimensional portrayals of the world. Buoyed by these skills, bricoleurs appreciate the multilogical nature of humanness and all that such multiplicity implies in the effort to interpret and make sense of the world. In this complex, power-inscribed, and diverse context bricoleurs are forced to become the interdisciplinary border workers who labour continuously to understand and rearticulate the diverse scientific and imaginative lexicons they encounter at the boundaries. Such translation helps preclude the possibility that researchers will return to some monological and exclusive view of reality that answers all questions while soothing the furrowed brows of all knowledge workers. With their consciousness of complexity, bricoleurs turn their backs to the sirens of reductionism. In their piety they reject the formalist notion that there is one answer to any question and that one question in a domain has primacy over all others.

While they carefully examine compartmentalized knowledge, they refuse to be comforted by its 'objective' existence. The bricoleur's understanding that traditional disciplines fragment the world into these neat compartments is, after all, one of the primary reasons why she was originally drawn to the bricolage. When reductionistic researchers use their familiarity with the contents of the compartments to lay out unambiguous problems with unproblematic solutions, the bricoleur winces. Social, psychological, and educational problems are much too ambiguous and ill-defined to be recognized and solved so easily. It is the illusion produced by an inadequate epistemology that moves researchers to think that human problems can be conceptually isolated and solutions can be packaged in neat and tidy containers. There is no such thing as a problem that is merely psychological. The psychological domain is a social construction. When they mistake it for reality, researchers are ensnared in the trap of rationalism (Lomax and Parker, 1996; Tarnas, 1991).

On the Road with the Bricolage: Reporting from behind the Epistemological Curtain

Research is always a contested act. In every body of knowledge there is a history of conflict, set of power-related decisions about the process of research. In the move toward a more rigorous form of research bricoleurs maintain that the record of these contradictions be preserved. Epistemological, ideological, value-related conflicts shape the questions we ask, the decisions we make about the knowledge we produce. We should not be embarrassed by these conflicts but instead document them as testimony to the complexity of knowledge work. An important dimension of the bricolage involves learning to deal with conflict and ambiguity. Bricoleurs have to negotiate emerging situations, complex processes, multiple contexts, and accelerating social change. Importantly, they must operate in these vexing circumstances while protecting themselves from becoming immobilized in light of the complexity of it all.

In this conflictual context bricoleurs understand that the weight of history is on their side: researchers, no matter how hard many may try to force them, can never return *en masse* to a simplistic correspondence epistemology. Complexity subverts the notion once and for all that rigorous research reflects an objective reality. The processes of knowing and producing knowledge are no longer viewed as abstract individual processes but as cultural phenomena. The old epistemology is dead even though some governmental agencies, academic institutions, and institutes for research continue their attempt to revive it. Behind the formalist epistemological curtain the old order is crumbling. Indeed, no matter how hard rationalist and reductionists may try, they simply cannot get around researchers' need to interpret data and to apply it in the unique historical context of contemporary life. Interpretation and application by their nature rest in the domain of complexity.

With these ideas in mind bricoleurs pursue their most important goal. At the same time that they develop the scholarly rigour to address the long-repressed complexity of the world, they democratize the process of knowledge production. Here rests the magic of the bricolage: as researchers come to understand the multiple influences shaping their daunting task, they bring previously excluded people and categories of people into the process. 'Damn these usurpers', the blind monks of reductionism exclaim. Research in the bricolage is always viewed as one aspect of a larger political process involved with apportioning power and resources. The bricoleur knows that marginalized peoples have little to do with such a process. Once research is viewed as a humanly constructed process and not a transcultural and transhistorical universal enterprise, bricoleurs contend that diverse and conflicting perspectives can be viewed as a resource.

Culturally different knowledges, subjugated knowledges, indigenous knowledges help bricoleurs get beyond the limitations of their own local perspectives. The insights gained from these perspectives are central to their growth and development as knowledge producers. On numerous levels bricoleurs are dedicated to questioning and learning from the excluded. This is one of numerous ways that questions of moral judgement intersect with epistemological and research-based concerns. In this complex process of integrating the political, the epistemological, and the moral the agency of the researcher to make judgements and construct new knowledges is highlighted. Bricoleurs understand that they have more freedom within the process of knowledge production and knowledge application than was ever imagined behind the epistemological curtain. A key element of rigour in the bricolage involves the ability to use this freedom wisely and for socially and educationally compelling purposes (Blackler, 1995; Lomax and Parker, 1996; Richardson and Woolfolk, 1994; Williams, 1999).

Thus, in the pursuit of rigour in complexity bricoleurs expose the mechanistic ontologies that view the world as a fixture with moving parts. In their place they study fractals, questioning how such entities might extend the interpretative frameworks of social, psychological, and educational research. The concept of fractals emerged in the effort to confront the complexity of the physical world – in particular, the irregularity of the geometric shapes found in the natural world. The phenomenal aspect of fractals is that they are found not only in the whole of the entity under study but also in the smaller and smaller parts of the entity in question. Thus, the parts of a structure, at any level, are similar to the shape of the structure as a whole. Biologists, for example, find this property of self-similarity throughout nature as larger patterns repeat themselves over and over again at diverse scales (Lepani, 1998; Capra, 1996). Sociologists, for example, may be able to apply fractal geometry to the study of society in a refracted way as they examine the inscriptions of macro-social structures at the level of the group or the individual. Psychologists might apply such a concept to the study of the organization and structure of 'mind' at the micro level of the individual to larger patterns of collective manifestations of intelligence.

Thus, moving beyond the machine metaphors of Cartesianism to the complexity of fractals may help connect researchers from diverse fields to the complex ontology of the lived world. In this context the construction of the bricolage is in part an evolutionary process that connects human knowing and knowledge production to the zone of complexity (Lepani, 1998). In this process new levels of awareness are produced that can be deployed to produce new social arrangements and new ways of being human. Bricoleurs are excited by the possibilities posed by this new rigour in research. As new information technologies provide us unimagined access to data, new modes of writing and communication emerging in the technologies presently used in video games, and new cognitive skills associated with the multitasking involved with attending simultaneously to diverse electronic media, bricoleurs take note. All of these dynamics are relevant in the effort to develop new forms of rigour in the research act.

3

Questions of disciplinarity/ interdisciplinarity in a changing world

Joe L. Kincheloe

For those of us committed to theorizing and implementing the bricolage, there are some profound questions that need to be answered as we plot our course. As we think in terms of using multiple methods and perspectives in our research and attempt to synthesize contemporary developments in social theory, epistemology, and interpretation, we must consider the critiques of many diverse scholars. At the core of the deployment of bricolage in the discourse of research rests the question of disciplinarity/interdisciplinarity. Bricolage, of course, signifies interdisciplinarity – a concept that serves as a magnet for controversy in the contemporary academy. Researching this book, I listened to several colleagues maintain that if one is focused on getting tenure, one should eschew interdisciplinarity; if one is interested in only doing good research, one should embrace it.

Implicit in the critique of interdisciplinarity and thus of bricolage as its manifestation in research is the assumption that interdisciplinarity is by nature superficial. Superficiality results when scholars, researchers, and students fail to devote sufficient time to understanding the disciplinary fields and knowledge bases from which particular modes of research emanate. Many maintain that such an effort leads not only to superficiality but also to madness. Attempting to know so much, the bricoleur not only knows nothing well but also goes crazy in the misguided process (McLeod, 2000; Palmer, 1996; Friedman, 1998). I respect these questions and concerns but argue that given the social, cultural, epistemological, and paradigmatic upheavals and alterations of the last few decades, rigorous researchers may no longer enjoy the luxury of choosing whether or not to embrace the bricolage (McLeod, 2000; Friedman, 1998).

The Great Implosion: Dealing with the Debris of Disciplinarity

Once understanding of the limits of objective science and its universal knowledge escaped from the genie's bottle, there was no going back. Despite the best efforts to recover 'what was lost' in the implosion of social science, too many researchers understand its socially constructed nature, its value-laden products that operate under the flag of objectivity, its avoidance of contextual specificities that subvert the stability of its structures, and its fragmenting impulse that moves it to fold its methodologies and the knowledge they produce neatly into disciplinary drawers. My argument here is that we must operate in the ruins of the temple, in a post-apocalyptic social, cultural, psychological, and educational science where certainty and stability have long departed for parts unknown.

In the best sense of Lévi-Strauss's concept, bricoleurs pick up the pieces of what is left and paste them together as best they can. The critics are probably correct, such a daunting task cannot be accomplished in the timespan of a doctoral programme; but the process can be named and the dimensions of a lifetime scholarly pursuit can be in part delineated. Our transcendence of the old regime's reductionism and our understanding of the complexity of the research task demand the lifetime effort. It is this lifetime commitment to study, clarify, sophisticate, and add to the bricolage that this essay advocates.

As bricoleurs recognize the limitations of a single method, the discursive strictures of one disciplinary approach, what is missed by traditional practices of validation, the historicity of certified modes of knowledge production, the inseparability of knower and known, and the complexity and heterogeneity of all human experience, they understand the necessity of new forms of rigour in the research process. To account for their cognizance of such complexity bricoleurs seek a rigour that alerts them to new ontological insights. In this ontological context they can no longer accept the status of an object of inquiry as a thing-in-itself. Any social, cultural, psychological, or pedagogical object of inquiry is inseparable from its context, the language used to describe it, its historical situatedness in a larger ongoing process, and the socially and culturally constructed interpretations of its meaning(s) as an entity in the world (Morawski, 1997).

Rigour in the Ruins

Thus, the bricolage is concerned not only with multiple methods of inquiry but also with diverse theoretical and philosophical notions of the various elements encountered in the research act. Bricoleurs understand that the ways these dynamics are addressed – whether overtly or tacitly – exert profound influence on the nature of the knowledge produced by researchers. Thus, these aspects of research possess important lived world political consequences, as they shape the ways we come to view the social cosmos and operate within it (Blommaert, 1997). In this context Douglas Kellner's (1995) notion of a 'multiperspectival cultural studies' is helpful, as it draws upon numerous textual and critical strategies to 'interpret, criticize, and deconstruct' the cultural artefacts under observation.

Employing Nietzsche's notion of perspectivism to ground his version of a multimethodological research strategy, Kellner maintains that any single research perspective is laden with assumptions, blindnesses, and limitations. To avoid one-sided reductionism, he maintains that researchers must learn a variety of ways of seeing and interpreting in the pursuit of knowledge. The more perspectival variety a researcher employs, Kellner concludes, the more dimensions and consequences of a text will be illuminated. Kellner's multiperspectivism resonates with Denzin and Lincoln's bricolage and its concept of 'blurred genres'. To better 'interpret, criticize, and deconstruct' Denzin and Lincoln (2000) call for bricoleurs to employ 'hermeneutics, structuralism, semiotics, phenomenology, cultural studies, and feminism' (p. 3). Embedded in Kellner, Denzin, and Lincoln's calls is the proto-articulation of a new rigour – certainly in research, but with implications for scholarship and pedagogy in general.

This rigour in the ruins of traditional disciplinarity connects a particular concept – in contemporary education, for example, the call for educational standards – to the epistemological, ontological, cultural, social, political, economic, psychological, and pedagogical domains for the purpose of multiperspectival analysis. In the second edition of their *Handbook of Qualitative Research*, Denzin and Lincoln (2000) maintain that this process has already taken place to some extent; they refer to it as a two-way methodological diaspora where humanists migrated to the social sciences and social scientists to the humanities. Ethnographic methodologists snuggled up with textual analysts; in this context the miscegenation of the empirical and the interpretative produced the bricoleur love-child.

Thus, in the early twenty-first century disciplinary demarcations no longer shape, in the manner they once did, the way scholars look at the world. Indeed, disciplinary boundaries have less and less to do with the way scholars group themselves and build intellectual communities. Furthermore, what we refer to as the traditional disciplines in the first decade of the twenty-first century are anything but fixed, uniform, and monolithic structures. It is not uncommon for contemporary scholars in a particular discipline to report that they find more commonalities with individuals in different fields of study than they do with colleagues in their own disciplines. We occupy a scholarly world with faded disciplinary boundary lines. Thus, the point need not be made that bricolage should take place – it already has and is continuing. The research work needed in this context involves opening an elastic conversation about the ways such a bricolage can be rigorously developed. Such cultivation should not take place in pursuit of some form of proceduralization but in an effort to better understand the beast and to realize its profound possibilities (Young and Yarbrough, 1993; Palmer, 1996; Friedman, 1998).

Bricolage and the Dialectical View of Disciplinarity

Questions of disciplinarity permeate efforts to theorize the research bricolage. Exploring such inquiries, one notes a consistent division between disciplinarians and interdisciplinarians: disciplinarians maintain that interdisciplinary approaches to analysis and research result in superficiality; interdisciplinary proponents argue that disciplinarity produces naive overspecialization. The vision of the bricolage promoted here recognizes the dialectical nature of this disciplinary and interdisciplinary relationship and calls for a synergistic interaction between the two concepts. Before one can engage successfully in the bricolage it is important to develop a rigorous understanding of the ways traditional disciplines have operated. I maintain the best way to do this is to study the workings of a particular discipline. In the context of becoming a bricoleur such a study would not take place in the traditional manner where scholars learned to accept the conventions of a particular discipline as a natural way of producing knowledge and viewing a particular aspect of the world.

Instead, such a disciplinary study would be conducted more like a Foucauldian genealogy where scholars would study the social construction of the discipline's knowledge bases, epistemologies, and knowledge-production methodologies. As scholars analysed the historical origins of the field, they would trace the emergence of various schools of thought, conflicts within the discipline, and the nature and effects of paradigmatic changes. In this genealogical context they would explore the discipline as a discursive system of regulatory power with its propensity to impound knowledge within arbitrary and exclusive boundaries. In this context scholars would come to understand the ideological dimensions of the discipline and the ways knowledge is produced for the purposes of supporting various power blocs.

It is not contradictory, I assert, to argue in a dialectical spirit that at the same time as this genealogical analysis is taking place, bricoleurs would also be studying positive features of the discipline. Even though the discipline operates in a power-saturated and regulatory manner, disciplinarians have often developed important models for engaging in a methodical, persistent, and well-coordinated process of knowledge production. Obviously, there are examples not only of genius within these domains but also of great triumphs of scholarly breakthroughs leading to improvements in the human condition. The diverse understanding of these types of disciplinary practices empowers bricoleur to ask compelling questions of other disciplines they will encounter. Such smart questions will facilitate the researchers' capacity to make use of positive contributions of disciplines while avoiding disciplinary parochialism and domination.

As bricoleurs pursue this dialectic of disciplinarity, gaining a deep knowledge of the literature and conversations within a field, they would concurrently examine both the etymology and the critique of what many refer to as the disciplines' arbitrary demarcations for arranging knowledge and structuring research. In a critical context bricoleurs would develop a power literacy to facilitate their understanding of the nature and effects of the web of power relations underlying a discipline's official research methodologies. Here bricoleurs would trace the ways these power dynamics shaped the knowledge produced within the disciplinary research tradition. Learning multiple lessons from their in-depth study of the discipline in particular and disciplinarity in general, the bricoleurs becomes expert in the relationships connecting cultural context, meaning-making, power, and oppression within disciplinary boundaries. Their rigorous understanding of these dynamics possibly makes them more aware of the influence of such factors on the everyday practices of the discipline than those who have traditionally operated as scholars within the discipline (Friedman, 1998; Morawski, 1997; Lutz *et al.*, 1997).

Disciplines as Discourses

Disciplinary histories and discursive analyses are irrelevant to formalists, rationalists, and positivists. A historically grounded discursive analysis of a field to such Cartesian researchers is merely a quaint chronicle of accomplishments in which old truths are simply replaced by contemporary new truths. There are no disjunctions, no fissures to such a chronicle, as the discipline develops in a linear process. Through continued experimentation truth is discovered and all that came before it is relegated to the elephant burial grounds of disciplinary history. In the bricolage's rigorous dialectic of disciplinarity, historical analysis is an ongoing project within research. Such historical work is not a mere ornament that exists apart from the 'real work' of the discipline. It is a necessary everyday dimension of rigorous and complex scholarship, as such analysis helps researchers identify the discourses that have shaped particular ways of collecting data, interpreting (both consciously and unconsciously) data, constructing narratives, and critiquing one another's scholarship.

Awareness of these dynamics creates a meta-level consciousness of the ways unexamined assumptions shape both research in the discipline in general and one's own inquiry in particular (Madison, 1988; Gee *et al.*, 1996). Bricoleurs with this historically informed discursive under-standing of a discipline know a field in the context of how it has been used in the world and who used it and for what purposes. In light of our notion of the dialectic of disciplinarity, bricoleurs understand diverse aspects of a discipline, in the process coming to understand the cognitive, epistemological, political, and ontological limitations of a field of study.

We are defining this as a profound act of rigour in the work of a researcher. Indeed, what bricoleurs are studying here are a discipline's rules of construction. Always aware of the complexity permeating knowledge production, bricoleurs understand that in order to survive, disciplines had to embrace particular features and structures at specific historical points in their development. Often such dimensions live on in new epochs of disciplinary history, serving no pragmatic purpose other than to fulfil the demands of unconscious tradition. When the bricoleur's historical and discursive study uncovers such anachronistic dynamics, they can be removed as part of the effort to facilitate more rigorous and pragmatic research.

Only when researchers understand the etymology of particular dis-ciplinary values and specific disciplinary research practices can they gain the freedom to innovate in ways that make a difference. Indeed, the construction of the bricolage is simply not possible without previous decades (nay, centuries) of such etymological work. In these efforts the purpose is not the necrophilic fetishization of the glorious past or of our exalted forefathers. Disciplinary origins are multilogical in character – they come from many locales and involve many individuals. Also, dis-ciplines do not emerge amidst balloons, fireworks, and parades. Dis-ciplines emerge in murky, unnoticed, and often quite lowly places. In this context naive notions of truth fade into their horizons, as bricoleurs find the long-lost DNA of disciplinary history. In light of such evidence the 'progress' enabled by a discipline's unfolding of truth does not look so progressive. Indeed, that viewed as truth reveals its discursive con-struction as bricoleurs make distinctions between correspondence and construction. What has passed as the truth of the discipline is less a correspondence to an objective conception of reality than a construction by particular knowledge workers operating in a particular discursively produced language game.

In these activities bricoleurs engage in a political analysis of a discipline's role in the world. What difference does a discipline make? What is its mark on the world? What is its relationship to other disciplines around it? Does it imitate them? Do they imitate it? What is the discipline's relation to practice? These are the types of questions bricoleurs seek to answer about the knowledge traditions on which they draw and about their own knowledge work itself. Moreover, in the social and behaviour sciences, for example, the answers to such questions help bricoleurs understand how particular moral norms, specific modes of public behaviour, and certain belief systems shaped and were shaped by these knowledge traditions. Such knowledge in a critical context is emancipatory, as it empowers bricoleurs to make informed decisions about the conduct of their lives and their work. As Foucault argued, it is in the often overlooked practices of the disciplines that researchers understand the way power works to oppress and regulate (Foucault, 1980; May, 1993). Bricoleurs pay close attention to these ostensibly insignificant disciplinary dynamics.

Disciplines and Paradigms

Another analytical tool bricoleurs use in their study of disciplines is the paradigm. Over the last 40 years researchers in the social, psychological, and educational domains have come to examine disciplinary work via the application of Thomas Kuhn's (1962) concept of paradigmatic change. In this context these paradigms or models of making sense of the part of the world a discipline engages are uncovered in different moments in a discipline's historical development. Aware of paradigms, researchers turn their attention to 'scientific crises' and the ways such problems are resolved using prevalent definitions of 'progress' employed in the discipline. Operating as formal discourses, diverse paradigms shape both knowledge production in the field and the professional lives of those researchers who work in the area.

The emergence of these diverse paradigms has been influenced by the perception of a breakdown of influential narratives of dominant Western culture during the last third of the twentieth century. During this period many scholars posited the existence of a 'postmodern condition' characterized by a cultural logic that resisted the efficacy of the 'grand narratives' of Western culture. As a result of these diverse paradigms, researchers operating in differing theoretical domains have found it increasingly difficult to communicate across the conceptual chasms. Awareness of the paradigmatic dimensions of disciplines has moved knowledge workers to question whether science is a universal practice driven by objective rules and procedures or a socially constructed practice shaped by the worldviews of individuals living in a particular place and time.

In this paradigmatic context bricoleurs ask numerous questions. If a researcher, for example, becomes aware of different cultures and different historical periods and the models for viewing domains covered by the social, psychological, and educational sciences found therein, what impact does this awareness have on the 'normal science' of the disciplines? Could such cultural and historical diversity be extended by awareness in the realms of gender, socio-economic class, religion, sexuality, and so on? Extrapolating from these understandings, bricoleurs maintain that all paradigmatic modes of disciplinarity and research are both constructed and legitimated by larger social and cultural practices.

This adds a layer of complexity not appreciated before the emergence of the conversation about paradigms. Indeed, paradigmatic awareness, bricoleurs maintain, has served to alert researchers to the regressive tendencies of normal sciences. For example, the tradition Cartesian paradigm in the social, psychological, and educational domains served to turn researchers' attention away from studying problems that were not easily reduced to the form of a puzzle. Old paradigm sociologists, for example, often did not possess the disciplinary and analytical tools to articulate ill-defined and non-puzzle-like problems (Kuhn, 1962; Shaker and Kridel, 1989).

Paradigmatic analyses of a discipline create a meta-awareness, an insight into the construction of its approaches to perceiving and operating in the world around it. In the transformed paradigms that emerged in the 1970s and 1980s researcher attention began to be focused not as much on observation statements, theories, and generalizations, but rather on larger overviews of research traditions. A research tradition is a constellation of assumptions concerning the 'appropriate methods' students of a discipline use in a their studies and the procedures they employ for developing theories about the area (Haggerson, 2000). Science educator Koshi Dhingra (2004) articulates this notion in the domain of pedagogical research and practice:

> Is science a collections of facts or truths or is science a dynamic body of tentative knowledge claims which depend upon social negotiation and which may change depending upon the operating research paradigm and the socio-political climate under which science works? The former depiction is in keeping with positivist notions of science in which knowable truths about the world are directly accessed by our senses. The latter depiction is in keeping with a range of postpositivist philosophies of science, all of which have in common the notion that knowledge is constructed by

people, whose interpretations are affected by their situations. I propose that that this latter, more complex set perspectives is the vantage point of the critical thinker. What implications does such a position have on one's views on the nature of scientific theories, laws and the so-called scientific method?

In this same context Francisco Varela (1999) writes about a long-overdue paradigm shift in cognitive science. Moving away from objective notions of disciplinary work that in their disinterestedness produce pure theoretical knowledges untainted by the biases of context or researcher perspective, Varela's concept of a paradigm shift emerges:

> there are strong indications that within the loose federation of sciences dealing with knowledge and cognition – the cognitive sciences – the conviction is slowly growing that this picture is upside down and that a radical paradigm shift is imminent. At the very center of this emerging view is the conviction that the proper units of knowledge are primarily *concrete*, embodied, incorporated, lived; that knowledge is about situatedness; and that the uniqueness of knowledge, its historicity and context, is not a 'noise' concealing an abstract configuration in its true essence. The concrete is not a step toward something else; it is both where we are and how we get to where we will be. (p. 7)

Picking up on these ideas, the bricolage seeks a complex transgressive relationship to disciplinarity and paradigmatic change. Realizing that pristine, virginal knowledge does not exist and that disciplinary practices are not developed in a rational, linear and fully conscious manner, bricoleurs are looking for a *modus operandi* in this epistemological sea of chaos. Since paradigmatic change is inevitable and what we are writing here will be seen as quaint and dated in 2063, advocates of the bricolage resist grandiose claims for the knowledge they produce. Bricoleurs are not the crazed transgressors but the chroniclers of difference and its never-ending presence and influence. As such bricoleurs are cat burglars who 'appropriate' paradigm theory's notion 'normal science' for the transgressive purpose of never allowing their work to be sucked into its life-disaffirming black hole. This move is not an attempt to 'vogue' the role of avant-garde theorists and position oneself as a matinee scholar. Indeed, it is just the opposite – an effort never to let the ego gratification of the limelight dull the transgressive duty to expose the unexamined paradigmatic assumptions of the new normality.

Disciplinary work in the paradigmatic comfort of normal science weakens the researcher's resolve to bring to the surface tacit methodological and ontological assumptions. It undermines a researcher's concern with locating the source of a discipline's choice of research problems and the objectives of its programme of inquiry. Indeed, normal science subverts the researcher's interest in examining the role of the researcher in the act of inquiry. Does she stand at the periphery of the action and employ her research instruments to measure particular aspects of what is happening? Or does she jump in, celebrate her subjective relationship to the scene at hand, and attempt to make a positive change in it? Does she seek difference in the form of subjugated knowledges, counter-paradigmatic perspectives, and non-Western vantage points? Does she study linguistic constructions of the act of inquiry, analysing the difference between the world itself and the linguistic representation of it? Discursive and paradigmatic understandings of disciplines enhance the bricoleur's ability to move beyond the norm, to engage in unprecedented forms of knowledge production.

Disciplines, Paradigms, and New Forms of Relationship

This effort to engage in unprecedented forms of knowledge production is directly connected to what we are referring to as a new rigour in research. Picking up on the best ideas emerging from the new disciplinary paradigms of the last forty years, bricoleurs pursue this rigour via such concepts as the importance of relationship in epistemological and ontological frameworks. From so many domains – such as physics, theology, and popular culture – numerous individuals have articulated a desire for a more connected vision of self, vocation, and scholarship. Some of these articulations have been trite and fatuous, while others have raised serious possibilities for rethinking everything from cognition to knowledge production. The much-documented alienation of the modern psyche has motivated modern individuals to engage in activities that reconnect them to both the cosmos and each other. This relational cosmology suggests the integrated nature of the universe itself with its wide variety of life forms. Such a notion can lead a lesser scholar to the hell of spiritual claptrap with its facile pronouncements that we are all one – 'we are the world . . .' On the other hand, a well-informed bricoleur can separate the wisdom in such understandings from the intellectual chaff, the profundity from the frippery (Tarnas, 1991; O'Sullivan, 1999).

In the basic spirit of the bricolage this is not an all-or-nothing situation. Taking a cue from the work of many feminist theorists over the past couple of decades, bricoleurs pick and choose carefully from the paradigmatic grab-bag of the disciplines. Though it is associated with the new and the innovative, the bricolage is unembarrassed in its selection of what might be called 'modernist concepts'. Bricoleurs clearly see the possibilities existing within modernist conceptions of human agency, justice, and democratic politics. No babies are floating in streams of bathwater here. Even as it interrogates modernism's propensity for constructing universal laws of history or human development, the bricolage is sifting through the modernist rubble to poach modernist genius. In this context bricoleurs flatly reject some simple binarism between a decontextualized notion of modernism and postmodernism. It is more complex that that. Any insight into new paradigmatic notions of the power of relationship must be firmly grounded in a political project to address human suffering with its obligatory literacy of power before it can be brought into the bricolage (Giroux, 1997; McLaren, 2001).

Thus, viewed from the complex vantage point of our no-nonsense politics of agency, justice, and democracy, the multidimensional quest for relationship can get past the tendency for trivialization. In this context we can begin to understand the ecological base of our concept of relationality and the ways it can help us rethink disciplinarity and the knowledge work it supports. Monological forms of information produced in reductionistic disciplines are typically unconnected modes of knowledge alienated from other ways of knowing and being. An autistic epistemology is at work here that operates best when all parties work in isolation, within the closed boundaries of monolithic and self-sufficient disciplines. When things are proceeding as they should, abstract individuals produce data about the fragment of the world the discipline is authorized to examine. The proper ontological state in this context is solitary. Even the polity in which these *solitary men* live is described as a contractual arrangement of 'social atoms'. Even the *concept* – not to mention the lived *enaction* – of community in this context is truncated.

In this isolation – this absence of relationship – Westerners have ignored difference. They have often produced an arrogant knowledge that ignores ways of perceiving inscribed with cosmological consequence. Bricoleurs, aware of these Cartesian failings, seek relationship and dialogue with those who see the world differently. The point is not to romanticize such individuals and appropriate their knowledges but to generate new edified perspectives and more sophisticated ways of knowing and inquiring (Giroux, 1997; O'Sullivan, 1999). Bricoleurs believe that this generative process takes place when present perspectives are connected to larger structures and supersystems. As individuals and groups come to see their assumptions in light of diverse epistemologies, ontologies, and cosmologies, they begin to imagine other ways of thinking about everyday life and the quest to make sense of it. Drawing upon my work in postformalism, Ray Horn (2000) writes about this process. Rarely do professionals and various types of knowledge workers

> engage in reflective thinking that entails a consideration of the origins of their culture, the way their knowledge is produced (etymology), the deeper, more complex systemic realities of their

situation (pattern), the apparent certainties of their professional lives (process), and the intricate context of their setting (contextualization). When educational change or an educational problem occurs, how often does the community that must engage the problem pause and converse about the relationship of their culture to the problem, the ways in which the problem is embedded or will affect the sub-systems in the schools system, the need to rethink what they believe to be certain, or the importance of place and time to the change or problem? (pp. 84–5).

The concerns Horn raises here are central to the notion of relationship in the bricolage. Moreover, I like the way he uses the example of an educational practitioner to illustrate his point – the implication being that a wide variety of individuals from diverse backgrounds can make use of the research orientations of the bricolage in their everyday vocational lives. In the ideological spirit of its genesis the bricolage is not only for high theorists and researchers operating in the arcane confines of research universities. As we think about our relationships with the planet and the ecological dimensions of such connections (cosmology), with knowledge and the way we view the world (epistemology), and with the notion of being itself and ways we define humanness (ontology), we begin a process that John Dewey (1916) referred to as 'reconstructing our experience'.

In this context we transcend the age of mediocrity that subverts efforts to develop better ways of making meaning and being/becoming human. In an age of mediocrity, efforts to push past the rationalistic and reductionistic boundaries that contain our imagination are often viewed as an attack on all that western societies hold sacred. The bricolage uses its synergistic relationships to cultivate the art of imagination within the social, psychological, and educational domains. In this context the importance of the disciplines has more to do with their relationships both to one another and to these larger questions. Bricoleurs see the power of disciplines not in the truths they own but in their kinetic possibilities that emerge in relationship.

Knowing this, bricoleurs are ready to consider the development of alternative rationalities grounded on a critically inscribed notion of relationship. Understanding that the 'fundamentalist rationalist' view that the disciplines will provide a comprehensive solution to all our problems is moribund, bricoleurs seek a new complex terrain of rigorous analysis. Bricoleurs are not satisfied that the rationalism of traditional Western disciplinarity is the ultimate expression of human possibility. Indeed, there is even an irrationality operating in some aspects of the mainstream social, psychological, and educational disciplinary view of intelligence and reason. A key aspect of producing reason and intelligence involves excluding those others who are 'unreasonable' and 'unintelligent'.

As we have examined these individuals excluded from the community of the rational throughout the history of many of these disciplines, they consistently seem to be those people who are culturally, racially, sexually, genderly, and/or economically different from the experts creating the classification system. This is disciplinary power operating at its regulatory 'best'. Thus, a basic feature of a rigorous alternate rationality involves the recognition that the traditional disciplines tended to designate an individual or a group as sophisticated to the degree that they reflected the disciplinarians' view of themselves. Bricoleurs maintain that researchers can do better than this.

Expanding the Concept of Relationship in the Bricolage: Symbiotic Hermeneutics in the Disciplines

While we will explore interpretation and hermeneutics in more detail in Chapter 4, a brief hermeneutic detour is in order in this discussion of disciplinarity in a changing world. As previously mentioned in both Chapters 1 and 2, hermeneutics is a central dimension of the bricolage. In Chapter 1 we discussed the importance of critical hermeneutics, while in Chapter 2 we alluded to the necessity of hermeneutic interpretation in all research. Here we introduce the concept of symbiotic hermeneutics, or relational hermeneutics, in the effort to develop the importance of relationality in all forms of disciplinary work. In their attempt to push disciplinary boundaries bricoleurs maintain that the quest for relationships results in the revelation of new contexts in which to view a phenomenon.

In symbiotic hermeneutics the process of interpretation and meaning-making is directly tied to exposure of relationships. In no way are bricoleurs looking for 'a correct relationship'. There are always multiple relationships, and as time passes new relationships will be discerned that were occluded in a different episteme or *Zeitgeist*. Thus, Cartesian notions of finality are avoided as cultural logics are always changing and producing new ways of making meaning (Grondin, 1994; Capra *et al.*, 1991; Vattimo, 1994; Madison, 1988). In this context disciplinary knowledge is contingent, always in process, and not universally true for all time. It must always be updated and re-energized in light of new times. Again, knowledge work and research are seen as more complex than scholars originally posited.

In the first decade of the twenty-first century the capacity to establish relationships with difference is enhanced by a couple of factors. Symbiotic hermeneutics, as used by bricoleurs, sees great possibility in global communications that potentially allow everyone to communicate with everyone else. No discipline should remain isolated in such a context. Also, such hermeneuts see great prospect in the continuing but always contested anti-colonial rebellion that emerged in Africa, Latin America, and many parts of Asia in the 1940s and 1950s. This rebellion conceptually framed and catalysed the civil rights movement, the women's movement, the anti-Vietnam War movement, and the gay rights movement in the USA in the 1960s and 1970s.

All of these movements, including indigenous peoples' movements around the world, can be connected to a more general postcolonialism that signifies their origins in these global liberation movements. Both of these factors allow for forms of interaction unimaginable before their occurrence. Bricoleurs urge scholars in the disciplines to study the impact of global communications via the Internet, TV, and radio on knowledge work. They also encourage scholars to examine what happens when global communications intersect with the postcolonial movements. In this symbiotic relationship new insights and new ways of thinking about knowing and researching emerge. The ecological consciousness produced by an awareness of the infinite ways phenomena are connected rests at the heart of symbiotic hermeneutics. Disciplines cannot remain the same when finding generative relationships is viewed as a basic dimension of knowledge work. This pursuit of relationality becomes a central effort to engage in rigorous scholarship in the ruins of traditional disciplinarity.

Attention to the ecumenicalism of the bricolage's concern both with multiple perspectives and with symbiotic hermeneutics' focus on the relationships connecting such diverse viewpoints profoundly changes the work of disciplines. This relational ontology causes us to focus not on things-in-themselves or simply on abstract individuals. In such a context symbiotic hermeneutics helps bricoleurs understand that the way human beings develop their identity is not by isolating themselves to find their 'true nature', but through their relationships with others. The ontological principle at work here involves not only the cultivation of human subjectivity but also the production of all living beings and inanimate objects.

The internal features of all patterns in both the physical and the social worlds are not simply intrinsic but emerge in relationship to other patterns and processes. This reveals itself in various types of research. In historical research, for example, an effort to study a historical event outside of the multiple contexts that shape it or the social, cultural, economic, and political processes of which it is a part will produce trivial research. The historical event obtains its meaning and significance in relation to these other dynamics. The historian finds deeper and more revealing meanings for an event, as she uncovers more and more previously unexplored relationships (Rosen, 1987; Capra *et al.* 1991; Jardine, 1998; Smith, 1999).

Thus, symbiotic hermeneutics maintains that all people, places, and things are parts of greater unities. The multiperspectival nature of the bricolage helps researchers reveal relationships and tune into these larger unities. Individuals become fully human by revealing these processes in their own lives. Research develops a higher degree of rigour by revealing these processes in the world of ideas and information. In this way the relational ontology pushes the boundaries of Newtonian science, as it refutes the notion that more than one object can occupy the same space. Relationships by their nature position objects in the same space. We are together in this relationship – we occupy it together. These two historical events share a relationship. These six social forces share a relationship that conceptually brings them together.

Such relationality forces the emergence of a new paradigm, a new focus for research. Indeed, the relationships are symbiotic, as they mutually enhance their parts. To use the cliché, the relationship is greater than the sum of the parts (Kogler, 1996; Rapko, 1998; Capra *et al.*, 1991). As bricoleurs explore these dynamics they connect the ecological and the ecumenical to the critical. Emphasizing the numerous common bonds connecting human beings, the physical world, and the political domain, bricoleurs emphasize the human responsibility to work toward egalitarianism and justice. Research in this context can never be disinterested or important simply for its own sake. There are too many critically grounded goals toward which it is directed that affect us all in our interconnection. The disciplines are liberated from their cloisters.

Einstein as Bricoleur: Symbiotic Hermeneutics and the Discipline of Physics

With these points made, bricoleurs move symbiotic hermeneutics into the domain of physical science. We have stayed away from the 'hard sciences' in the construction of the bricolage, but make one short foray into the domain here to illustrate both the multiple influences that shape the bricolage and the diverse locales where it can be applied. The distrust of the physical sciences has grown dramatically in the wake of the anti-colonial rebellions over the past sixty years. There is frustration with such science's frequent dismissal of its responsibility in areas such as

- the misuse of non-renewable resources,
- the exploitation of people living in non-industrial societies,
- the production of private, concentrated wealth,
- the careless use of technology,

- the environmentally destructive disposal of waste,
- the construction of war machines.

Around the globe people are hungry for a more responsible, smarter science. Obviously, the ecumenical spirit of the bricolage can help physicists, biologists, chemists, engineers, geologists, and other physical scientists gain broader perspectives on the nature of their research activities. Employing our symbiotic hermeneutics, scientists from these disciplines begin to rethink the boundaries of, say, chemistry. In this context chemists who combine their study of the discipline with work in economics, philosophy, and human geography are viewed as rigorous scholars, not dilettantes. In their pursuit of multiple perspectives they realize they can never go back to a chemistry that rests simply in an isolated and monological space. Relational hermeneutics has permanently changed the discipline.

Using the bricolage, physical scientists can begin to address public misgivings about their work. As critical cultural workers they transcend Cartesian modes of seeing the world and their disciplines as simply 'as they are or appear to be'. In the spirit of criticality they view them in their immanence; they construct the world and their disciplines in the dialectic relationship between being and becoming. The critical vision of the bricolage moves them to make themselves, their disciplines, and the world anew. In this context the bricolage follows in the footsteps of Albert Einstein (Kincheloe et al., 1999b) and his initiation of a paradigmatic explosion in physics. The revolution he initiated in 1905 takes researchers to new domains. Sometimes these new domains are places in which the researcher may not feel very comfortable – as was the case of Einstein as the revolution in physics evolved. In this context the bricolage pressures the guardians of the disciplines to join a cognitive and intellectual revolution taking place in the detritus of disciplinarity (Kovel, 1998; Woods and Grant, 1998; Peyton, 1996).

Drawing upon symbiotic hermeneutics, this revolution confronts some of the basic assumptions of the physical sciences. The meaning of empiricism, with its concept of sensory knowledge forming the epistemological basis of science, for example, is brought into question. Indeed, symbiotic hermeneutics unabashedly focuses on relationships that typically cannot be heard, smelled, viewed, felt, or tasted. Einstein employed what we are calling symbiotic hermeneutics in his work in physics, often focusing on the 'no-thing' of physical reality rather than things-in-themselves. For example, his general theory of relativity put to rest the notion that gravity was a thing. For a quarter of millennium physicists since Newton had debated whether gravity was a particle (a graviton) or a wave. The general theory of relativity pointed out that it was neither, *and* neither was it a thing or, more in the lexicon of philosophy, a substance. Gravity, Einstein proclaimed, resulted from a *relationship* among mass, space as a fabric, and time. His famous rubber sheet experiment provided the explanatory mechanism, as he placed bowling balls, billiard balls, and buckshot (which he called BB shot) on a taut rubber sheet to illustrate the interaction of the parts.

Stretching a rubber sheet over a large baking dish, Einstein demonstrated that when a bowling ball or a BB is placed on it the sheet is bent or warped around the objects. This distortion, he argued, exemplifies what massive objects such as the sun or the moon do to the fabric of space. The rubber sheet is flat when no objects are place on it. Einstein referred to this as the absence of gravity. When the bowling ball depresses the sheet, the curvature around the depression represents a gravitational field. A BB rolled along the sheet will fall into the trough just as an asteroid will fall to Earth if it gets too close to it. The more massive the object, the greater the bending of space. The bowling ball will distort the sheet, bend space, more than the BB.

The general theory of relativity is all about the power of relationship. Cartesian ways of thinking in the discipline of physics had focused physicists' attention on things-in-themselves for 250 years. Always the genius, Einstein understood the implications of his work for researchers in general. Thinking in an epistemological context, he once argued that the more relationships one can find, the more powerful the impact of one's theory (Peyton, 1996). Still, in the first decade of the twenty-first century the epistemological and ontological dimensions and implications of Einstein's work are not generally understood, even in academia.

Thus, a central task of bricoleurs is to search for new relationships that provide insights into new dimensions of the lived world. In their aversion to the unconnected disinterestedness of forms of positivistic and rationalistic modes of analysis, bricoleurs are careful not to turn to a nebulous intuitionism or a corrupt relativism. Neither do they seek the comfort of unexamined warm and interconnected mystical feelings about their oneness with the world. There is too much injustice, too many people in pain, and much cultural work needed to address these dark realities (Bookchin, 1995).

As an alternative to the shortcomings of Cartesianism, bricoleurs seek a more rigorous path. In this context bricoleurs develop principles of selection not only of research-orientations but also of what interconnections they attend. They choose particular interconnections because of their relevance to the alleviation of human suffering and the cultivation of the intellect. Thus, they seek both social and personal change. The better the researcher I become, the more valuable I am in the effort to promote democracy and ease pain. Indeed, individual understanding and critical social change are synergistic, not antagonistic. Thus, in the pluralistic logic of the bricolage we seek large-scale interconnections in the political, aesthetic, social, cultural, economic, moral, psychological, philosophical, cognitive, and educational domains.

Indigenous Knowledges and Disciplinarity: Studying Models of Interconnectedness and Difference

Always looking for insight in diverse places, bricoleurs examine disciplinarity and interconnectedness via the lens of indigenous knowledges. Many systems of indigenous knowledge illustrate the *enaction* of interconnectedness and raise profound questions about the ways Western scholars have defined disciplinary knowledges. While there is great diversity in these so-called indigenous knowledges, most assume that humans are part of the world of nature. Extending this holism, many indigenous scholars maintain that the production and acquisition of knowledge involves a process of interactions among the human body, the mind, and the spirit (Dei, 1995). Mosha (2000) writes that among the East African Chagga people knowledge that is passed along to others must further the development of morality, goodness, harmony, and spirituality. Indeed, he continues, in the Chagga worldview it is impossible to separate these domains. Such fragmentation simply does not make sense to the Chagga. Embedded in every Chagga child is a part of the divine dimension of reality, illustrating the interconnectedness of all aspects of reality. Thus, knowledge production cannot take place outside this intricate web of relationships.

In Cartesian–Newtonian modes of disciplinary thought the interrelationships cherished by the Chagga are not as *real* as their individual parts. For example, in Cartesian psychology consciousness is often reduced to neural and chemical dynamics. Researchers in this context often study nothing outside the narrow confines of brain chemistry from graduate school to retirement. The notion that the understanding of human consciousness might be enhanced by anthropological, theological, or philosophical investigations rarely, if ever, occurs to such researchers over the decades of their research.

Making use of indigenous knowledges and the theological insights of Buddhism in this domain, the cognitive theorist Francisco Varela employs the bricolage to develop a dramatically different concept of consciousness. Understanding the indigenous notion that the individual cannot be understood outside the community of which she is a part, Varela posits that human consciousness *emerges* from the social and biological interactions of its various parts. This understanding may over the next couple of decades revolutionize the fields of cognitive science, psychology, and even pedagogy. When scholars grasp the multilogical, interrelated nature of the bricolage, possibilities emerge for dramatic changes in the ways disciplines operate. Using the indigenous metaphor, knowledge *lives* in the cultures of indigenous peoples. As opposed to the disciplinary knowledges of Cartesian–Newtonianism which are often stored in archives or laboratories, indigenous knowledges live in everyday cultural practices (Woodhouse, 1996; Dei, 1995; Maurial, 1999).

Bricoleurs ask hard questions of indigenous knowledges. They know that folk knowledges – like Western scientific knowledges – often help construct exploitation and oppression for diverse groups and individuals. With this caution and resistance to essentialism in mind, bricoleurs study the ways many indigenous peoples in Africa construct the inter-relationships of their inner selves to the outer world. This indigenous tendency to avoid dualisms that, when unacknowledged, undermine the balance of various relationships is important to bricoleurs. For example, the dualism between humans and nature can wreak havoc in an indigenous social system. In many indigenous African conceptions humanness is viewed as a part of nature, not separate from it. Unlike for scholars in the Cartesian–Newtonian disciplines, the world was too sacred for humans to study and dominate or conquer. Once humanness and the environment were viewed as separate entities, forces were unleashed that could destroy the delicate eco- and social systems that sustained the indigenous culture. Thus, to accept the dualism between humanness and nature in the minds of many African peoples was tantamount to committing mass suicide.

Another example of indigenous culture whose knowledges bricoleurs deem valuable is the Andean peoples of South America. Everyone and everything in traditional Andean culture is sentient – for example, the rivers and mountains have ears and eyes. Acting in the world in this cultural context is a dimension of being in relationship to the world. In her actions within the physical environment, an Andean individual is in conversation with the mountains, rivers, trees, lakes, etc. This language of conversation replaces in Andean culture a Western traditional disciplinary language of knowing. A profound epistemological shift has taken place in this replacement. In Andean culture the concept of knower and known is irrelevant. Instead humans and physical entities engage in reciprocal relationships, carrying on conversations in the interests of both.

These conversations have been described as mutually nurturing events, acts that enhance the evolution of all parties involved via their tenderness and empathy for the living needs of the other. Thus, the epistemology at work here involves more than simply knowing about something. It involves tuning oneself in to the other's mode of being – its ontological presence – and entering into a life-generating relationship with it (Apffel-Marglin, 1995). Bricoleurs take from this an understanding of a new dimension of epistemology. Those working in the academic disciplines of Western societies must enter into relationships with that which they are studying. Such relationships should be enumerated and analysed. How am I changed by this relationship? How is the object of my study changed or potentially changed by the relationship?

Great change occurs as a result of the Andean's conversation with nature. Nature's voice is heard through the position and brilliance of planets and stars; the speed, frequency, colour, and smell of the wind; and the size and number of particular wild flowers, to mention only a few. Such talk tells Andeans about the coming weather and various dimensions of cultivation and they act accordingly. Because of the overwhelming diversity of ecosystems and climates in the Andes mountains and valleys, these conversations are complex. Interpretations of meanings – like any hermeneutic acts – are anything but self-evident. Such conversations and the actions they catalyse allow the Andeans to produce an enormous variety of cultivated plant species that amazes plant geneticists from around the world. Apffel-Marglin (1995, p. 11) describes this diversity:

> The peasants grow and know some 1,500 varieties of quinoa, 330 of kaniwa, 228 of tarwi, 250 of potatoes, 610 of oca (another tuber) and so forth ... The varieties differ according to regions, altitude, soils, and other factors. Such incredible diversity cannot only be due to ecological diversity. The manner in which peasants converse with plants and all the other inhabitants of the world, be they animate or inanimate, with not only an infinite attention to detail but with a receptive, open, and direct or embodied attitude is at the heart of such diversity.

The Andeans actually have a word for those places where conversation between humans and the natural world take place. *Chacras* include the land where the Andeans cultivate their crops, the places where utensils are crafted, and the places where herds and flocks live and graze. According to the Andeans these are all places where all entities come together to discuss the regeneration of life. The concept of interrelationship is so important in the Andean culture that the people use the word *ayllu* to signify a kinship group that includes not only other human beings but also animals, mountains, streams, rocks, and the spirits of a particular geographical place. Bricoleurs adapt these indigenous Andean concepts to the rethinking of the disciplines, as they identify the methodologies, epistemologies, ontologies, cultural systems, social theories, etc. that they employ in their multilogical understanding of the research act. Those who research the social, psychological, and educational worlds, bricoleurs conclude, hold a special responsibility to those concepts and to the people they research to select critical and life-affirming logics of inquiry. Symbiotic hermeneutics demands that relationships at all levels be respected and engaged in ways that produce justice and new levels of understanding – in ways that regenerate life.

Rethinking Disciplinarity in the Bricolage

Learning from difference in so many diverse domains, bricoleurs are unrelenting in their efforts to rethink the nature of and the process of research promulgated by traditional disciplines. Picking up on the genealogical dynamics mentioned earlier in this chapter, it is important to note that rigorous disciplinary work in the bricolage not only develops new ways of perceiving the world but also explores the baggage all knowledge brings with it – the knowledge produced by bricoleurs included. Thus, bricoleurs always arrive at the disciplinary roundtable with questions about the research strategies of the experts and the unexamined mores and folkways of the disciplinary culture. In the spirit of difference and interconnectedness, bricoleurs push those associated with the discipline to consider differing disciplinary frameworks, viewpoints of cultural workers from different social domains along axes of class, race, culture, gender, sexuality, and religion, and scholars who hold different value structures. By examining Einsteinian physics, the perspectives on manufacturing from workers operating an assembly line, and/or scholars of pedagogy who do not accept the need for organized schooling, a bricoleur gains ways of approaching a study she could find in few other places.

Such activities force traditional scholars to confront the problems that emerge from 'territorial' conceptions of disciplines that exclude everyone but a certified few from engaging work in a particular discipline. In this context hierarchies are established and disciplines and researchers who work in particular disciplines are rank-ordered in status. At the top of the hierarchy rest physics and the physicists, followed by the other physical sciences, the social sciences, the practical sciences, and the professions. Coming from education, I bring with me the subjugated knowledge derived from operating at the bottom of the disciplinary food chain. Nevertheless, all researchers – even those of us in the low-status domains – can become bricoleurs who learn the parameters of disciplines, the nature of the certified practices employed in them, the knowledge and skills they designate as foundational, and what they define as problems. Of course, bricoleurs argue that researchers can and should learn these dynamics in a wide variety of disciplines.

In such disciplinary work bricoleurs, of course, seek to uncover relationships between different disciplinary configurations. Often, as in any other confrontation with difference, they will uncover conflicts between disciplines. Importantly, in this context they do not attempt to resolve or synthesize all disagreements. Many times simply being aware of conflict will generate new insights in the study of the tensions that emerge between different perspectives. While syntheses often come out of the exploration of conflicts, such an outcome is not necessarily the goal of all such analyses. Indeed, the conflict itself may help bricoleurs uncover unexplored assumptions shaping disciplinary activity, generate new insights about the topics at hand, and develop new modes of research (Weinstein, 1995; Bereiter, 2002; Burbules and Beck, 1999). When Einstein, for example, confronted the conflict in physics between those who saw gravity as a particle and those who viewed it as a wave, he made no effort to resolve this particular conflict. If he had moved in this direction, he may never have arrived at the general theory of relativity. The goal of bricolage is not conflict resolution. Indeed, his research demonstrated that the conflict was not resolvable – an insight that changed the history of physics.

Thus, in confronting the regressive dynamics of mainstream disciplinarity bricoleurs push those within the disciplines to consider modes of understanding that fall outside the traditional conventions. Drawing upon critical theory, bricoleurs work toward an evolving criticality that melds several social-theoretical traditions in the effort to understand the way power operates to perpetuate itself. In this context modes of oppression are uncovered and the traditional disciplines' complicity in maintaining the political status quo is interrogated. By the way disciplines fragment knowledge, they subvert the free flow of information to people who need it the most in their political struggles against dominant power. The bricolage in its most simple articulation helps overcome this fragmentation.

In this context bricoleurs maintain that any rigorous knowledge about a particular entity – given all the contexts and relationships that shape it – forces researchers to apply numerous disciplinary ways of seeing in an integrated manner. Phenomena of the world always overlap numerous disciplines, refusing to deport themselves in accordance with the folkways of rationalism. The traditional disciplines are inexorably connected to the truncated perspectives that Western researchers have historically constructed in the effort to understand particular fragments of the world around them. The traditional disciplines have become particularly adept at providing partial knowledges about isolated segments of the cosmos. Such knowledge, of course, is profoundly inadequate when directed toward the solution of ill-defined social, psychological, and educational problems.

These realities bring us to the doorstep of interdisciplinarity – we had to get there eventually. Bricoleurs want to be sure that when they knock on the interdisciplinary door they are ready to ask difficult questions of the concept and not just accept its usefulness in an uncritical way. Of course, there is great possibility for the bricolage in interdisciplinarity, but it is no panacea. Bricoleurs recognize the complexity of the interrelationships between disciplines. They understand that there are conflicts, congruences, and overlaps among disciplines, and any notion of mixing and matching them must begin with a sophisticated overview of their relationships along numerous axes. In this complex context bricoleurs seek the help of those with special insights into the problem.

Academic librarian James Marcum (1998) is insightful in this domain. Representing a group of scholars who have multidisciplinary experience and are attuned to the fragmentation of the disciplines, Marcum writes about the ways he must make connections among diverse fields in order to pursue his professional work. Such work involves helping faculty and student researchers connect and integrate similar concerns with knowledge producers in other fields. Of course, what Marcum is writing about here is a central dimension of the bricolage – the promotion of cross-disciplinary work and the collaboration among researchers with similar concerns and interests.

In many ways it is amazing that we need to look for specialists such as Marcum to help us in this scholarly pursuit. Bricoleurs should be at work in every discipline, in a variety of spaces in both the academy and the society-at-large. In pre-modernist scholarship before the Scientific Revolution in seventeenth-century western Europe scholars were less concerned with fragmented and isolated aspects of physical and social phenomena. After the birth of science few researchers crossed the borders of the disciplines – a *modus operandi* that rendered their work far more parochial than it needed to be. Insights that could have emerged from such border crossings were lost and questions that could have led to unimaginable innovations were never asked. This disciplinary segregation cast a pall over Western scholarship that undermines its rigour into the twenty-first century. Questions concerning the integration of knowledge were cast aside as irrelevant, as specialists devoid of spirit and a sense of larger purpose controlled the disciplines (Allard, 2002; Marijuan, 1994; May, 1993; O'Sullivan, 1999).

An Ontology of Complexity: Implications for the Bricolage

I have alluded several times in the discussion of relationship to a complex ontology in the description of the bricolage. Because of the importance of this concept, it is useful to specifically describe this notion before moving into new dimensions of the bricolage. As bricoleurs prepare to explore that which is not readily apparent to the ethnographic eye, that realm of complexity in knowledge production that insists on initiating a conversation about what it is that qualitative researchers are observing and interpreting in the world, this clarification of a complex ontology is needed. This conversation is especially important because it has not generally taken place. Bricoleurs maintain that this object of inquiry is ontologically complex in that it cannot be described as an encapsulated entity. In this more open view of the object of inquiry it is always a part of many contexts and processes, it is culturally inscribed and historically situated. The complex view of the object of inquiry accounts for the historical efforts to interpret its meaning in the world and how such efforts continue to define its social, cultural, psychological, and educational effects.

In the domain of the qualitative research process, for example, this ontological complexity undermines traditional notions of triangulation. Because of its in-process (processual) nature, inter-researcher reliability becomes far more difficult to achieve. Process-sensitive scholars watch the world flow by like a river where the exact contents of the water are never the same. Because all observers view an object of inquiry from their own vantage points in the web of reality, no portrait of a social phenomenon is ever exactly the same as another. Since all physical, social, cultural, psychological, and educational dynamics are connected in a larger fabric, researchers will produce different descriptions of an object of inquiry depending on what part of the fabric they have focused on – what part of the river they have seen. The more unaware observers are of this type of complexity, the more reductionistic the knowledge they produce about it. Bricoleurs attempt to understand this fabric and the processes that shape it in as thick a way possible (Blommaert, 1997).

The design and methods used to analyse this social fabric cannot be separated from the way reality is construed. Thus, ontology and epistemology are inextricably linked in ways that shape the task of the researcher. The bricoleur must understand these features in the pursuit of rigour. A deep interdisciplinarity is justified by an understanding of the complexity of the object of inquiry and the demands such complications place on the research act. As parts of complex systems and intricate processes, objects of inquiry are far too mercurial to be viewed by a single way of seeing or as a snapshot of a particular phenomenon at a specific moment in time.

In social research the relationship between individuals and their contexts is a central dynamic to be investigated. This relationship is a key ontological and epistemological concern of the bricolage; it is a connection that shapes the identities of human beings and the nature of the complex social fabric. Thus, bricoleurs use multiple methods to analyse the multidimensionality of this type of connection. The ways bricoleurs engage in this process of putting together the pieces of the relationship may provide a different interpretation of its meaning and effects. Recognizing the complex ontological importance of relationships alters the basic foundations of the research act and knowledge-production process. Thin, reductionistic descriptions of isolated things-in-themselves are no longer sufficient (Foster, 1997; Zammito, 1996).

What the bricolage is dealing with in this context is a double ontology of complexity: first, the complexity of objects of inquiry and their being-in-the-world; second, the nature of the social construction of human subjectivity, the production of human 'being'. Such understanding opens a new era of social research where the process of becoming human agents is appreciated with a new level of sophistication. The complex feedback loop between an unstable social structure and the individual can be charted in a way that grants human beings insight into the means by which power operates and the democratic process is subverted. In this complex ontological view bricoleurs understand that social structures do not *determine* individual subjectivity but *constrain* it in remarkably intricate ways. The bricolage is acutely interested in developing and employing a variety of strategies to help specify the ways subjectivity is shaped.

The recognitions that emerge from such a multiperspectival process bring analysts beyond the determinism of reductionistic notions of macro-social structures. The intent of a usable social or educational research is subverted in this reductionistic context as human agency is erased by the 'laws' of society. Structures do not simply 'exist' as objective entities whose influence can be predicted or 'not exist' with no influences over the cosmos of human affairs. Once again fractals enter the stage with their loosely structured characteristics of irregular shape – fractal structures. While not *determining* human behaviour, for example, fractal structures possess sufficient order to affect other systems and entities within their environment. Such structures are never stable or universally present in some uniform manifestation (Varenne, 1996; Young and Yarbrough, 1993). The more we study such dynamics, the more diversity of expression we find. Taking this ontological and epistemological diversity into account, bricoleurs understand there are numerous dimensions to the bricolage (Denzin and Lincoln, 2000). As with all aspects of the bricolage, no description is fixed and final and all features of the bricolage come with an elastic clause.

Questioning the Social Construction of Interdisciplinarity

With these ontological dynamics in mind bricoleurs are ready to enter the interdisciplinary terrain. Operating within what was described earlier in the chapter as the dialectic of disciplinarity, bricoleurs gain an in-depth understanding of the 'process of disciplinarity', adeptly avoiding any superficiality that might result from their interdisciplinary pursuits. At the same time such researchers possess the insight to avoid complicity in colonized knowledge production designed to regulate and discipline. Such subtle expertise illustrates an appreciation of the complexity of knowledge work to which bricolage aspires. Understanding disciplinary processes and models of expertise while recognizing the elitist dimensions of dominant cultural knowledge technologies involves a nuanced discernment of the double-edged sword of disciplinarity. Concurrently, bricoleurs subject interdisciplinarity to the same rigorous perusal. Accordingly, bricoleurs understand that interdisciplinarity is as much a social construction as disciplinarity. Just because bricolage is about interdisciplinarity, bricoleurs must not release the notion from the same form of power analysis used to explore disciplinarity.

In addition, bricoleurs must clarify what is meant by interdisciplinarity. A fuzzy concept at best, interdisciplinarity generally refers to a process where disciplinary boundaries are crossed and the analytical frames of more than one discipline are employed by the researcher. Surveying the use of the term, it quickly becomes apparent that little attention has been paid to what exactly interdisciplinarity implies for researchers. Some uses of the concept assume the deployment of numerous disciplinary methodologies in a study where disciplinary distinctions are maintained; other uses imply an integrated melding of disciplinary perspectives into a new methodological synthesis. Advocates of bricolage must consider the diverse approaches that take place in the name of interdisciplinarity and their implications for constructing the bricolage.

In light of the disciplinary implosion that has taken place over the last few decades and the 'no going back' stance previously delineated, I feel no compulsion to preserve the disciplines in some pure, uncorrupted state of nature. While there is much to learn from their histories, the stages of disciplinary emergence, growth and development, alteration, and devolution and decline, the complex view of bricolage I am presenting embraces a deep form of interdisciplinarity. A deep interdisciplinarity seeks to modify the disciplines and the view of research brought to the negotiating table constructed by the bricolage. Everyone leaves the table informed by the dialogue in a way that idiosyncratically influences the research methods they subsequently employ.

The point of the interaction is not standardized agreement as to some reductionistic notion of 'the proper interdisciplinary research method' but awareness of the diverse tools in the researcher's toolkit. The form such deep interdisciplinarity may take is shaped by the object of inquiry in question. Thus, in the bricolage the context in which research takes place always affects the nature of the deep interdisciplinarity employed. In the spirit of the dialectic of disciplinarity the ways these context-driven articulations of interdisciplinarity are constructed must be examined in light of the power literacy previously mentioned (Blommaert, 1997; Pryse, 1998; Young and Yarbrough, 1993; Friedman, 1998).

Bricolage as Deep Interdisciplinarity: The Synergy of Multiple Perspectives

With these disciplinary concerns in the front of our mind, I will now focus attention on the intellectual power of the bricolage. It does not seem a conceptual stretch to argue that there is a synergy that emerges in the use of different methodological and interpretative perspectives in the analysis of an artefact. Historians, for example, who are conversant with the insights of hermeneutics, will produce richer interpretations of the historical processes they encounter in their research. In the deep interdisciplinarity of the bricolage the historian takes concepts from hermeneutics and combines them with historiographical methods. What is produced is something new, a new form of hermeneutical historiography or historical hermeneutics. Whatever its name, the methodology could not have been predicted by examining historiography and hermeneutics separately, outside the context of the historical processes under examination (Varenne, 1996). The possibilities offered by such interdisciplinary synergies are limitless.

An ethnographer who is conversant with social theory and its recent history is better equipped to transcend certain forms of formulaic ethnography that are reduced by the so-called 'observational constraint' on the methodology. Using the X-ray vision of contemporary social-theoretically informed strategies of discourse analysis, poststructural psychoanalysis, and ideology critique, the ethnographer gains the ability to see beyond the literalness of the observed. In this manoeuvre the ethnographer-as-bricoleur moves to a deeper level of data analysis as he or she sees 'what is not there' in physical presence, what is not discernible by the ethnographic eye. Synergized by the interaction of ethnography and the social-theoretical discourses, the resulting bricolage provides a new angle of analysis, a multidimensional perspective on a cultural phenomenon (Dicks and Mason, 1998; Foster, 1997).

Carefully exploring the relationships connecting the object of inquiry to the contexts in which it exists, the researcher constructs the most useful bricolage his or her wide knowledge of research strategies can provide. The strict disciplinarian operating in a reductionistic framework chained to the prearranged procedures of a monological way of seeing is less likely to produce frame-shattering research than the synergized bricoleur. The process at work in the bricolage involves learning from difference. Researchers employing multiple research methods are often not chained to the same assumptions as individuals operating within a particular discipline. As they study the methods of diverse disciplines, they are forced to compare not only methods but also differing epistemologies and social-theoretical assumptions. Such diversity frames research orientations as particular socially constructed perspectives – not sacrosanct pathways to the truth. All methods are subject to questioning and analysis, especially in light of so many other strategies designed for similar purposes (Denzin and Lincoln, 2000; Thomas, 1998; Lester, 2001).

This defamiliarization process highlights the power of the confrontation with difference to expand the researcher's interpretative horizons. Bricolage does not simply *tolerate* difference but *cultivates* it as a spark to researcher creativity. Here rests a central contribution of the deep interdisciplinarity of the bricolage: as researchers draw together divergent forms of research, they gain the unique insight of multiple perspectives. Thus, a complex understanding of research and knowledge production prepares bricoleurs to address the complexities of the social, cultural, psychological, educational domains. Sensitive to complexity, bricoleurs use multiple methods to uncover new insights, expand and modify old principles, and re-examine accepted interpretations in unanticipated contexts. Using any methods necessary to gain new perspectives on objects of inquiry, bricoleurs employ the principle of difference not only in research methods but also in cross-cultural analysis. In this domain bricoleurs explore the different perspectives of the socially privileged and the marginalized in relation to formations of race, class, gender, and sexuality (McLeod, 2000; Young and Yarbrough, 1993; Pryse, 1998).

The deep interdisciplinarity of bricolage is sensitive to multivocality and the consciousness of difference it produces in a variety of contexts. Described by Denzin and Lincoln (2000) as 'multi-competent, skilled at using interviews, observation, personal documents', the bricoleur explores the use of ethnography, Pinarian currere, historiography, genre studies, psychoanalysis, rhetorical analysis, discourse analysis, content analysis, and so on *ad infinitum*. The addition of historiography, for example, to the bricoleur's toolkit profoundly expands his or her interpretative facility. As bricoleurs historically contextualize their ethnographies, discourse analysis, semiotic studies, they tap into the power of etymology. Etymological insight (Kincheloe and Steinberg, 1993; Kincheloe, *et al.*, 1999a) involves an understanding of the origins of the construction of social, cultural, psychological, political, economic, and educational artefacts and the ways they shape our subjectivities. Indeed, our conception of self, world, and our positionalities as researchers can only become complex and critical when we appreciate the historical aspect of its formation. With this one addition we dramatically sophisticate the quality and depth of our knowledge work (Zammito, 1996).

Expanding the Boundaries: The Search for New Forms of Knowledge Production

Operating as a form of deep interdisciplinarity, bricolage is unembarrassed in its effort to rupture particular ways of functioning in the established disciplines of research. One of the best ways to accomplish this goal is to include what might be termed 'philosophical research' in the bricolage. In the same way that historiography ruptures the stability of particular disciplinary methods, philosophical research provides bricoleurs with the dangerous knowledge of the multivocal results of humans' desire to understand, to know themselves and the world. Differing philosophical/cultural conventions have employed diverse epistemological, ontological, and cosmological assumptions as well as different methods of inquiry. Again, depending on the context of the object of inquiry, bricoleurs use their knowledge of these dynamics to shape their research design. It is not difficult to understand the epistemological contention that the types of logic, criteria for validity, and methods of inquiry used in clinical medicine as opposed to teacher effectiveness in teaching critical thinking will differ.

In making such an assertion the bricoleur is displaying philosophical/epistemological/ontological sensitivity to the context of analysis. Such a sensitivity is a key element of the bricolage, as it brings an understanding of social theory together with an appreciation of the demands of particular contexts; this fused concept is subsequently used to examine the repertoire of methods the bricoleur can draw upon and to help decide which ones are relevant to the project at hand. Practising this mode of analysis in a variety of research situations, the bricoleur becomes increasingly adept at employing multiple methods in concrete venues. Such a historiographically and philosophically informed bricolage helps researchers move into a new more complex domain of knowledge production where they are far more conscious of multiple layers of intersections between the knower and the known, perception and the lived world, and discourse and representation. Employing the benefits of philosophical inquiry, the bricoleur gains a new ability to account for and incorporate these dynamics into his or her research narratives (Bridges, 1997; McCarthy, 1997; Fischer, 1998; Madison, 1988).

This is what expanding the boundaries of knowledge production specifically references. In the particularities of the philosophical interactions with the empirical in a variety of contexts bricoleurs devise new forms of rigour, new challenges to other researchers to push the methodological and interpretative envelopes. As bricoleurs study the subjective meanings that human beings make, for example, they use their philosophical modes of inquiry to understand that this phenomenological form of information has no analogue in the methods of particular formalist forms of empirical research. Thus, in an obvious example, a choice of methods is necessitated by particular epistemological and ontological conditions – epistemological and ontological conditions rarely recognized in mono-logical forms of empirical research (Haggerson, 2000; Lee, 1999).

I want to be as specific as possible about the nature of these epistemological and ontological conditions. While we have made progress, much of the research that is devoid of the benefits philosophical inquiry brings to the bricolage still tends to study the world as if ontologically it consists of a series of static images. Entities are often removed from the contexts that shape them, the processes of which they are a part, the relationships and connections that structure their being-in-the-world. Such ontological orientations impose particular epistemologies, specific ways of producing knowledge about such inert entities. In this ontological context the task of researchers is reduced, as they simply do not have to worry about contextual insights, etymological processes, and the multiple relationships that constitute the complexity of lived reality. In a reductionistic mode of research these dynamics are irrelevant and the knowledge produced in such contexts reflects the reductionism. The bricolage struggles to find new ways of seeing and interpreting that avoid this curse, that produce thick, complex, and rigorous forms of knowledge (Karunaratne, 1997).

In this thick, complex, and rigorous context bricoleurs in the social, cultural, psychological, and educational domains operate with a sophisticated understanding of the nature of knowledge. In order to be well prepared, bricoleurs must realize that knowledge is always in process, developing, culturally specific, and power-inscribed. They are attuned to dynamic relationships connecting individuals, their contexts, and their activities instead of focusing on these separate entities in isolation from one another. In this ontological framework they concentrate on social activity systems and larger cultural processes and the ways individuals engage or are engaged by them (Blackler, 1995).

Bricoleurs follow such engagements, analysing how the ever-changing dynamics of the systems and the processes alter the lived realities of participants; concurrently, they monitor the ways participants operate to change the systems and the processes. The complexity of such a mode of inquiry precludes the development of a step-by-step set of research procedures. Bricoleurs know that this inability to proceduralize undermines efforts to 'test' the validity of their research. The researcher's fidelity to procedure cannot simply be checked off and certified. In the complex bricolage the products of research are 'evaluated'. The evaluation process draws upon the same forms of inquiry and analysis initially delineated by the bricolage itself (Madison, 1988). In this context the rigour of research intensifies at the same time the boundaries of knowledge production are stretched.

Life on the Boundaries: Facilitating the Work of the Bricoleur

The bricolage understands that the frontiers of knowledge work rest in the liminal zones where disciplines collide. Thus, in the deep inter-disciplinarity of the bricolage researchers learn to engage in a form of boundary work. Such scholarly labour involves establishing diverse networks and conferences where synergistic interactions can take place as proponents of different methodologies, students of divergent subject matters, and individuals confronted with different problems interact. In this context scholars learn across these domains and educate inter-mediaries who can build bridges between various territories. As dis-ciplinary intermediaries operating as bricoleurs facilitate this boundary work, they create conceptual and electronic links that help researchers in different domains interact. If the cutting edge of research lives at the intersection of disciplinary borders, then developing the bricolage is a key strategy in the development of rigorous and innovative research. The facilitation and cultivation of boundary work is a central element of this process.

There is nothing simple about conducting research at the inter-disciplinary frontier. Many scholars report that the effort to develop expertise in different disciplines and research methodologies demands more than a casual acquaintance with the literature of a domain. In this context there is a need for personal interaction between representatives from diverse disciplinary domains and scholarly projects to facilitate these encounters. Many researchers find it extremely difficult to make sense of 'outside' fields, and the more disciplines a researcher scans the harder the process becomes. If the scholar does not have access to historical dimensions of the field, the contexts that envelop the research methods used and the knowledge produced in the area, or contemporary currents involving debates and controversies in the discipline, the boundary work of the bricolage becomes exceedingly frustrating and futile. Proponents of the bricolage must help develop specific strategies for facilitating this complicated form of scholarly labour.

In this context we come to understand that a key aspect of 'doing bricolage' involves the development of conceptual tools for boundary work. Such tools might include the promotion and cultivation of detailed reviews of research in a particular domain written with the needs of bricoleurs in mind. Researchers from a variety of disciplinary domains should develop information for bricolage projects. Hypertextual projects that provide conceptual matrices for bringing together diverse literatures, examples of data produced by different research methods, connective insights, and bibliographic compilations can be undertaken by bricoleurs with the help of information professionals. Such projects would integrate a variety of conceptual understandings, including the previously mentioned historical, contextual, and contemporary currents of disciplines (Palmer, 1996; Friedman, 1998).

Doug Kellner (1995) is helpful in this context with his argument that multiperspectival approaches to research may not be very helpful unless the object of inquiry and the various methods used to study it are situated historically. In this way the forces operating to socially construct all elements of the research process are understood, an appreciation that leads to a grasp of new relationships and connections. Such an appreciation opens new interpretative windows that lead to more rigorous modes of analysis and interpretation. This historicization of the research and the researched is an intrinsic aspect of the bricolage and the education of the bricoleur. Since learning to become a bricoleur is a lifelong process, what we are discussing here relates to the lifelong curriculum for preparing bricoleurs.

Also necessary to this boundary work and the education of the bricoleur are social-theoretical and hermeneutical understandings. Social theory alerts bricoleurs to the implicit assumptions within particular approaches to research and the ways they shape their findings. With grounding in social theory bricoleurs can make more informed decisions about the nature of the knowledge produced in the field and how researchers discern the worth of the knowledge they themselves produce. With the benefit of hermeneutics, bricoleurs are empowered to synthesize data collected via multiple methods. In the hermeneutic process this ability to synthesize diverse information moves the bricoleur to a more sophisticated level of meaning-making (Zammito, 1996; Foster, 1997). Life on the disciplinary boundaries is never easy, but the rewards to be derived from the hard work demanded are profound.

Redefining and interpreting the object of study

Joe L. Kincheloe

A central dimension of the bricolage involves the interpretative act, making sense of the complexity of everyday life and the data it constantly throws at us. In the previous three chapters I have referred to this hermeneutic process several times, using the terms 'critical hermeneutics' to designate an understanding of how power inscribes the word and the world and 'symbiotic hermeneutics' to describe a form of interpretation grounded on the importance of relationship. In this chapter we will explore various dimensions of the interpretative process in relation to the bricolage. We start with the premise that all being in the world of human beings is an interpreted form of being. This holds profound epistemological implications, as all knowledge is socially constructed in a dialogue between the world and human consciousness. Bricoleurs who understand that knowledge and interpretation are inseparable terms work to enhance their interpretative ability. Indeed, the ability to generate rich and compelling interpretations is a key to producing more rigorous forms of research. Thus, such an ability is central to our construction of the bricolage.

Interpretation in the Bricolage: The Centrality of Critical Hermeneutics

The research bricolage as articulated here is grounded in a critical notion of hermeneutics. Long concerned with the theory and practice of interpretation, hermeneutics is a form of philosophical inquiry that focuses on the cultural, social, political, and historical nature of research. In this context hermeneutics maintains that meaning-making cannot be quarantined from where one stands or is placed in the web of social reality. Thus, in a hermeneutic context interpretation is denaturalized in the sense that certain events and/or phenomena do not imply a particular interpretation of their meaning. Interpretation is far more complex that assumed, far more a product of social forces than admitted.

Thus, bricoleurs focus great attention on the act of interpretation in research, appreciating the distinction between describing a phenomenon and understanding it. In this context bricoleurs informed by herme-neutics understand that any act of rigorous research involves:

- connecting the object of inquiry to the many contexts in which it is embedded;
- appreciating the relationship between researcher and that being researched;
- connecting the making of meaning to human experience;
- making use of textual forms of analysis while not forgetting that living and breathing human beings are the entities around which and with which meaning is being made;
- building a bridge between these forms of understanding and informed action.

Too often in mainstream forms of research, bricoleurs maintain, these interpretative understandings are deemed irrelevant.

The form of hermeneutics employed here is a critical hermeneutics – critical in the sense that it has engaged in a dialogue with the tradition of critical theory. Critical theory is always concerned with the ways power operates, the ways various institutions and interests deploy power in the effort to survive, shape behaviour, gain dominance over others, or, in a more productive vein, improve the human condition. Realizing that power is not simply one important force in the social process, critical theory understands that humans are the historical products of power. Men and women do not emerge outside the process of history. Human identities are shaped by entanglements in the webs that power weaves. Critical hermeneutics emerges in the dialogue between hermeneutics and critical theory's concern with power and social action (Jardine, 1998; Kincheloe *et al.*, 1999c; Smith, 1999; McLaren, 2000).

In this hybrid context critical hermeneutics pushes interpretation in research to new levels, moving beyond what is visible to the ethno-graphic eye to the exposure of concealed motives that move events and shape everyday life. As critical hermeneutics observes the intersection of power and omnipresent, pre-reflective cultural meanings, a sensitive and rigorous understanding of the social world begins to take shape. Critical hermeneutics takes the concept of historicity to a new conceptual level, as it specifies the nature of the historicity that helps produce cultural meaning, the consciousness of the researcher, the construction of the re-search process, and the formation of human subjectivity and transform-ative action. In this interpretative context critical theoretical concerns with praxis-based notions of social change are more easily addressed, as social action informed by thick description and rigorous understanding of a social and political circumstance is made possible (Lutz et al., 1997; Zammito, 1996).

I Walk the Line: Empowered Subjects and Rigorous Analysis

In this critical hermeneutic context bricoleurs are concerned with the empowerment of the subjects of research and the voice to the subjugated and the marginalized. Such efforts raise numerous questions about the research process. For example, do the acts of empowerment and giving voice involve simply highlighting the specific words of the research subjects? Do they mean featuring the interactions of the participants and the researcher as the most important dimensions of the research narrative? While in no way dismissing the importance of these dimensions of the empowerment process in the criticality of the bricolage, bricoleurs informed by critical hermeneutics worry that sometimes in highlighting the specific words of participants and featuring research participant interaction rigorous insights can be lost.

In the specifics of the process, interpretation emerging from the interaction of the particular with macro-social configurations can be set aside in the focus on the personal. Concurrently, psychologistic representations of abstract individuals can crowd out the contextual concerns of the hermeneutically informed bricolage. In such cases the rigour of complexity is displaced not by scientific reductionism but by an excessive fascination with unsituated personal experience. As Johnny Cash once put it, one must 'walk the line'; in this case the line separates the decontextualization of the idiosyncrasy of the personal from the unreflective, authoritarian voice of truth of the reductionistic researcher.

Bricoleurs operating in a critical hermeneutical framework work to record the voice of the subjugated but to expand its meaning by engaging in the hermeneutic circle of interpretation. Even subjugated voices are better understood when studied in relation to numerous social, cultural, political, economic, philosophical, historical, psychological, and pedagogical dynamics (Dicks and Mason, 1998). I attempt to walk this line in my recent book, *The Sign of the Burger: McDonald's and the Culture of Power* (Kincheloe, 2002). As I highlight the voices of my ethnographic research subjects, I always contextualize their perspectives within the frames of macro-social, political, and economic concerns, the insights of social theory, and the discernment of critical hermeneutics. The rigorous demands of the bricolage insist that researchers engage in these deliberations and struggle with their implications for every project they undertake.

Researchers in this struggle draw strength from the multiple perspectives of the bricolage. Such multiperspectivalism is enhanced by critical hermeneutics and the interpretative collisions it promotes in the hermeneutic circle – hermeneuts often refer to this dynamic as the fusion of horizons. Here we return to the very basis of bricolage, learning from the juxtaposition of divergent ideas and ways of seeing. Metaphors abound in this context as the work of the bricoleur is compared to that of a jazz musician, quilt maker, and the producer of pictorial montage. In all of these processes different dynamics are brought together in ways that produce a synergistic interaction – the whole is greater than the sum of the parts. The hermeneutic fusion of horizons helps bricoleurs consider numerous representations of reality simultaneously. In this context the concept of simultaneity is important, as it takes precedence over more traditional research concerns with sequence and linearity. As hermeneutically grounded bricoleurs watch these conceptual collisions, they adeptly sidestep the danger of liberal eclecticism. Here in the hermeneutic circle they chart the ways that the divergent representations both inform and transform one another (Pryse, 1998; Paulson, 1995; Denzin and Lincoln, 2000; Kellner, 1995).

The Bricolage, Interpretation, and Complexity

We all have experience with the complexity of interpretation in everyday life. In their book on the US Educational Testing Service (ETS), Owen and Doerr (1999) provide an excellent example of the conflict between the complex nature of interpretation and the rationalistic reduction of the concept. They examine the following SAT question:

> A customer is seated in a fancy restaurant. The clumsy waiter spills soup in his lap. The customer exclaims:
> A.   You could not pay attention, no?
> B.   The soup is delicious!
> C.   What good service!
> D.   I would like a spoon!

In order to answer the question 'correctly', the test taker has to understand the mind-set of the test maker. Not known for their keen sense of humour, the operatives at ETS probably are not looking for B, C, or D. I could easily see a customer at a restaurant with a lap full of soup make good use of any of those three answers in such a circumstance. Knowing the *subjectivity* of the parties involved is essential to providing the 'correct' interpretation of the question. Thus, interpretation here depends on a variety of factors, including the nature of the test takers' cultural experience and its relationship to the test makers. There is nothing simple or direct in such a process nor, I would argue, does it have much to do with objectivity or genetic intelligence. Profound implications emerge from the notion that interpretation has to do with factors such as understanding the subjectivity of the test maker. The ante of complexity has just been profoundly raised, as analysts and researchers have to look at the meaning-making process in terms of the interrelationships and the web of interdependent concepts in which all knowledge is ensnared.

Thus, bricoleurs understand that any act of interpretation involves tapping into an ontological organic process that is ever changing, ever moving toward new articulations. Without rigorous ontological and epistemological grounding, researchers who employ rationalistic methods designed to pick out micro-features of isolated systems will produce meaningless knowledge with little use value in the lived world. As the result of their efforts, they will offer up a collection of discrete factoids unconnected to larger contexts and processes. Consumers of their research will confuse these factoids with reality. Such a reality can only be discerned when it is anaesthetized, held motionless, and vivisected. The reality 'constructed' in such a process is reduced to a static state in its fragmentation. The ontological process that gives life to the physical and social worlds emerges from such manipulations as an inert thing-in-itself. Thus, the work of bricoleurs is to transcend such rationalism and to produce interpretations of phenomena that involve both identifying complex processes and understanding the ways diverse individuals view the world from differing vantage points within these processes (Madison, 1988; May, 1993; Mayers, 2001; Pickering, 1999; Berry, 2001; Korn, 2004).

Despite all the talk about the importance of knowledge work emanating from the contemporary globalized world of commerce and the halls of academia over the last decade, these basic understandings about the complexity of interpretation are rarely discussed. Knowledge is reduced to either data found in one's head or data found in the world or both. Without the rigour of the epistemological and ontological understandings that bricoleurs must confront, the individuals who lead these conversations about knowledge are lost and the knowledges their organizations produce usually fall into the inert things-in-themselves category.

In these corporate notions of research and knowledge work, a naive realism subverts the long march toward complexity. In this context the articulable and the visual are deemed to have a consistent and preordained relationship to one another. In such epistemological naivety the articulable occupies the same relation to the visible as language has to sense data in positivism. It is a simple mirror of reality. A complex hermeneutics insists that the articulable is not a reflection of reality, nor does the world control what can be spoken about its nature. Bricoleurs employing this complex hermeneutics come to understand that discourse trumps 'reality'. In other words, the articulable dominates the visual, as it constructs the form of information ascribed to the visual. We live, bricoleurs remind us, in a discursive universe.

Thus, in the discursive universe – as we have argued throughout these first four chapters – the world is more complex that it appears at first glance. As previously maintained, the activities of human beings are not produced by social or physical forces but by intentional states. Understanding human behaviour and producing knowledge about it that matters is an extremely difficult and complex task. Successful execution of such a task demands a profoundly sophisticated interpretative ability. Of course, all human knowledge is an interpretation. In contemporary Western societies the interpretative dimension of this human knowledge is not generally recognized as the interpretation is confused with a description of an objective reality. The key move for bricoleurs involves bringing this process of interpretation to the front burner of consciousness so that it may be analysed and better understood. An important dimension of the research bricoleurs engage in has to do with interpreting why individuals, oneself included, construct the interpretations that they do.

Every aspect of human knowing – a.k.a. interpretation – is linguistically filtered, contextually grounded, power-saturated, implicated in a particular social process, shaped by particular narrative forms, and inscribed by tacit theories about the nature of reality. The smell of complexity permeates these dynamics. We cannot make contact with the world without the mind as our escort – and our escort has already established a particular relationship with the world. Thus, despite the best efforts of rationalists to put us directly in contact with the world, all our observations of it are shaped by prejudgements and unseen inscriptions. Researchers can operate in a state of reductionistic unconsciousness about such matters and claim objective truth for their explanations of reality; or they can understand the existence of these unseen dynamics and make more humble claims for their interpretations. Thus, bricoleurs may end up with multiple and sometimes unreconciled interpretations of the same phenomena. The fact that they are unable to produce one final, monological interpretation should not be held against them. The complex world has room for diverse interpretations coexisting in a productive tension (Bruner, 1996; Bereiter, 2002; Tarnas, 1991; Richardson and Woolfolk, 1994; Gadamer, 1989; Burbules and Beck, 1999).

Interpretation and Explanation

In the first decade of the twenty-first century we are far more acquainted with these interpretative dynamics than we were before the linguistic turn in academia four decades ago. Many scholars understand the argument put forward in this paradigm shift that there is a distinction between the world and our linguistically driven interpretative perception of it. Nevertheless, bricoleurs maintain, while the academic worm turned for many scholars in diverse disciplines, such a change should by no means be seen as universal. There is still tremendous resistance to such a new way of thinking about knowledge. In the twenty-first century in the USA in particular situations such resistance has overwhelmed any gains made by the paradigmatic change. Importantly, even among those who accept many of the premises of the change, the implications of what the shift implies for the specific enactment of the research act are still fuzzy. This is why a clear understanding of interpretation in the bricolage is so important. Hermeneutics in this context becomes a central tool in the bricoleur's toolkit, as researchers are forced to make a distinction between rationalistic explanation and interpretive understanding.

Hermeneutics promotes a dialectical notion of understanding that seeks to free knowledge production from the authoritarian explanations of the certified experts – whether they are the religious elite of the medieval period or the scientific elite of modernity. In the modernist context hermeneutics resists scientific explanations that reduce the world to what is objectifiable, i.e., expressible in mathematical terms. This focus on understanding and interpretation rejects unilateral experiences of all kinds that too often eventuate in oppression via the functionalization and hyperrationalization of lived experience. Such explanations are couched in the monologic of correct and incorrect answers – a way of researching that subverts critical analysis as it imposes meanings. Such material is packaged for easy consumption. No interpretive activity is necessary, just throw it in the explanatory microwave, heat, and insert into one's memory.

Hermeneutic understanding, unlike rationalist explanation, does not launch a pre-emptive strike against other ways of producing knowledge. When I argue in *The Sign of the Burger* that McDonald's can be understood as a semiotic phenomenon in its strategic deployment of cultural signifiers, this does not mean that George Ritzer's McDonaldization thesis (Ritzer, 1996) is wrong. Indeed, the two ways of interpreting McDonald's seem to me quite synergistic. Hermeneutics of the complex, critical, and symbiotic varieties discussed in the bricolage believes that meaning is consistently multiple in nature (Reason and Bradbury, 2000; Madison, 1988; Lester, 2001). In a culture infiltrated with the ideology of the superiority of scientific explanation such multiplicity seems to many inherently lacking in standards.

Student: But, Professor Kincheloe, what is the correct answer?

JLK: There may be many answers here depending on the context in which the phenomenon is viewed, the questions we ask about it.

Student: So, do you mean you don't know the answer?

Thus, bricoleurs informed by hermeneutics become rigorous researchers of context, perspective, and discourse. They understand that they must use multiple research traditions and theoretical tools to understand the way these factors influence how we make sense of the world around us. Bricoleurs appreciate that any research that fails to account for these dynamics cannot produce a complex, thick, and textured picture of a phenomenon. Empirical, quantitative studies that take these factors into account move toward the criteria of rigour. Thus, explanation and understanding are not necessarily incompatible if the proponents of explanation are willing to explore the forces that shape their assumptions (Bruner, 1996).

Redefining and Interpreting Phenomena: Restoring Lost Meaning

Bricoleurs are obsessed with recovering meanings about the physical, social, political, psychological, and educational worlds that have been lost, that have fallen through the disciplinary cracks of modernism. Such losses are especially severe in the domains of the ecological, the emotional, the unconscious, the ideological, and the cultural, as many research orientations are simply not prepared to produce knowledge within these areas. Such research orientations have a history of focusing on inert material that no longer lives in various processes and contexts. As its connections with the world are severed, it becomes far easier to analyse. In this context it could be configured as a piece of the cosmic jigsaw puzzle and put in its proper place. On completion, the puzzle would give researchers a portrait of reality. Such a picture could be described as a sum total of the puzzle pieces, but not an integrated whole. Unless researchers transcend the one-dimensionality of the puzzle, the portrait created is a reductionistic representation of the multi-dimensionality of the world.

There is no one final picture of the world with all of its puzzle pieces in their correct places. The inertness implicit in such finality is disturbing in its rejection of the 'in-process' nature of the lived world. Equally disturbing is the exclusive aspect of such a finalized picture of reality – there are no other realities, this is the only one (Karunaratne, 1997; Horn, 2001). Bricoleurs are comfortable with the unfinished, unresolved nature of the multidimensional, ever-changing constructions of reality they produce. When faced with such complexity many researchers from the monological tradition become paralysed, as the single predetermined path to knowledge production closes down. Unaccustomed to ambiguity and diversity, they lose their confidence and their epistemological compass. Bricoleurs insist that researchers must learn to navigate an ever-shifting and mutating terrain of knowledge (Weil, 2001). Without such skills researchers will eventually be lost at sea, set adrift in the changing epistemological tides and the daunting ontological currents. In the process, meanings central to the understanding and reconceptualization of social, cultural, political, psychological, and educational life will be lost.

Despite all the criticism of positivism and the emergence of qualitative studies in the last several decades, the desire for final pictures and formalist explanations of phenomena still shapes much of what passes for research. 'What did the interviewee really mean?' is a common question in contemporary ethnography. Again, some final delineation of an individual's meaning is as elusive as a final picture of the world. Meaning is not simply a rational matter, as spoken language is always accompanied by gestures, inflections, intonations, accents, bodily movements, forms of eye contact, etc. What is the final meaning of my sarcasm? As a respondent to your questions about my education in the mountains of Southern Appalachia, did you catch my inflections that just might have signalled my irritation at what I perceived to be your socio-economic class condescension? Or did you (or I) just imagine that? Obviously, these subtle but all-important fugitive knowledges are central in the meaning-making process (Thomas, 1998). I do not believe that formalistic and rationalistic methods of inquiry are capable of dealing with them.

Thus, in this context bricoleurs interested in the complex nature of interpretation in research must work diligently to open communication with the fugitive knowledges in order to better access the domains of the symbolic, irrational, corporeal, and relational. Too often these are the desperadoes who make off with meaning under the cloak of epistemological darkness. Reductionistic and rationalistic researchers issue a sigh of relief, as they are glad to get rid of them. Bricoleurs, in the spirit of complexity, track them down. Hermeneutics in the bricolage plays a central role in this dragnet for meaning, as it convinces the posse that it is not searching for the desperadoes as much as it is constructing them. Thus, the tracking process shifts to an alternate universe as the fugitives are tracked in another dimension of reality. The bricoleurs are still on the lookout, but unlike the rationalists and reductionistic bounty hunters before them they operate in a virtual world where fugitive knowledges are constructed as well as flushed out.

Interpretation in the bricolage destroys the objective world. In such a world all phenomena are things-in-themselves that wait passively like antebellum southern belles at the ball for a knowing subject to recognize them. Such recognition involves the formation of a mental representation of them – a reflection in the mirror of the mind. The closer to reality such a reflection appears, the greater the rigour of the research process. The objective world's things-in-themselves abhor creativity and the multiple ways of seeing of the bricolage. Such orientations subvert the stability of such a world and threaten to reveal the status quo as merely one way of being in multiple universes of possibility. Such revelations are hard on power wielders who have created hegemonic and ideological certainties about who *we* are as a society and what *we* believe as good people – certainties that exist for the purpose of winning consent for their power. Mind and matter – knower and known – are always connected, and the idea that phenomena are simply things-in-themselves is not compatible in the hermeneutics and the critical ontology of the bricolage.

If in no other way, phenomena are not things-in-themselves simply because of the role of the mind in creating them. They cannot be viewed in isolation because of the mind's complicity in their construction. Mind and matter are particular phases in a larger process, as mind constructs matter and matter produces mind. Ignoring these connections, modernist researchers devoted their time and energy to the analysis of things-in-themselves, fetishizing the *ultimate* things-in-themselves – the smallest building blocks of matter and life. In physics the search for the atom, electron, and quark, and before Einstein the gravitron, while in biology the isolation of the gene dominated work in these disciplines for long periods of time. Such disciplinary orientations undermined the search for connections and processes that ultimately unlocked doors to meanings unimaginable inside the frames of the search for the basic building blocks of reality (Madison, 1988; Reason and Bradbury, 2000; Pickering, 1999).

Cartesian researchers working in quantum mechanics received a group electroshock treatment with the discovery that even the physical world cannot be fragmented into discrete basic units. The more they studied sub-atomic phenomena, the more they realized that the physical cosmos is less an accumulation of elementary building blocks and more an integrated web of relationships forming an interconnected whole. It is this ontological insight that shapes the meaning of the title of this chapter – *redefining* the object of inquiry. Thus, bricoleurs move from parts to wholes, study schools, psyches, social organizations, the forces of power *in relation to* other phenomena looking for the interconnections that shape all of the parts. Interpretation in the bricolage cannot take place without the understanding of both a relational ontology and a symbiotic hermeneutics. As radical as such notions may sound to the modernist ear, it is interesting to note that such concepts are not new but have been expressed by scholars, poets, griots, and storytellers in a variety of civilizations.

Thus, in their redefinition and reinterpretation of the object of study bricoleurs move from the isolated factoid of reductionism to what Andrew Murphie (1998) labels the objectile. Conceived in a relational ontology, an objectile is a substanceless entity characterized by its ever-moving and ever-changing qualities and by the phenomena it connects. The objectile operates in bricoleurs' alternative universe, the ontological reality that exists beyond the fragmented people, places, and things of modernism. In this universe individuals cannot be separated from their historical contexts, research procedures are not transhistorical and transcultural objective practices, and knowledge emerges in the dynamic interplay connecting self and other, centre and margin, before and after, and past and present.

In its impermanence the world takes shape in the interaction of diverse processes in the physical, social, psychological, and educational arenas. Ancient peoples developed numerous discourses for signifying these activities. It could be argued that the ancient Greeks used the interaction of the gods of Olympus, ancient Indians the Maha-Bhuta (Krishna's description of the make-up of all matter), and numerous native American tribes the conversations among the animal spirits to represent the concept. Thus, moving to its new universe the object of inquiry moves from the 'some-thing' of substance to the 'no-thing' of relationship. In the process lost meanings are restored (Richardson and Woolfolk, 1994; Capra, 1996; Karunaratne, 1997).

Confronting the Power of Monological Empiricism: Perspectivism, Dialectics, and Polysemy

Bricoleurs are very concerned with the way that rationalists and formalists classify discursively informed, relationship-oriented, and interpretation-centred research as non-empirical. Simply put, the bricolage produces empirical research, if empirical research is defined as the production and analysis of data about the world and people's experience of it. Bricoleurs operate to make sure that their form of empirical knowledge work avoids many of the mistakes that have been made in the empirical arena over the centuries. Such mistakes often involve insufficient analysis of the nature and meaning of these data about the world and the researcher's relationship to it.

A central feature of the bricolage involves rethinking how this knowledge of the world acquires meaning in the world. This, of course, is a key idea in our discussion of interpretation in the bricolage. Empirical truth claims, we are arguing, are more complex than traditionally thought. As bricoleurs examine the language of empirical science they find that language games and narrative devices subvert any claim that language is a neutral instrument that reflects the world around us. Thus, all empirical knowledge claims are ideologically inscribed and dependent on a variety of contexts. Bricoleurs in this context seek an empiricism informed by the complications, a more cautious empiricism that understands its own limitations.

The empiricism of the bricolage is guarded by the notion of perspectivism. Contrary to the radical empiricism of positivism, perspectivism denies that something can be completely and finally known. It is not possible, according to perspectivism, to produce a complete theory of anything or to produce an understanding that accounts for every fact relevant to a phenomenon. The multilogical nature of the bricolage draws upon perspectivism, positing that every description of the world is an interpretation and there are always new interpretations to encounter. Such a view may not sit well with traditional empiricists, but holding it does not make bricoleurs anti-empiricists. My hope is that it would make bricoleurs smart empiricists (Fischer, 1998; Ward, 1995; May, 1993).

Humans always view the world from a perspective, from a point within the web of reality. As self-aware as we can become, there will always be a new way to view an event or a text. Many eighteenth-century male poets who wrote about the nature of their love for one of their male friends did not anticipate that more than two centuries later their work would be examined within the discursive context of queer theory. What seemed commonplace to them would be seen by succeeding generations as manifestations of larger socio-cultural impulses. Even death fails to curb the emergence of new perspectives from which to view our data. Indeed, the effort to make sense of empirical data never ends and doubts about particular explanations and interpretations are never erased. Human beings always speak in the domain of feelings, desires, repression, customs, and discourses. A central point in hermeneutics involves the appreciation of the instability of language and the elusiveness of understanding (Richardson and Woolfolk, 1994; Thomas, 1998). Empiricists who do not take note of these complications will find the rigour of their research compromised. Bricoleurs work to increase the rigour of research by ridding empirical researchers of their delusions of clarity and perfect explanations.

As they explore these complex interpretative dimensions of empirical research, bricoleurs examine the tradition of dialectics. Emerging in the ancient Greek scholarship of the sophists and the rhetoricians, dialectics has always harboured a suspicion of monological forms of both philosophy and knowledge production. In its simplest articulation dialectics wants to substitute monologue with dialogue. Such an act, dialecticians maintain, emancipates us from the power-driven assertions of the political, religious, social, cultural, educational, and scientific elite who believe their expertise moves them to a new stratum of authority. Thus, in the critical eyes of the bricolage dialectics has always been deliciously subversive.

Thus, knowledge in this tradition is viewed as dialectical, not propositional. This implies that there is more than one answer to any inquiry and there exists no one question that is primary in the production and analysis of data about a phenomenon. In this orientation dialectics operates to question common sense, to subvert deference to the proclamations of the powerful, to interrogate the ease with which particular data gain the imprimatur of fact, and to expose contradictions within certified knowledges. Dialectics lends the word, 'tentative' to the bricolage – the knowledge produced by bricoleurs is tentative rather than final. In this context bricoleurs do not allow a single understanding of the world to shut down analysis. Bricoleurs know that they will always conduct research-in-action, inquiry in living and evolving contexts. Diversity and complexity are the watchwords of the bricolage, and difference always plays a central role in the process of knowledge production. Difference as it is employed in this context is always treated with dignity, is not fetishized or exoticized, and is accounted for in every act of research engaged (Lomax and Parker, 1996; Madison, 1988; Giroux, 1997; Burbules and Beck, 1999).

In their concern with difference, bricoleurs engage a critical polysemy as a hermeneutic concept seeking even greater interpretative depth. Avoiding manipulative uses of polysemy, bricoleurs employ the concept to open up for examination tensions within data that may lead to previously unconsidered interpretations. In its more elementary form a critical polysemy, like dialectics, is suspicious of monological forms of research and interpretation and maintains that a text with multiple meanings does not simply result from a problem of miscommunication. Oppressed people or their allies can use a critical polysemy to uncover repressed readings of a text that subverts the power-inscribed meaning of the dominant interpretation. In the hands of gay activists, for example, Barbie and Ken dolls can be reinterpreted not as representations of heterosexual normativity but as gender-bending subversive icons. In this manoeuvre traditional sexual power relationships are turned on their head as new meanings, both humorous and gay-friendly, rise to the surface. Thus, polysemy may be used in both in the creation and the reception of meaning.

It is important to note that the resistant interpretations of polysemy may be used for regressive purposes. Skilful political figures may use polysemy in their speeches to inscribe different ideological messages to diverse groups for the purpose of winning their consent to oppression. Bricoleurs evaluate the specific uses of polysemy on the basis of the power relations – whom does it benefit? – and the ethical principles involved. Bricoleurs frequently use polysemy in a hermeneutic context to challenge the meanings given to certain texts and social artefacts by experts from the dominant culture. My book, *The Sign of the Burger*, presents polysemous resistant readings of the social role of McDonald's. Not content with perspectives positioning McDonald's as little-company-made-good achieving the American Dream, I wanted to present interpretations of McDonald's that questioned the socio-political effects of McDonald's American success story.

My effort was not to prove that McDonald's is *not* an American success story – it is. Instead, I provided other interpretations that might cause readers to rethink the meaning of such a story. Throughout the book these diverse meanings of McDonald's engage in a dance. My hope as the author is that the dance, like a hula dance, tells a story. As a bricoleur I want it to enrich our understanding of McDonald's as a socio-political and pedagogical phenomenon in a way that leads to progressive social action. Bricoleurs employ polysemy to keep discussion open around particular phenomena, knowing that authoritarianism operates best when analysis is finalized (Ceccarelli, 1998; Marcum, 1998).

The Creative Nature of Interpretation

Interpretation is always a creative activity open to the hermeneutical expertise of the researcher. Reductionists and rationalists operate on the different premise that interpretation operates in a confined space, and, given the mimetic nature of knowledge, the researcher has little prerogative in the act of meaning-making. Understanding that knowledge is not mimetic, that it is far more complex than a reflection of a true reality, bricoleurs proclaim that interpretation is a productive, not a reproductive, activity (Gadamer, 1989). As a productive activity interpretation involves seeing the world anew, from a different perspective. In this context the most mundane situation in the gaze of an adept bricoleur may be viewed as mysterious and full of lived possibility.

Too often I have worked with fellow researchers who told me they were not going to complete a book or article they were writing on a particular topic because someone else had already done it. A bricoleur understanding the open and creative dimension of interpretation would never entertain such a thought. Upon seeing a new book or essay on the topic they were researching, bricoleurs read it, note the perspectives of the author and then either reframe their book to respond critically to the interpretations or employ their own conceptual frameworks to ask different questions of the phenomenon under scrutiny. Such flexibility is possible when interpretation is viewed as an active process, an active organization of experience. In the case of my colleagues their passive view of interpretation as dictated only by the phenomenon itself rendered them immobile in the headlights of a newly published work. Clio after all is the Muse of poetry *and* history, indicating that the ancient Greeks understood the complexity of interpretation and the active and creative nature of its employment (Mayers, 2001; Chandler, 1998; Bruner, 1996).

Returning for a moment to Francisco Varela and Humberto Maturana's notion of emergence and autopoiesis referenced throughout the preceding chapters, bricoleurs discern the convergence of these concepts with the hermeneutic insights we are addressing here. Maturana and Varela refuse to look at knowledge as an inert entity produced by the experts and 'learned' by isolated students (see Tara Fenwick, 2000, for a challenging extension of these concepts). Analysing the pedagogical dimensions of enactivism, Dennis Sumara and Brent Davis (1997) maintain that human beings enter into the learning or interpretative act as a part of the system under study. This interaction, Maturana and Varela contend, results in a series of structural couplings. When these couplings take place a larger relationship is formed that creates meanings and identities that could not have emerged in isolation.

The hermeneutic circle operates in the realm of knowledge (epistemology), as do the structural couplings of enactivism in cognition. The hermeneutic circle shifts the attention of the interpreter back and forth between systems levels, constructing the 'structural couplings' of what might seem to some as unrelated ideas. In enactivism when the parts come together in these structural couplings, they become integrated wholes characterized by properties possessed by none of the parts. These properties emerge from the systemic relation of the parts, from a constellation of particular interactions. In the hermeneutic circle the meaning of a phenomenon begins to emerge as parts and wholes are examined in relation to one another. Textual meaning in this context *emerge*s only in the relationships connecting particular aspects of a phenomenon. Ultimately the meaning of each of the parts depends on its relationship to the whole. A text's parts must become part of the 'living system' created by the text as a whole. As in enactivist studies of life and cognition, this textual whole, this living system possesses properties exhibited by none of the textual parts.

Thus, when the hermeneutic circle connects parts to parts and parts to wholes, a profound process takes place that enhances the creativity of the researcher. Bricoleurs consider this process to be central to rigorous and creative research. Amazing things happen when bricoleurs step into the hermeneutic circle. The meanings that emerge in the relationships the bricoleur creates are often compelling in their unpredictability. In my own research I eagerly set up these hermeneutic circles in order to watch what happens when dissimilar parts and parts, and parts and wholes, collide. In this context the bricolage helps me draw upon concepts and ideas that are not typically 'structurally coupled'. Bricoleurs are quick to point out that there is nothing magical or supernatural about the emergence of meaning in these contexts. Nevertheless, very interesting things can happen when different concepts intersect with one another in the circle (Fenwick, 2000; Capra, 1996; Bruner, 1996).

Numerous scholars have pressed hermeneuts to develop a more systematic set of methods for interpretation and to proceduralize the operation of the hermeneutic circle. Give us a method, more rationalistic fans of hermeneutics have insisted, that shows us specifically how to do this. Referencing the creative dimension of the interpretative process, hermeneuts such as Hans-Georg Gadamer argued that all meaning-making is historically and culturally specific. As such the purposes and the perspectives of different interpreters are never the same, and, accordingly, different steps and procedures need to be developed for use in divergent circumstances. In addition, hermeneutics is empty if it is not connected with the vicissitudes of everyday life and human struggle. If a hermeneutic method were to be proceduralized, our interpretations would become increasingly disconnected from the lived world (Richardson and Woolfolk, 1994). They would degenerate into abstractions worthy of a dusty repository, abandoning their status as a living form of knowledge connected to the most important issues facing contemporary individuals.

An important dimension of this creative aspect of interpretation involves the use of aesthetics in the hermeneutic process. In this context let us return momentarily to Andrew Murphie's (1998) conception of the objectile as an ever-changing and moving entity that operates to connect various concepts and phenomena. Art has always served an objectile function, as it catalyses the production of unique interactions and insights in a variety of domains. Indeed, art's objectile quality induces researchers and analysts of various stripes to gain new awareness, ask new questions, and address complexity in ways that would have been more difficult outside the aesthetic domain (Carter and Villaverde, 2001). An understanding of hermeneutics in relation to art provides researchers with new lenses through which to view power. In the discipline of aesthetics and art criticism hermeneuts can begin to discern the ways social, cultural, and political forces shape the way art is viewed.

Carefully observing such processes, bricoleurs transfer the understanding of such dynamics into areas outside the aesthetic domain. From the outside it is sometimes easier to discern how power wielders in the artistic community shaped the interpretation of paintings and sculpture in ways that reflected dominant values and ways of seeing than in the discipline or disciplines in which one routinely operates. When bricoleurs expose the connections and ideological commitments of such arbiters of taste and meaning, the processes by which interpretations are often made become transparent. No matter how much the artistic elite may insist that the essential form of a painting determines its aesthetic value, bricoleurs operating in the hermeneutic domain can always reveal a variety of contextual and ideological forces at work in the evaluation. Such is the nature, hermeneuts point out, of interpretation in general. Thus, art in this context serves a meta-objectile function, making connections that illustrate the relationship of art, aesthetic evaluation, power, ideology, modes of representing reality, definitions of realism, and the creativity of the interpretative act.

Power and Interpretation

Rigorous interpretation in the bricolage accounts for the important role of power in shaping the ways texts are produced and understood. The difficult aspect of tracing the impact of power involves the silent and invisible ways that power operates via structures, narratives, and meta-narratives to constrain our understandings of the world. In this context such understandings typically legitimate particular socio-political interests while delegitimating others. Bricoleurs aware of these dynamics structure their research to look for what is not there. Hiding in the taken-for-granted, the ostensibly banal dimensions of the lived world are the forces of power that shape how and what we see. Particular cultural forms perpetuate specific forms of power that sponsor a certain view of culture or history. If bricoleurs are not vigilant in becoming researchers of power, they risk producing knowledge that unknowingly reflects dominant interests. In the effort to confront and expose the regressive nature of certain practices, they may unwittingly reflect the assumptions of dominant power – assumptions that quietly operate to maintain an unjust status quo (Mayers, 2001; Fernandez-Balboa, 2004; Mayers and Field, 2003; Bruner, 1996).

This concern with power, of course, reflects the critical hermeneutic dimension of the bricolage discussed in Chapter 1 and in the first section in this chapter. In this context bricoleurs understand that social relations of power enacted through discourses, language, and an infinite number of other means are always implicated in constructions of knowledge. Here we learn that power and knowledge cannot be conceptualized as two separate entities but are always melded together to the point that we do not know where one ends and the other begins. It is this insight that constructs the by now clichéd observations that knowledge is power and power is knowledge. Thus, in the bricoleur's quest to analyse the way power shapes knowledge, they devise interpretations that are deemed resistant because of such exposure. Power prefers to hide in the shadows, and efforts to reveal its presence and influence are often not looked upon kindly.

But power-conscious bricoleurs simply cannot help themselves. Understanding the centrality of power in the interpretative act, bricoleurs have to go after it in their research. The way all researchers select what some refer to as 'the facts' and others call 'the findings' is always restricted by the conceptual matrices their culture has provided them. Marginalized members of the culture do not shape these matrices, the most powerful do. The interpretative aspects – how one chooses to tell the story – in this production of the facts or the findings demands particular value judgements be made by researchers. Such value judgements do not, as the old theory purported, spontaneously generate like maggots from meat.

Instead, they are profoundly shaped by dominant cultural constructions of value. Indeed, the topics researchers choose to study are shaped by these same dynamics (Williams, 1999; Fenwick, 2000; Ceccarelli, 1998). Men, for example, rarely have to face breast cancer. Thus, when men predominately populated the medical profession, the topic of breast cancer was relegated to a low priority on the research agenda. The power of patriarchy shaped not only interpretative dynamics but also what problems were deemed worthy of study in the first place. The footprints of power are discernible at every step in the research process. In their understanding of this notion bricoleurs studiously avoid appropriation by power blocs promulgating regressive ideologies.

Thus, the bricolage promotes a meta-understanding of power that is aware of the ways all frames of reference and all approaches to research are shaped by dominant ideologies, discourses, and values. The articulation of such power forces will change from historical era to historical era and from culture to culture. Particular ideologies will be more influential in specific 'regimes of truth' than others. A central task of the bricoleur is to trace these ever-mutating forms of power. When such evidence of the effects of power is presented, bricoleurs are quick to follow it up with alternative modes of meaning-making and interpretation. This is why bricoleurs must be knowledgeable of multiple ways of knowing and producing data. A central dimension of learning to become a rigorous researcher involves developing a deep awareness of alternative ways of understanding and operating in the world.

In this situation there is no way to avoid offending some power wielders and apologists for status quo power arrangements. If a researcher consistently manoeuvres to evade this possibility, it shows. Research that is designed to placate power becomes moribund and gradually slides into irrelevance. Thus, power-literate knowledge produced by bricoleurs is always dangerous, always places the researcher in a risky position. Bricoleurs must be ready to face the political dissonance their research will eventually evoke. In an era where power has increased its capacity to shape the world as models of checks and balances on the influence of power have been systematically destroyed, the vulnerability of the bricoleur is greater than ever (Malewski, 2001; May, 1993; Roberts, 1998; Bruner, 1996; Goodson, 1999). In this contemporary context the job of the bricoleur becomes even tougher than it originally was.

Choosing Interpretations: Considering Principles of Selection

Bricoleurs accept the responsibility that comes with the interpretative process. Knowledge production always involves multiple acts of selection, and these choices of methods, theoretical frameworks, and interpretative strategies must be defended. Bricoleurs become experts not only in discerning the selections other researchers make, but also in explaining their own choices in the effort to make sense of a phenomenon. The consideration of our principles of selection in choosing interpretation inevitably leads bricoleurs to the question of validity. Rejecting positivistic notions of internal and external validity, bricoleurs seek new ways of justifying their interpretative choices. In this counter-positivistic tradition they cannot appeal to the notion that their interpretation is the 'most true one'. Thus, bricoleurs develop a set of elastic criteria, tentative principles for selecting particular interpretations over others.

A few considerations are in order before delineating these criteria – considerations of the inherent complexity of the interpretative act. The multilogical nature of the bricolage obviously complicates matters, as the production of different perspectives is always necessary. In this context judgement becomes more complex, as the researcher must attend to numerous concepts simultaneously. Add to this recipe complexity theory's insights into impermanence with its ever-changing interrelationships and the stew thickens. If reality is shaped by the interaction of countless factors, then how can the bricoleur account for them all? At least the answer to this question is simple. There is no way to account for them all and no way the bricoleur should attempt such a Sisyphean task. Only a radical reductionist would claim such a feat is possible in her quest for a singular and universal truth (Villaverde, 2004; Gabriel, 2004; Willinsky, 2001).

The bricoleur's principles of selection would include, but not be limited to, the following. A particular interpretation is chosen because it:

• *provides a richer insight into the text than did others.* Is the interpretation thorough in answering all the inquiries it raises about the

phenomenon? Is it sensitive to the complexity in which all phenomena are embedded? Does it expand our consciousness in relation
to the phenomenon?

- *constructs an interconnected and cohesive portrait of the phenomenon.* Does
  it delineate diverse interrelationships that produce the phenomenon? Does it illustrate the ways these interrelationships shape the
  form the phenomenon takes?

- *grants access to new possibilities of meaning.* Does it raise new questions
  and suggest new types of research into the phenomenon? Does it
  help in the construction of future insights?

- *benefits marginalized groups in their struggle for empowerment.* Does it
  elucidate the role of power in shaping the lives of those connected to
  the phenomenon? Does it identify where individuals are situated in
  the socio-political web of reality? Does it uncover the ways ideology
  operates to undermine individuals' desire for both self-direction and
  interconnectedness?

- *fits the phenomenon under study.* Are the questions raised and
  answered in the interpretation appropriate to the topic explored? Is
  there coherence between the analysis and the phenomenon being
  researched?

- *accounts for many of the cultural and historical contexts in which the
  phenomenon is found?* Does it use these contexts in the effort to make
  sense of the phenomenon? Does it identify the multiple processes of
  which the phenomenon is a part and how they shape it?

- *considers previous interpretations of the phenomenon in question.* Does it
  point out their strengths and deficiencies? Does it place itself in this
  history of interpretations so the reader understands its relationship
  to other interpretations? Does it examine the motives of those who
  have offered diverse interpretations of the phenomenon?

- *generates insight gained from the recognition of the dialectic of particularity
  and generalization, or wholes and parts.* Does it make use of the hermeneutical circle? Does it question the relationship between the
  abstract and the concrete, between socio-historical forces and individual lives? Does its engagement in the hermeneutic circle help
  create new metaphors that move analysis out of clichéd modes?
  Does it reveal the impact of the unconscious use of metaphors on the
  interpretative process?

- *indicates an awareness of the forces that have constructed it.* Does the
  interpretation explore the place in the web of reality from which it
  emanates and the impact of this dynamic on the form it assumes?
  Does it raise questions of self-understanding, for example, the nature
  of the relationship of the producer of the text to the phenomenon in
  question? Does it indicate an awareness of the discourses, values,
  and ideologies that have shaped it?

- *makes use of perspectives of multiple individuals coming from diverse social locations.* Have these voices been examined in relation to the social, linguistic, cultural, and ideological forces that shape them? Does it make use of subjugated knowledges?
- *catalyses just, intelligent, and worthwhile action.* Does it engage its subjects to better conceptualize the world so they can transform it? Does it recognize the spectres of action implicit in the data produced (Madison, 1988; Lather, 1991, 1993)?

These principles of selection get us started in the quest for more rigorous interpretations and more beneficial forms of research. In the following chapters Kathleen Berry takes us through specific examples of how the bricolage might be put into action, of how we might enter the bricolage.

5

Structures of bricolage and complexity
Kathleen S. Berry

What Counts as Structure

Bricolage has structure. One of the major features, as stated in the previous chapters, is that there are no methods or procedures to constructing knowledge through bricolage as research. That does not mean, however, that doing the bricolage is without structure. The structure of bricolage works inwardly, playfully, complexly and rigorously. The chapters that follow are about doing bricolage as research. After reading the previous chapters about the theoretical features and arguments, one might wonder if indeed it is at all possible to do, to put in to motion, to research using the bricolage.

The question which a bricoleur faces is how to engage the bricolage without falling back on positivistic, empirical, monological structures or depending on well-known research discourses and methodologies. Beginning bricoleurs feel overwhelmed – many feel paralysis – by the plethora of issues and lack of explicit directions, linear steps or structure. In the past, direction and structure were provided by research courses in both qualitative and quantitative design and methodology. Students tracked their questions and field using either quantitative or qualitative methodologies with the occasional crossbreeding of data called complementarity. Whatever method or methods were chosen, however, research followed a set course. The research process and writing seemed to unfold as a sequence of steps: first, the identification of questions and sub-questions, the significance and limitations of the study; second, a review of the theory and previous research findings related to the field being researched; third, a discussion of the methodology, data-collecting procedures and research strategies; fourth, a report of the data findings and analysis; and finally, a reporting of the findings with implications for further research and application. No matter what methodology and techniques were used, whether from quantitative or qualitative approaches, the researcher followed a narrow highway with the destination predetermined as to what counted as research. In this same process the discursive practices of science legitimized what counted as knowledge and truth. Members of thesis/dissertation and funding committees looked for evidence of these features and empirical structure. Implicitly they decided what counts as research, truth, knowledge and rigour. Students, with the guidance of a supervisor, proceeded with the doing.

As the borders of traditional quantitative and qualitative research shift with the influence of other technologies such as computers and with challenges to these formally legitimized research discourses, new means and ways of structuring knowledge, truth, and value are surfacing. These structures, in some ways, are new and in other ways they have not yet been recognized or legitimized as research. Bricolage, in its quest to use the tools at hand, identifies the availability of new technologies and structures in addition to new ways of using traditional research tools. It would be like a carpenter who discovers new tools to build the structure of a house at the same time as incorporating traditional structures and tools she/he had used for years.

Problems of Using a Monological Research Structure

Many of the complaints that are issued against monological, linear research exist mainly in theory. Actual examples of the problems internal to the structure of empirical, positivistic research are prevalent but not necessarily obvious. What is missing is difficult to track and examine, as is what data/knowledge is presented. What counts as research and knowledge is questionable under the lens of the bricolage. What follows are two examples, with pseudonyms and ethical changes, to demonstrate some of the issues of monological, empirical research.

A graduate student was researching how teachers perceived their professional development in pursuing an academic degree. He used grounded theory research in its purest sense. As a grounded theory piece of research it was excellent work. As the research progressed it became evident, however, that grounded theory research only covered a limited range of knowledge about these teachers and not necessarily the complexity behind the original research question or data collection. The impact on the research subjects' lives as they conduct their daily affairs at home and workplace in addition to managing a university degree in professional development is very complex – politically, historically, economically, socially and intellectually. A reduction of this complexity to a set of grounded theory categories had, in turn, a limited impact on understanding their world. In the twenty-first century, diversity, plurality and multiple readings, inclusiveness and other concepts cannot be ignored, especially in research that informs institutional policies, structures and practices. Doing the research as a monological methodology limited production of knowledge to that field alone.

The study might have benefited from a different kind of rigour and research process – an application of several fields of study such as feminist and Marxist theories of research (yes, teaching is still dominated by women as third-'class' workers); race studies that would have situated the research findings in a context of whiteness (no one thought of this as problematic); different genres of research, from phenomenology to ethnography, that would capture the patterns and subjective voices of the research subjects in the taken-for-grantedness of their everyday life; and perhaps a partial inclusion of archaeological genealogy that would expose the history of hegemonic practices that produced particular subjects and subjectivities through discursive practices at the institutional and societal levels of both academia and schools. A bricoleur would argue that the empiricism of using one methodology or even one single theory presents only a partial answer to the original research question. Also there exists the potential of linearity of monological research to reproduce the political, economic, societal, historical, and intellectual issues and problems that led to the study in the first place.

In another study, a researcher collected stories of parents living in conditions of poverty. In an attempt to understand their everyday situations and the connections to their child's literacy at school, the researcher collected extremely lively stories of what everyday life was like for these parents. The purpose of the study was to have the stories transform classroom practices about literacy. To interpret the stories, narrative analysis was used with a hint of action research. The interpretation was limited, however, by the categorical borders of narrative and the unrecognized positionality of a middle-class, white researcher to decentre. Without other elements, such as those available in the bricolage, the interpretations remained in the mainstream middle-class categories and assumptions of what counts as home literacy. Other areas of the bricolage, including that of critical positionality and axiology, might have assisted the researcher to decentre the privileged middle-class reality from which she spoke. She might have noted the way her conflicting interpretation reflected the conflicting knowledges, truths, and values promoted by middle-classed schooling of parents living in poverty.

These preceding examples are not a criticism of the researchers' work or of monological research or even methodological research. The examples are presented to indicate how and where bricolage changes what counts as research. They are not put forward to suggest that bricoleurs naively think that they have answers; this would contradict the very premise that bricolage espouses. So instead of answers, conclusions, and questions for further research, as traditional research approaches and methods proclaim, bricolage generates knowledge that is used for social action that transforms grand narratives and discourses, and traditional procedural research methodologies. Is it bricolage to include all voices and ideologies, for example, and thus make claims that this is now research for social justice, inclusiveness, equity and democracy? Is it bricolage when the knowledge produced is a pot-pourri of discourses, challenges and resistance to the status quo? Is it bricolage that blurs the boundaries between traditional, dominant academic disciplines and research methodologies? Is bricolage just another wardrobe of 'the emperor's new clothes' and cultural capital for the authors and economic capital for publishers? What structures can overcome the linear, single-voiced, scientific rationality of the traditional, dominant empirical research of both quantitative and qualitative methodologies and discourses? The last question is the focus of this chapter.

We have chosen to develop the process of employing bricolage as if meeting students new to bricolage but also new to the field of research in general. Therefore, we attempt to use language that will provide workable metaphors and manageable frameworks to equip a beginning or seasoned researcher to start the process. More importantly, several possibilities are suggested to enable the researcher to continue through the labyrinths and webs of complexity and chaos. Furthermore, our intentions are to map out the research journey in a manner that avoids the very pitfalls and practices of positivistic research. The purpose of using the complexity of the bricolage is like a marriage of modern research with research in the postmodern where conflicting discourses remain but where no one area becomes restrained by conceptual borders and where no one area becomes dominant over another.

A Plurality of Structures

In line with the spirit of bricolage, it is possible to select from a host of structures and indeed create your own. To avoid linear, monological, hierarchical, empirical, and structuralist formats, the bricoleur can turn to poststructural configurations and current computer technologies. Other sources could include different realms such as: the dream time and culturally different consciousness of indigenous peoples (see Smith, 1999) and Eastern world cultures; the maieutic circle of hermeneutics and women's ways of knowing; encyclopedias of literary, postmodern, and other contemporary terms; structures of complexity borrowed from current studies in sciences; and the structuring devices of computers such as hypertext and the Internet. The list of possibilities is unlimited and only constrained by the bricoleur's access to varied sources and technologies and the ubiquitous limits of bureaucratic time.

In this chapter we present some possible frameworks and areas of study which could be used to examine and construct a research text with bricolage. The structures and processes presented are meant as guides, not as directives or methods. The bricoleur is guided through these structures with the help of the theoretical threads that are discussed in Chapters 1–4. In many cases, the bricoleur diverges from the highway of efficiency and procedures of traditional monological research to engage different perspectives, readings, structures, processes, discourses, theories, methods, genres and so forth. The permutations and combinations are unlimited but not impossible to engage. There is as much an unlearning of the traditional methods of research as there is learning the bricolage. Bricolage in some manner deploys the traditional at the same time as it employs the plurality of postmodern research. This epistemological paradox is the very challenge and question of research in an era of postmodernism, computer programs and policies of inclusion, equity, plurality, and social justice. Engaging the bricolage is one of many actions that addresses these paradoxes.

The question persists about where to begin the bricolage process. We debated about the order in which to present the theories and practices of bricolage. At the same time, we wanted to profile issues and difficulties unique to bricolage. In the end we decided to present the potential frameworks and maps of possible processes which would allow the research to be set in action. Discussions of issues and difficulties could then be considered as the bricoleur moves back and forth between theories and practices. This sets up a pattern of activity similar to DVD technology or computer hypertext where the bricoleur is in control of the movement (self-organization). The bricoleur can create, pause, return, visit and revisit, access, and withdraw from the process as needed while combining both the epistemological, ontological, and axiological architecture of the bricolage. In order to conceptualize the process, numerous ideas are borrowed from the principles and discourse of complexity theories (Coveney and Highfield, 1995; Prigogine and Stengers, 1984; Ruelle, 1993). A partial range of concurrent theories in the arts and humanities are included in encyclopedic lists and also five dimensions of organization. Chapter 6 involves potential questions and issues that act as the dynamics to push the bricoleur forward and deeper into the text being examined. Chapter 7 presents examples of how other authors apply these multiple areas and structures of the bricolage. In addition, work of graduate students actually engaged in the bricolage process with their professors is included.

Structure of Complexity and Rigour

In many ways it is easy to get started doing the bricolage. There are several ways to start and many directions to travel once the bricoleur moves from the point of entry text (henceforth POET) and threads through the field. Selection of a discourse, discipline, principle, or genre is the decision of the bricoleur, often in consultation with colleagues and professors. Once the process begins, the elements of complexity propel the bricoleur forward. The following frameworks allow the beginning bricoleur to proceed in a random fashion, sometimes toward familiar areas and sometimes unfamiliar territories. Although the choices and directions will vary with each bricoleur, the emergent pattern evolves as the butterfly effect of complexity (see Figures 2 and 3). To accomplish the journey, the bricoleur will be faced with several principles of complexity: self-organization, far-from-equilibrium conditions, feedback looping, randomness, spontaneity, and bifurcations. While moving through the field, certain features of complexity will be present and produce a structure unique to each bricoleur.

The Point of Entry Text

The POET acts as the pivot, the axis for the rest of the application of the bricolage (see the axis of the butterfly effect in Figure 3). It is anything that has or can generate meaning – a picture, a book, a photograph, a story, a theory, a newspaper article, a social issue, a history, a healthcare flyer from the doctor's office, a classroom, a movie. As one student said – borrowing from Paulo Freire – the world's a POET in bricolage.

There are several metaphors that best frame the bricolage process.

1. *Trees and forest.* The POET is poststructural. There is no constant beginning, middle or end, as in modernist texts such as books and film. Other ways of thinking, believing, knowing, valuing and being, slip in and out of the POET, sometimes revising or adding to or destroying the original text. It remains there for the reader to apply the possibilities of different readings, different layers of the text. Each threading through from the different areas of the bricolage map challenges the truths, knowledge of the original POET but never destroys it. Each threading through of any one or many of the areas of the bricolage map exposes in the original POET the complicity, conflicts, contradictions, exclusions, injustices and so forth of the knowledge, beliefs, values, discourses and the representations and practices they produce. New knowledge, truths, are foregrounded. Changes in discourse and practices are implied and hopefully change.

2. *Overhead transparency* (remember that technology?). The POET is the bottom text. Another transparency is overlaid to change, but not erase, the meanings of the original POET. Another and then another transparency from the bricolage map is overlaid, each one with different discourses, knowledges and so forth that exposes the hegemonic forces at play in the creation of the original text. The layers of transparency always see through to the hidden dimensions of the original text. In addition, the different layers can be moved, shifted, or discarded for future use. Each layer, each shifting changes the meanings in the original POET, but each layer is always available for recovery.

3. *Hypertext*. The POET is linked and webbed to a variety of sources, areas of the bricolage, discourses and so on. The author generates multiple possible readings of the text, the reader can 'click' on any text page, any discourse, follow any link, retrace and so on as one can do when producing and using a hypertext program. The original POET is foregrounded and backgrounded, depending on the reader/ user.

4. *DVD*. The structure here is obviously similar to the others, keeping in mind that the structure eventually plays out as a growing map of complexity. To build the complexity does indeed require a different kind of rigour than that of sequential, linear, logical positivism and scientific rationality. Again, like the structure of a DVD movie, authors and readers can go to different areas of the bricolage 'menu' (map), and access authors' notes, deletions and changes from the original POET. The structure is different each time but again the POET is exposed for complicities, conflict between knowledges, exclusion of certain societal and institutional values.

What follows is only one possible way to begin, to proceed, and to finish. Each journey will be different and proceed, seemingly, as a route of randomness. New constructions of knowledge, truths, values and practices act as a compass while the bricoleur seeks to expose the multiple possibilities, connections, depth and complexity of the original POET. Eventually the complexity of life is also illuminated.

Figure 1 is one possible map beginning with a POET. After a brief browse through the map, a discussion will follow. Once the students glance at Figure 1, they are ready to begin the bricolage. We use a threading metaphor as a means to visualize the process as non-linear, which increasingly unfolds as the butterfly image of complexity theory (see Figures 2 and 3). Imagine the bricoleur starts at the POET with a large needle and limitless thread. The bricoleur decides what area of the map to visit first, such as 1 or 13 or 24 or any of the others. The researcher then threads through the discourses and practices delineated

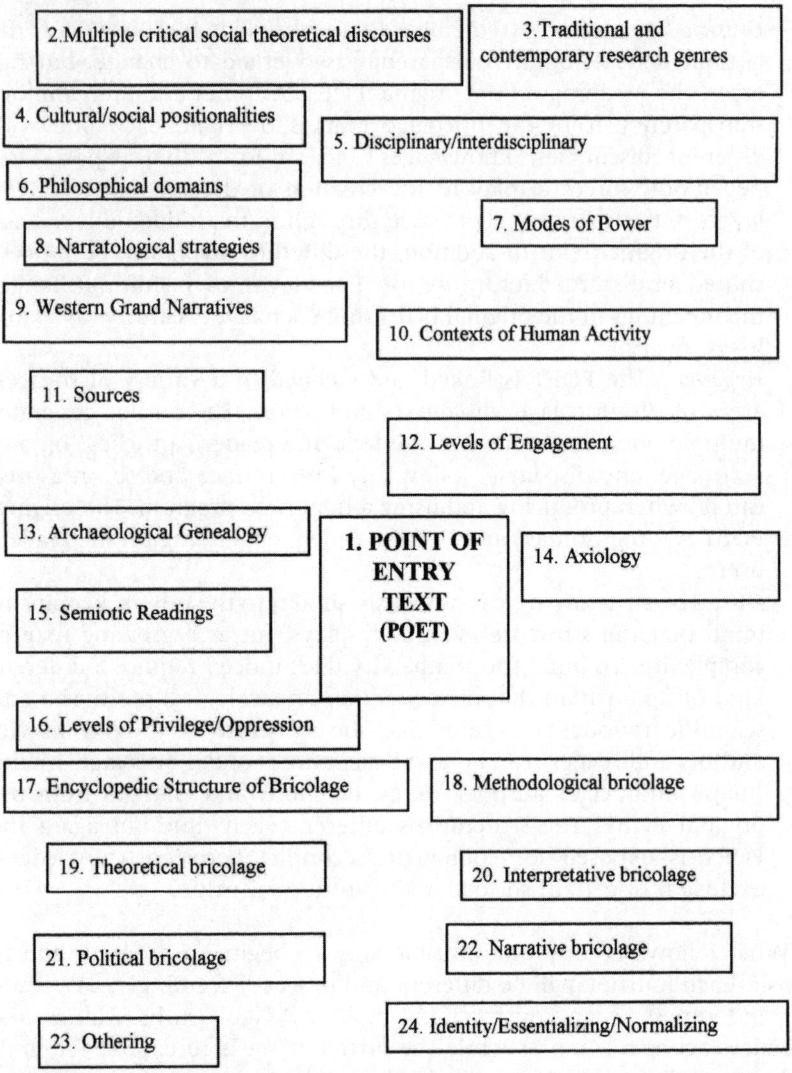

2.Multiple critical social theoretical discourses	3.Traditional and contemporary research genres

4. Cultural/social positionalities

5. Disciplinary/interdisciplinary

6. Philosophical domains

8. Narratological strategies

7. Modes of Power

9. Western Grand Narratives

10. Contexts of Human Activity

11. Sources

12. Levels of Engagement

13. Archaeological Genealogy

1. POINT OF ENTRY TEXT (POET)

14. Axiology

15. Semiotic Readings

16. Levels of Privilege/Oppression

17. Encyclopedic Structure of Bricolage

18. Methodological bricolage

19. Theoretical bricolage

20. Interpretative bricolage

21. Political bricolage

22. Narrative bricolage

23. Othering

24. Identity/Essentializing/Normalizing

Figure 1 Point of entry and bricolage map

in the lists, focusing on a particular relevant one. Then he or she threads back to the initial text. The threaded return acts as a feedback loop to the initial text and changes, expands, clarifies, modifies, and challenges the existing knowledge. In the process new perspectives and knowledge about the text are produced. The bricoleur can then repeat the process by threading through a different feature of the lists and again looping back to the original text. This process can be repeated several times, each rethreading enhancing the texture of the knowledge produced. The

constant interactions between the original text and the feedback loops
build a multimode of research that requires rigour and complexity and
thus engages the concept of doing bricolage. The final map looks like the
butterfly shape (see Figure 3) produced by the Lorenz attractor, and as
Coveney and Highfield (1995) state, 'the more information is exchanged,
the more feedback processes occur and thus, in general the more
complexity'.

Figure 2 illustrates the process of how one bricoleur created the butterfly effect of complexity. She started at the POET and then threaded
through the various areas of the bricolage map as follows:

(1) started at POET (2) threaded through archaeological genealogy
and semiotic readings (3) back to POET (4) threaded through
axiology (5) back to POET (6) threaded again through archaeological
genealogy and semiotic readings after changing initial interpretation
of POET (7) back to POET (8) used different sources to add or
challenge original POET in addition to once again threading through
semiotic readings and archaeological genealogy (9) revised POET
again (10) added two new areas of the bricolage map, interpretative
and methodological bricolage, in addition to threading some points
and principles of axiology back to (11) the POET and finally ended
(12) in political bricolage for gathering more understanding of this
area to eventually feedback to the POET.

In Figure 3, the increase in complexity is evident as the bricoleur visits
and revisits possible areas of the bricolage map to revise and rethink the
original POET. The map has been overlaid with an actual diagram of
Lorenz's butterfly effect.

Threading through the Landscape

The POET (see Figure 1) is the starting point. It acts as point of origin
through which all the different areas of the bricolage are threaded. The
original text changes in content as well as structure once the volume of
bricolage threads increases with each feedback looping. For every bricoleur the starting point is different. In one graduate research course
with twenty students, there were twenty different POETs. Although only
one text is used to model the process at the beginning of the course,
individual texts gradually appear as a wide and diverse range of topics,
questions, and sources. In the case of Sadie (discussed in Chapter 7), her
POET arose out of a conversation about height discrimination; this was a
concern that was personal to her, but at the time she felt unworthy of
applying the bricolage. For some it might be a question like Nelson's on
why vocational education no longer existed; or Mary's on classroom
questioning; or Bridie's study of public school students living in

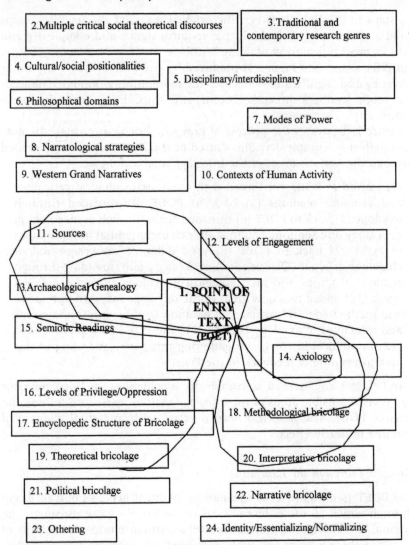

Figure 2 Bricolage map and the emergence of complexity

conditions of poverty. Diana used a policy document on school discipline as her POET. Mia's interest in how to teach her fifth grade students to do multiple readings of a children's novel served as her POET. Both Wally's photographs from 1930s' school records and Gordon's personal journey to some World War II veterans' reunions in Europe became topics for research. The possibilities are infinite, and with continuous application of the bricolage, an image of the butterfly structure of complexity eventually evolves (see Figures 2 and 3).

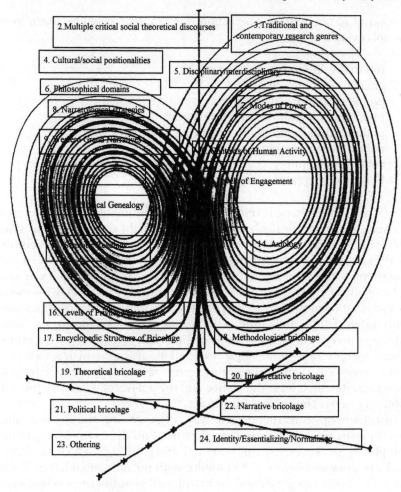

Figure 3 Butterfly image of complexity

Once the subject for the POET is chosen, the bricoleur turns to the areas of the bricolage that appear in Figure 1. Each area of the structure can be visited once, several times or not at all and threaded back to the POET. The areas mapped out in Figure 1 are only a few of the possible sites for the bricoleur to visit. There are plenty of areas that could appear, depending on what is needed or what is missing. To add to the intricacy and rigour of doing bricolage research, some components of an area can be extended even further. In area 3 for example, one research genre is hermeneutics, which consists of several possible theoretical variations. The bricoleur might use a general notion of hermeneutics to thread back through the POET. Or he/she might choose to draw upon a more specific version of hermeneutics. A selection, for example, could be made from the following list:

- rationalist hermeneutics;
- general hermeneutics;
- philological hermeneutics;
- phenomenological theory of meaning;
- philosophical hermeneutics (Mueller-Vollmer, 1988);
- radical hermeneutics;
- cold hermeneutics;
- hermeneutic phenomenolgy.

An astute or seasoned researcher could distinguish the difference between these versions. A novice bricoleur might only be able to skim their surface meanings. Both might be able to use the different versions to reveal similar or conflicting interpretations within or between the variations – thus the rigour of bricolage. The point is that even one component of an area has many possible threads for the POET – many threads that open the text to deeper, further, multiple, and contradictory knowledge, truths and, ultimately, social action. Whatever the case, bricolage breeds complexity if the original text remains open to multi-dimensionality or a multilogical orientation. This type of research prevents knowledge and humanity being reduced to simplicity and sameness. Research for social justice and the politics of difference meet in solidarity under the rubric of bricolage.

Bricoleurs can construct diverse ways of perceiving and conceptualizing. To assist the bricoleur in the effort to begin the examination of the complexity of the POET, the potential areas through which to thread back are expanded below in accordance with the numbered boxes. These are only partial categories and, as mentioned about hermeneutics, each one has possible internal versions. To prevent intellectual overload or paralysis, we suggest different groups of novice bricoleurs take a different area of the map and study it in depth (time permitting). Then it is suggested they apply each area to the same text. When each group has studied and implemented the different areas of the map to the same text, eventually each bricoleur can apply the specific area of the bricolage to his/her individual POET. To increase the complexity by application of other areas, each bricoleur consults with the other bricoleurs of the original group and they then work to provide feedback looping to each other's text using the different areas. In one graduate research course, we did this (see Chapter 7).

While passing through the various areas of the bricolage, the researcher enacts the principles of complexity. Self-organization, feedback looping, far-from-equilibrium, randomness, spontaneity, bifurcation points and other conditions of complexity push the bricoleur forward, drawn by knowledge known and the knowledge to be constructed. On the one hand, the bricoleur is surrounded by choices to make and most likely will start with the familiar area(s) that best serve the immediate quest. Guided by theoretical perspectives, critical pluralism (Schumaker, 1990), subjective voices, attentiveness to and inclusiveness of difference, the bricoleur reaches for knowledge and truths that will incite action for social justice. On the other hand, the increasing complexity cautions the bricoleur against slippage into logical positivism and artificial scientific realism. In other words, bricolage must problematize both the world and itself. These characteristics will be elaborated further in Chapter 6 with actual examples of interactions between professors and students. The following areas of the map are meant to be used in a manner consistent with the principles of complexity theory.

2. *Multiple critical social-theoretical discourses*: includes Frankfurt School critical theory, postmodernism, poststructualism, postcolonialism, critical pedagogy, constructivism/critical constructivism, complexity theory, ecological theory, etc. Each area can be applied to the POET in full with other areas of the map, or partially, or not at all. The difference in using them as bricolage, however, is that the bricoleur avoids totalizing in addition to recognizing conflicts, contradictions and limitations both within and between the discourses. Whatever discourse is employed, any echoes of logical positivism which appear throughout the analysis must be purged. Attention to this principle is necessary for all the areas of the bricolage map.

3. *Traditional and contemporary research genres/methodologies and their analytical tools*: borrows ideas, discourses and methodologies from traditional quantitative and qualitative analysis, case studies, action research, grounded theory research, ethnography, phenomenology, psychoanalysis, historiography, semiotics, textual analysis, hermeneutics, rhetorical analysis, discourse analysis, and contemporary analytical tools such as intertextuality, hypertext and multimedia. The obvious point for the bricoleur is to be aware of the complicity and contradictory principles and practices within and between the methodologies. Since each methodology releases its own internal logic, bricolage cautions against a totalizing, stabilizing and legitimizing epistemology of truth. Another concern of bricolage is the indeterminate openness of interpretation that leads to cultural relativism. To add to the growing complexity of bricolage research, reflection is required. However, unexamined reflection on the knowledge being produced using a singular or combination of genres and methodologies does not necessarily count as bricolage. Reflection is a theoretically informed action. Naming what theories the

bricoleur is using to reflect on the ideas and methodologies sets up a hall of mirrors. In this way, multi-reflections from the myriad of different perspectives and positionalities (see 4) add to the complexity. Butterfly wings flapped through the many areas of the map increase the epistemological complexity in the POET.

4. *Cultural/social positionalities*: recognizes that the researcher is positioned in the interpretation of the text through particular socializing processes, discourses and artefacts. These elements influence the position from which a researcher speaks, thinks, and acts; thus the knowledge, values, beliefs and practices that the researcher carries into the research text such as: race (e.g., Afrocentric analysis, indigenous studies, identity politics), class (e.g., materialism), gender (e.g., feminist studies, masculinity), sexuality (e.g., queer theory), ability studies, religion (e.g., Islamic studies, Judaic studies, liberation theology), etc. 'Individuals cannot separate where they stand in the web of reality from what they perceive [and include] ... [p]ositionality involves the notion that since our understanding of the world and ourselves is socially constructed, we must devote special attention to the differing ways individuals from diverse social backgrounds construct knowledge and make meaning' (Kincheloe and Steinberg, 1997, p. 206). Drawing upon cultural/social positionalities combined, for example, with archaeological genealogy (see 13) that analyses knowledge in historical and political contexts, bricolage continues to compile a text of increasing complexity and plurality.

5. *Disciplinary/interdisciplinary departmentalizations of knowledge*: combines and blurs modern constructions of disciplinary/academic knowledge such as history, philosophy, sociology, anthropology, political science, economics, geography, psychology, literary criticism, aesthetic criticism, theatrical and dramatic studies, cultural studies, paradigmatic knowledge, enactivist cognitive studies, etc. Under the rubric of bricolage, traditionally organized disciplinary knowledge is reorganized 'into new configurations and alliances, or forms of interdisciplinarity, when these old ways of thinking have come to seem stale, irrelevant, inflexible or exclusionary' (Moran, 2002, p. 1). United, for example, with modes of power (7) which exist in modes of thought and institutional practices, bricolage problematizes and disrupts, but does not eliminate, modern borders of knowledge organized as disciplines. Similar to interdisciplinary studies, bricolage 'represents ... a denaturalization of knowledge: it means that people working within established modes of thought have to be permanently aware of the intellectual and institutional constraints within which they are working, and open to different

ways of structuring and representing their knowledge of the world' (Moran, 2002, p. 187).

6. *Philosophical domains*: produces ideas about how and why the world is or should be such as how we come to know/be/act, what is knowledge (epistemology), being (ontology), axiology (the disputational contours of morality and value – see Figure 5), teleology, cosmology, and so forth. Bricoleurs realize that many of these ideas were produced by the growth and development of Western civilization and construct what counts as knowledge and being. Furthermore, these ideas remain as residuals of dominant systems, policies, and practices for Western civilization. The bricoleur examines and critiques texts; struggles to dismantle the manipulation and control of knowledge and being that, in the past, privileged and oppressed Self and the Other (see, for example, Said, 1979).

7. *Modes of power*: exposes different modes of power and relationships that are at play in research studies, ideas, discourses, canons, relationships, etc. and have come to be accepted as normal, commonsensical, natural and truthful. Among the invisible veins of power are hegemonic, ideological, regulatory, discursive, disciplinary, coercive, hierarchical, bureaucratic, assumed, privileged, and oppressive. Young (2000) names five faces of oppressive power as exploitation, marginalization, powerlessness, cultural imperialism and violence. Each type of oppressive power works in everyday life. Layering Young's discussion with locations of privilege and oppression (16) expands the investigation of modes of power to the individual, institutional, societal and civilizational levels. Analogous to stacking transparencies for overhead projectors on top of one another, the layering of any area of the bricolage map with another results in a transparent texturing to feed back to the POET.

8. *Narratological strategies*: utilizes romance, tragedy, satire, irony, comedy, absurdism, to massage the POET with personal and literary style, voice and conventions. These literary genres supply the bricoleur with a host of tools for the production of contradiction, paradoxes, divergence, randomness, surprise, dramatic poignancy, tension and possibilities for flexibility and unfamiliar structuring of text. Another amplification of complexity becomes apparent.

9. *Western grand narratives*: requires dismantling of dominant and totalizing theories and discourses such as capitalism, socialism, liberal humanism, Marxism, neo-Marxism, Christianity, democracy, conservativism, whiteness, heterosexuality, and patriarchy. These stories get told as logical, rational, objective and scientific. Other stories are either left untold or erased; many narratives are circulated as absolute truth and many stories are argued as power for the storytellers. Bricolage employs these grand narratives as a means to

debunk their mythologies produced in the name of rationality, truth and justice.

10. *Contexts of human activity*: surrounds knowledge, truths, beliefs and values with the following temporal and spatial contexts in which they were created, circulated and maintained: the historical, political, social, cultural, intellectual, economic, geographical (place), personal, regional, local, national, global, societal, institutional, civilizational, and tribal. Bricoleurs are constantly placing knowledge, truths, beliefs, values and practices in many of these contexts. At times, the different contexts are complicit with each other. The bricoleur's responsibility is to state, for example, the complicity of dominant policies and practices, while at the same time uncovering the contradictions and silences cloaked by decontextualized knowledge. In this way, knowledge and actions cannot be generalized, universalized, normalized and so on for all times, places and people. Threading the POET through multiple contexts requires a rigour not necessarily required by a decontextualized or a singular context.

11. *Sources*: accesses traditional canons and contemporary sources of knowledge and artefacts such as oral, printed, photographs, Internet, visuals, art works, cartoons, popular culture, media, policies, documents, history, daily life, books, journals, film, issues, and questions. The sources of knowledge available to the bricoleur draw on several sources ranging from pre-modern (oral) and modern (print) to postmodern (computer) technologies. The reporting and publication of knowledge is no longer dominated by print, books and academia. Other texts and sources, such as magazines and popular culture, are as much a resource as 'high culture'.

12. *Levels of engagement*: structures the process of engagement as the bricoleur employs the map. Knowledge shifts and increases through different levels of engagement from attraction to attention, interest, concern, investment, commitment, passion, and compassion, then maybe a bit of learning (Heathcote, 1984). According to Michael Polanyi (1958) and other philosophers of epistemology (Gleick, 1992; Kincheloe *et al.*, 1999b), researchers follow no particular method leading to discovery and breakthroughs, but after an initial attraction to the POET (issue, problem, question, etc.) engagement increases, driven by interest and sustained through passion (self-driven) and compassion (driven by passion for others). In part, informed intuition sorts out the leads and dead ends. The landscape of bricolage appears 'as an exciting engagement with difference: the challenge of "the other"; the disruption of certainties; the recognition of ambiguities within one's self as well as one's differences with others [knowledge, values, beliefs, practices etc.]' (Benhabib, 1996, p. 144).

13. *Archaeological genealogy*: offers an examination of a text based on the work of Foucault. It acts as a synthesis of his archaeological exca-

vation of text analysis that 'discerns how discourses constructed individuals for human regulation' and his locating of power relations within those discourses through a process of genealogical connections (Agnello, 2002). Archaeological genealogy, like bricolage, problematizes different aspects of text analysis such as the subject, power/knowledge, institutional discourses and policies, the author and notions of the self (Rabinow, 1984). Through her research on matters of whiteness, Frankenberg (1997) outlines a range of possible processes to include in archaeological genealogy. In no particular order, the bricoleur investigates the POET with theoretical features of Foucault's works including the considerations listed in Figure 4.

14. *Axiology*: asks what and whose values/morality counts. On a grid with epistemology and ontology, axiology refers to what and who counts as morality and value from a Western theological hermeneutic perspective. In bricolage, axiology adds configurations to the mapping out of the shifting centres of privilege and oppression measured along several axes with knowledge and other philosophical domains. Complexity emerges as the POET is scrutinized for shifting contexts, social histories of particular civilizations and within particular cultural groups within those civilizations (Scheurich, 1997). Bricolage constantly places the knowledge generated in the POET along axes of shifting values – centres of dominance and privilege and margins of oppression and exclusion. The following image (see Figure 5) is designed to help the novice bricoleur use axiology to thread possible questions and observations through the POET.

Imagine several dowels of the same length inserted into the centre of a polystyrene ball (the image's dimensionality is reminiscent of Tinker Toy building blocks or similar to that of a sea urchin). Each dowel is labelled with a cultural category such as race, gender, sexuality, religion, class, ethnicity, and so forth. The points of the dowels in the centre of the ball represent privilege and dominance, the other end of the dowel represents the margins and oppression. The bricoleur moves the discussion back and forth on the dowel, depending on what category is being investigated. If the discussion, for example, were about what/whose values/knowledge/beliefs count as good behaviour, good mothering, literacy, leadership, work, truth, administration, learning, childhood and so forth, the use of axiology would illustrate what definitions and categories lie at the centre and those that exist on the margins or are excluded depending on race, class, nationality, sexuality and the host of other possible culturally constructed categories. Even the centre is constantly shifting. Certain values or what counts as legitimate may exist at the centre when race is considered. Those definitions may

Figure 4   Process-oriented archaeological genealogy

tracking	How/when/where/why did the social/cultural construction being studied move from an everyday, informal existence into formal, institutional, dominant, political texts, artefacts, discourses and practices?
deconstructing	How are social constructions of Western thought, spirituality, race, gender, class, sexuality, etc. marked in literary, cinematic, scholarly, and other practices in ways that privilege and legitimize the producers?
examining	What/who is to be studied? Bricolage considers all texts as products of culture and thus open to examination for locations of power and oppression.
excavating (archaeology)	What constructions exist at certain temporal and spatial points that are carried forth unnoticed into the present and, without disruption, would be carried into the future? How/why does each layer reproduce the construction as a historically constructed system of differentiation, exclusion and belonging?
connecting (genealogy)	In what ways does the intellectual, political, economic, social, cultural, and historical climate discursively support the legitimization and dominance of the construction that produces inequities, social injustices and exclusions?
critiquing	What questions/insights can the bricoleur use to challenge the complicity, continuation and reproduction of domination?
articulating	What discourses, strategies, actions, policies, structures, practices can be developed that would move/transform societal, institutional, individual and civilizational discourses etc. toward social justice, inclusion, equity, democracy, and plurality?

shift towards the margins when viewed along the axes of class and other constructed categories. Whereas positivistic research reduces the information to homogeneous and singular knowledge by eliminating the variables, obviously the point of applying axiology to the POET is to track the movement of shifting centres depending on a multitude of variables such as race, education, sexuality, context,

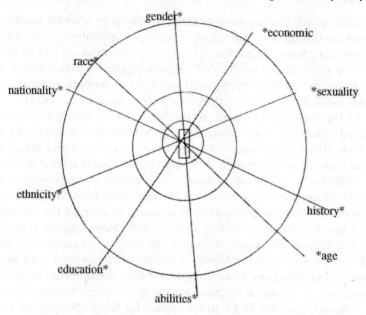

Box = centre of privilege/dominance
Smallest to largest circle = decreasing from culture of privilege to margins/oppression
* lines of shifting value

Figure 5 Axiological shifts

temporality, power base and so on. Tracking shifting centres supplies a charted grid that, when threaded through the POET, subverts hegemonic totalizing and artificial textual unity.

If a person were tracked throughout a routine day, for example, he/she might enter into several relationships and activities in which he/she could be found at the centre and on other occasions on the margins, dependent on race, gender, economic status, and other cultural constructs. If a pattern of privilege or oppression materializes as consistently dominant, then threading through another area of the map, such as discussed in 16, would contribute to the complexity of interpretation and understanding. In turn, the bricoleur constantly keeps in mind that the model is multidimensional. It operates in the multilogical context described in the previous chapters. Continuous scrutiny of truth, meanings and interpretation using axiology, like poststructuralism, characterizes the propensity of bricolage to decentre the dominant, the subject, and thus launch preconditions for transformative policies and practices.

15. *Semiotic readings*: continues multiple readings as a social reading of texts according to a threefold model (see Thwaites *et al.*, 1994). Borrowing from Stuart Hall (1980), the bricoleur questions if the text is reproducing embedded taken-for-granted assumptions and codes/signs/signifers/representations. Textual semiotic readings spin additional threads for the bricoleur to feed back to the POET.

    In the example in Figure 6, the bricoleur examines the text for coded symbolic representations of what counts as family in the 1950s. If the codes were relocated to other cultures and times, the readings of the text would shift and change. Each rereading would be different as the bricoleur moves the semiotic readings through the POET, at the same time conscious of the shifting contexts of time and space. An interesting epiphany that seems to emerge for the brico-leur involves the ways coding systems shift depending on numerous factors such as the reader, the times, the purpose or publication date. Lively discussions about whether the text is embedded with domi-nant, negotiated, or resistant codes often disrupt the bricoleur's tendency to assign a singular meaning or interpretation. Once a bricoleur opens the POET to colleagues for feedback looping, using the chart of semiotic readings in Figure 6, the movement of codings and representations produces opportunities for revelations of com-plicity, conflict and contradiction. As Thwaites *et al.* (1994) claim 'texts do not contain fixed ideas but are involved in people's nego-tiations with, and responses to, the social values and attitudes represented by dominant and preferred meanings' (p. 85).

16. *Levels of privilege/oppression*: scrutinizes, consistent with axiology and other areas of the bricolage map, the POET for fluctuating and consistent levels of privilege and oppression. To explore a text,

Figure 6 Semiotic readings

Semiotic reading as	Coding	How constructed in 1950s
Dominant	Dominant meanings and relationships are reproduced	Nuclear (heterosexual parents, married, middle class, etc.)
Negotiated	Some of the codes are questioned but the overall mythologies are accepted	Single-parent family (usually female)
Oppositional/ resistant	Connotations and codes are challenged and trigger conflicting mythologies	Homosexual parents

Scheurich (1997) provides an interesting structure which bricoleurs can adapt for threading through the POET. The levels are helpful when novice bricoleurs seem trapped at the personal and psychological level which restrict interpretation and understanding. With Scheurich's levels, bricoleurs are compelled to move beyond individualism in research that ignores the broader cultural locations of privilege and oppression (text as racialized, gendered, classed and so forth) at institutional, societal and civilizational levels. Bricoleurs labour concurrently with the four cultures to challenge 'prevailing ... assumptions, norms, concepts, habits, expectations that privilege one race [etc.] over another' (p. 136). Bricolage asks what makes privilege and oppression possible at the four levels. The most significant feature of Scheurich's categories, the civilizational culture in which the other three are embedded, complements bricolage by checking the very (racial, gender, etc.) bias that lies within the research text itself, within the bricoleur and the very methodology employed. Obviously these conditions add to the complexity and rigour of doing bricolage. The embedded levels, from the broadest to the smaller, are shown in Figure 7.

17. *Encyclopedic structure of bricolage*: arranges key terms and principles by alphabetic order. There are dozens of dictionaries and encyclopedias

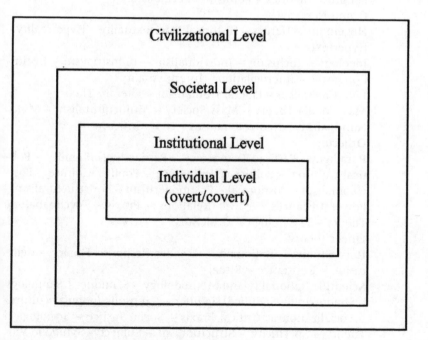

Figure 7   Scheurich's embedded levels of cultural values

that briefly introduce the rookie bricoleur to the terminology of contemporary theories and practices. The following are a few possibilities:

Archaeological Genealogy – Archetype – Articulating – Axiology

Bricolage – Binarisms – Biographical (Historical, New Historical Criticism)

Capitalism – Cartesianism – Challenging the Authority of the Text – Chaos and Complexity – Christianity – Communism – Complicity – Confessional Discourse – Constructions (of knowledge, value, truths, practices, gender, race, text) – Corporate Pedagogy – Critical Autobiography – Critical Pedagogy – Critical Theory – Critique of Representation – Cultural Criticism – Cultural Heritage – Cultural Imperialism

Dead White European Males – Deconstruction – Deliberative Democracy – Desire – Dialogical Theory – Discourse Discourses in Conflict – Disciplinary Knowledge – Discursive Structures – Diversity

Effective Histories – Elite Culture – Enlightenment – Equity – Examing – Excavating Critiquing – Exclusion – Existentialism

Far-from-Equilbrium – Feedback Looping – Feminist Criticism – Feminist Theories – Fordism – Formalism

Grand Narratives

Hegemony – Heroes – Historical Intertextuality – Hyperreality – Hypertext

Ideology – Inclusion – Individualism – Industrialism – Institutionalisms – Interpellation – Intertextuality

Late Capitalism – Liberal Humanism – Literary Theory

Mass Media Theory – Mass Society – Multiculturalism – Myth

Nationalism – Neo-colonialism – New Criticism

Othering

Paradigm – Partisan Democracy – Patriarchy – Plurality – Political Cultures – Politics of Difference – Popular Culture – Postcolonialism – Postformal – Postmodernism – Poststructuralism – Power Distances – Power Relations – Praxis – Psychoanalytic Theory – Psychological Criticism

Queer theory

Race Studies – Rationality – Reader-Response Theory – Reification – Resistance – Ritual

Scientific Rationality and Methodology – Semiotics – Semiology – Shadowing – Signified/Signifier – Simpsons (popular culture) – Socialization as Critical Praxis – Social Justice – Sociological Theory – Specificity – Structuralism – Subject – Symbolic Violence – Symbols

Textuality – Totalizing (narratives, logic) – Tracking – Truths –
Types of Democracy – Types of Feminism
Universalism
Value
Whiteness Studies

Areas 18–22 of the bricolage map were initially suggested in Denzin
and Lincoln (1994, 2000) and developed further by Joe Kincheloe. In
what follows, there are obvious and not so obvious overlaps and
redundancies with other areas of the bricolage. Synonymous with the
theories and practices of complexity, bricolage regards the repetition as
noise to be included. The noise of multiple variables, voices and principles extends the opportunities for the bricoleur to mark the complicities,
conflicts, contradictions and limits both between and within the different
areas of the map.

18. *Methodological bricolage*: employs numerous data-gathering strategies
    from the interviewing techniques of ethnography, historical research
    methods, discursive and rhetorical analysis of language, semiotic
    analysis of signs, phenomenological analysis of consciousness and
    intersubjectivity, psychoanalytical methods, Pinarian currere, to
    textual analysis of documents.

19. *Theoretical bricolage*: uses a wide knowledge of social-theoretical to
    positions – from constructivism to critical constructivism, enacti-
    vism, feminism, Marxism, neo-Marxism, critical theory, post-
    modernism, poststructuralism, postcolonialism, cultural studies, and
    queer theory – to situate and determine the purposes, meanings, and
    uses of the research act.

20. *Interpretative bricolage*: deploys a range of interpretative strategies that
    emerge from a detailed awareness of the field of hermeneutics and
    the ability to use the hermeneutic circle. In this context bricoleurs
    work to discern their location in the web of reality in relation to
    intersecting axes of personal history, autobiography, race, socio-
    economic class, gender, sexual orientation, ethnicity, religion, geo-
    graphical place, and numerous other dynamics. These various per-
    spectives are used to discern the role of self in the interpretative
    process. This process is combined with different perspectives offered
    by people located in diverse locations in the web in order to widen
    the hermeneutical circle and to appreciate the diversity of perspec-
    tives on a particular topic. These perspectives or interpretations are
    viewed in relation to one another and in relation to larger social,
    cultural, political, economic, psychological and educational struc-
    tures as well as the social-theoretical positions previously referenced.
    In this way the complexity and multidimensionality of the inter-
    pretative process is comprehended by the bricoleur.

21. *Political bricolage*: understands that all research processes hold political implications, are manifestations of power. No science, no mode of knowledge production is free from the inscriptions of power. In this context bricoleurs study the information they collect and the knowledge they produce to discern the ways tacit forms of power have shaped them. In light of such awareness bricoleurs attempt to document the effects of ideological power, hegemonic power, discursive power, disciplinary power, regulatory power, and coercive power.

22. *Narrative bricolage*: appreciates the notion that all research knowledge is shaped by the types of stories inquirers tell about their topics. Such story types are not innocently constructed but reflect particular narratological traditions: comedy, tragedy, and irony. The bricoleur's knowledge of the frequently unconscious narrative formula at work in the representation of the research allows a greater degree of insight into the forces that shape the nature of knowledge production. Thus, more complex and sophisticated research emerges from the bricolage.

23. *Othering*: realizes that all studies are about othering even when autobiographical or naming positionality. Bricoleurs, as producers of knowledge, beliefs and values about Other(ness), monitor their studies for the ways in which the Other(ness) is represented. Questions about whether the Other is being pathologized, victimized, stereotyped, silenced, or bashed by the interpretation and construction of knowledge are foregrounded and challenged in bricolage. For example, through research studies, reports, literature, film and academic writing, knowledge is constructed about mothering, parenting, masculinity, literacy, leadership, nursing, indigenous people, counselling the Other, education, law and the many possible worlds of Other(ness). How does the bricoleur ensure that these worlds inhabited by human beings are reported in a manner that keeps intact the dignity, freedom, and agency of the Other? Bricolage rigorously pursues knowledge in this manner – not an easy task given the dominance and validation of positivism and scientific methodology in the construction of knowledge and value about the Other(ness).

24. *Identity/essentializing/normalizing*: avoids reducing difference in identities and socially constructed categories and processes to simplistic notions such as biological naturalism. Because of the complexity of being human, social beings cannot be reduced for scientific manipulation and control. Bricoleurs monitor the discourses and practices they proclaim as truths, beliefs and knowledge. Examination of the knowledge and values produced by using several or all areas of the bricolage map does not necessarily prevent the reduction

of human agency, activity and consciousness to objective, scientific logic. With language as the major way we organize knowledge (oral, printed, visual, auditory, mathematical, musical and so on), it can be very convenient and comfortable to slip into the discourse of normalizing, essentializing, naturalizing, generalizing, neutralizing, assimilating, accommodating, universalizing, and decontextualizing. Through naivety or unchecked discourse, bricoleurs might unknowingly be reducing knowledge and values produced by their study. Statements such as 'boys will be boys' need to be flagged and examined for discourse of naturalizing. Narratives might be used to represent experiences of women or race but included in the research as speaking for all women regardless of race, sexuality and other culturally constructed difference; that there is some essence common to all women (essentializing). What counts as 'it's just common sense' or 'it's always been that way' knowledge is packed with a mythos that soon covers up, for example, practices and experiences of exclusion and discrimination; systemic and institutional abuses of individuals and groups and symbolic violence in popular culture and media. So to avoid essentializing and so on, bricoleurs perform cross-examination. While examining and critiquing the knowledge of a text/world/experience, they are also critiquing what they produced as knowledge about the text being examined.

Bricolage in a Computer Age

The computer age has changed the way we construct knowledge. If bricolage seems impossible or so difficult to even entertain as a way of thinking about and organizing knowledge, computer technology helps to relieve that situation. The capabilities and features of computers, such as the structuring devices of hypertext, storage capacity, linking and webbing, the speed of threading through multiple domains, in addition to the theoretical discourse, premises, and multiplicity of doing bricolage, makes it possible to engage in complexity. While we are not suggesting that books and other technologies should be tossed aside, we recognize that computer technology can assist the doing of bricolage in ways that would have been considered impossible two or three decades ago. Since complexity theories have been created, in large part, on the back of computer developments, engaging bricolage as complexity and rigour is assisted by computer metaphors and technologies. No technology, however, can substitute for the sensitivity and passion of the bricoleur to produce knowledge for social change and justice.

6
Feedback looping for increasing complexity
Kathleen S. Berry

Introduction

As bricoleurs continuously thread the initial POET with a multiplicity of knowledges and structures, discourses and premises, questions and practices taken from the different regions of the bricolage map, increasing conditions of complexity develop. Although the overall image of the structure of complexity, that of Lorenz's butterfly effect, is presented in Chapter 5, the minute details of doing bricolage are not evident. As the details of bricolage are added to the POET, a clear delineation of the threads disappears. The situation is similar to a surveyor's map, for example, that depicts the coastline of Newfoundland, Canada, in kilometres, so that the outline of the province is general. If, each time, the same coastline is measured with smaller units such as metres, decimetres, centimetres, and so on, the details of the coastline become almost impossible to record or image. This is a condition of complexity. In bricolage, details of complexity are created mainly by feedback looping. How feedback looping works in bricolage is, like the smallest measures of a coastline, the focus of this chapter.

In bricolage, where the POET is subjected to multiple readings, conflicting discourses, fragments of an area, articulations of positionality, mixed genres of epistemology and methodologies, discursive ideologies and so forth, to describe feedback looping in detail is parallel to measuring the coastline of Newfoundland in centimetres. The documentation of complexity and rigour works with such a deep unconventional structure researchers might question the validity of bricolage and finally resort to simple and traditional structures of logical positivism established by the binary and linear approaches of both quantitative and qualitative research genres. To accomplish retreat, feedback looping is a major element for increasing complexity; that is, adding details to the mapping-out process of doing bricolage.

Inundated with the diversity of knowledge and the non-linearity of the structure, feedback looping in bricolage meets the requirements of increasing complexity. In addition to the feedback looping from the different areas of the map to the POET, bricoleurs receive additional feedback from professors, colleagues, and self. The intellectual, social, political, historical, and funding contexts in which the research is conducted also act as feedback looping. Together, these strands produce several conditions that are major features of complexity. Feedback looping in bricolage, however, is not prescriptive responses or comments requesting elaboration or clarification to the author's text. Feedback looping acts as a disruption of totalization of thought, words and deeds. Feedback looping does not mourn the loss of simple structures and processes. To meet these expectations, bricoleurs play with the POET through feedback looping, never resting at a point of completion. Several major functions of feedback looping in bricolage are:

- to include all the variables, the possibilities, the contradictions, the inconsistencies, the conflicts, the complicity with dominant centres of knowledge, beliefs, values, and practices;
- to expose the invisible locations of power and dominance, hegemonic processes and practices;
- to challenge taken-for-granted assumptions hidden in language, knowledge, traditions of grand narratives of Western, modern civilization;
- to decentre positions of authority and privilege;
- to confront discomforting truths about legitimized knowledge and practices inherited from pre-positivistic and scientific positivism;
- to contest, deliberate, disrupt, unmask, reclaim, and track the past that has been misinterpreted, marginalized, colonized, silenced, or lost.

In others words, feedback looping in bricolage demands a constant state of turbulence – a healthy and necessary feature of complexity, a necessary aspect of Varela's enactivist autopoiesis.

These types of interventions in the thoughts of the bricoleur and in the analysis of the POET possess qualities of spontaneity, randomness, self-organization, disequilibrium, time horizons, novelty, diversity, difference, far-from- and near-equilibrium, bifurcation, sensitive dependence on initial conditions, and the noise of variables complicit and in conflict with one another.

In many cases, realities created by these qualities of complexity are unimaginable. They do not match with current or traditional constructs of truth, knowledge, research, society, institutions, texts, policies, history,

actions and other worldly realities. Since one of the fundamental premises of bricolage research is to transform realities, truths, policies, etc.
that privilege the few and marginalize and/or oppress many, feedback
looping purposely works to evoke imaginary, virtual spaces; that is, spaces
that are packed with infinite possibilities to create new realities that are
inclusive, diverse, socially just, equitable, and respectful of agency and
democratic, equal participation. A surmountable task is the claim of bricolage. Feedback looping is the catalyst.

Features of Feedback Looping

Perhaps the most frequent comments in response to a professor's feedback looping include:

- 'Am I on the right track?'
- 'I don't know what to say.'
- 'Tell me what to do next.'
- 'What method should I use?'

These comments tend to suggest that the speakers are either unaccustomed or scared to proceed without explicit directions from the
feedback. Or they have preconceived notions about what counts as
research, meaning 'what methodology do I follow?'. Predictability and
provability, linearity (sequencing of steps/methods), truth as right and
wrong answers, textbook knowledge and research experts as authority,
equilibrium (as familiar, safe, comfortable), the political, institutional,
and cultural values of decision-makers, and the empirical control and
reduction of variables are only a few of the expectations of these
speakers. Raised on a diet of logical positivism from previous schooling/
education, the conditions of feedback looping to build complexity must
seem like the imposition of a monster. When shifts and changes in
familiar and legitimized knowledge, beliefs, and practices are in motion,
retreat and backlash are ways of resisting. It seems, when this appears to
be the point of paralysis, a discussion about the features of complexity is
timely.

On a grand scale, feedback looping is easy to follow according to the
mapping images introduced in Chapter 5. It is a way of getting started
and continuing as the bricoleur rigorously threads back (looped feedback) to the POET from the possible areas of the bricolage. Further
detailing, however, is essential as complexity increases with additional
feedback looping from professors, colleagues, readings, and self.

As mentioned previously, feedback looping in bricolage functions as
disruption, challenge, opposition, tracking, excavating, connecting, and
so on (Berry, 2004), to the invisible layers of meanings and practices

generated by dominant ideologies, discourses, policies and other culturally constructed worlds. The type of feedback looping to increase complexity is formulated many times in a *random* and *spontaneous* manner.
Without an assigned order to follow and with limited, if any, precedence
about how to organize the knowledge, the respondent to the POET,
whether it be professors, colleagues, cultural workers, or self cannot
predict in any traditional logical manner what will or will not present
itself. As professors providing feedback looping, orally or printed, we find
there is no consistent overall pattern of feedback looping even when the
bricoleurs are reading and writing about the same POET. Since bricolage
pays homage to the premise that knowledge is constructed in social,
political, intellectual, and historical contexts by certain groups or individuals who decide what and whose knowledge counts, we find that
feedback looping to each bricoleur's construction of knowledge occurs in
the reading of or in discussion about the POET. Even within one sentence
or paragraph, we find serendipitous moments where feedback looping
can disrupt the 'train of thought' of the bricoleur. Questions of 'Am I on
the right track?' (meaning am I right or wrong? Am I giving the professor
the right answers?) are shuffled to the background. Feedback looping
intervenes with certain questions, prodding and reflexivity. And these
interventions are political – not neutral statements asking for general
clarification, elaboration and accuracy – but radical disturbances in the
bricoleur's construction of knowledge/research truth/reality. Feedback
looping addresses the plurality of possible interpretations (2, 8, 20), the
multiplicity of theoretical discourses (2, 19), the inclusion of variables (3,
10), the non-linear directions (18), the semiotic readings of a word/
signifier/signified (15), the archaeological genealogy of concepts, institutional discourses and policies (13, 16), and more. Further investigation
initiated by the feedback looping might nudge the bricoleur in several
other directions and to several other sources (11). Feedback looping
might require the bricoleur to visit an area again or an area not yet
considered as available or necessary.

Self-organizing and Feedback Looping

For many novice and even seasoned bricoleurs, the most difficult aspect
of receiving intensive and rigorous feedback to loop back into the POET
involves the element of self-organization. With no precedence in for-
matting this style of research and with no categorical step-by-step
methodological directions, documenting the process and deciding on
directions is very spontaneous and, many times, on the verge of chaos. In
complexity theory, however, conditions of near-equilibrium and far-
from-equilibrium are expected. Indeed these situations are very healthy

as bricolage, like poststructuralism, embraces several theoretical discourses available for application to the POET. Poststructuralism's means of conducting an interrogation of language, subjectivity, and power relationships in the production of knowledge plays handmaiden to feedback looping in bricolage. Both modes practise disruption of monological knowledge and truth as fixed, unified, and totalizing (knowledge, subjects/identities, reality). Bricoleurs required to digress from the equilibrium of monologic knowledge and truth will find themselves, like poststructuralists, in near-equilibrium and in far-from-equilibrium conditions. Monological, linear, positivistic research such as practised by an empirical, logocentric analysis of text/phenomena as a single point, unlike the carnivalesque of bricolage, achieves equilibrium and thus stability. This state in turn is applied to subjects, policies, curricula, teaching, parenting, knowledge, value, and ethics – with the agenda of manageability, control, and manipulation.

Complexity can only emerge in far-from-equilibrium conditions. In an intellectual climate of near-equilibrium and far-from-equilibrium conditions, a bricoleur finds emancipatory practices possible. And it is feedback looping that plays a key role in destabilizing a state of equilibrium by randomly and spontaneously pushing bricoleurs into the richer territory of far-from-equilibrium conditions. When states of unity, stability, and equilibrium are disturbed by the non-linear spontaneity of questions, challenges, conflicts, and multidirectional possibilities of the type native to bricolage, feedback looping acts as the springboard to self-organization. The responsibility of the bricoleur to include and organize all the variables contained in the feedback looping continuously replenishes the far-from-equilibrium conditions, thus avoiding reductionism and simplicity.

Throughout the application process of feedback looping to and self-organization of the POET, complexity increases. Along the path, the bricoleur is confronted with a plethora of contradictions, unexpected results, inconsistent logic, bifurcation points, dissipative structures, diffusion, and unlimited opportunities to include or exclude knowledge. Each of these features presents itself in a manner expected of increasing complexity – randomly, spontaneously, diversely, and unpredictably. Bifurcations, for example, are unexpected points at which the bricoleur favours one response or strand of knowledge over another – in other words, novelty. In bricolage, however, the researcher acknowledges the options and discusses why he/she chose one option and not other possibilities. Bifurcations performed in bricolage remind us of the capabilities of recent DVD technology that allows the viewer to hear why the director elected to include or cut a scene from the film. In fact, current technologies such as DVDs and hypertext computer programs use principles and practices comparable to those of bricolage.

Self-organization by the bricoleur conjures up other features of complexity. The bricoleur is sensitive to the shifting and changing content of the POET with each re-entry and rethreading. Bricolage is not an excuse to simply create complexity for its own sake. Knowledge for knowledge's sake and the simple addition of knowledge is not the project of bricolage. In contemporary theories of reading and interpreting texts, the text and the reader are located in cultural, political, historical, and intellectual contexts, which thus makes reading an act of complexity. Similarly, bricolage is linked multidimensionally to the world outside the POET, not just to the words of the text. Bricoleurs are constantly sensitive to and dependent on the initial conditions that steered them to use bricolage in the first place. Bricolage works from these initial conditions to move the research to a 'higher' level of understanding through complexity. Bricoleurs are sensitive to a world seething with crisis, wars, conflicts, ecological disasters, hunger and poverty, and with social, cultural, political, historical and economic inequities, exclusions, injustices, and totalitarism at the individual, local, and global levels. Individual interventions in a POET are constantly related to global conditions that can only be understood through systems and practices of complexity. We echo Coveney and Highfield (1995, p. xi) who state:

> In intervention science, such as medicine [education, bricolage research, law and many other areas], it may be the complexities themselves that provide the key to the problem. In a [world] gone wrong . . . the more complexity we are aware of, the more numerous are the sites where intervention can take place.

Feedback looping is actually an organizational device for bricoleurs. To maintain the conditions necessary for complexity to build and to keep the bricoleur in a state of disequilibrium, feedback looping is the action that fuels the complexity of doing bricolage.

On a final note, to clarify the phenomenology of intervention by feedback looping, we call upon a metaphor that many parents have experienced. The complexity of the daily management of a household is in many ways parallel to the landscape of intervention by feedback looping. In both places, the number and quality of interventions are vast. In daily household activities, disruptions occur, usually unplanned, such as:

- babies to feed;
- children to get ready for school;
- eating;
- sleeping;
- cleaning;
- discussions about who is going where, when, how;

- unexpected interruptions by illness, deaths, anger, divorce, reloca-
tion, careers, friends;
- economic inconsistencies such as layoffs, cutbacks, raises, house
repairs, education funding;
- multiple voices demanding to be heard and valued;
- oh yes, the phone and the laundry.

These are only a few of the unpredictable interventions that happen in a
day. This constant feedback is both positive and negative. The members
of the household live in this complexity in near- and far-from-equilibrium conditions. Rare is the household in equilibrium, and sometimes
there are spaces that are in chaos. Whatever the state, family members as
a social unit are constantly organizing and reorganizing the feedback
looped back into their world of complexity. If a computer were to track
the number and pattern of household disruptions, it seems a map of
complexity would appear including invisible elements of the inner life of
relationships. The complexity of household life, like the complexity that
emerges in doing bricolage, is always there and we have been living in it
and with it. Social units, from the leaf on a tree to global eco-systems,
from family units to international relationships, are always in a state of
complexity. The project of bricolage is to examine, track, deconstruct,
excavate, connect, critique, and articulate this complexity (see area 13 of
Figure 1).

Theories and practices of complexity, of course, are not new. Several
fields of study, from physics to biology, from literature to business
management, from education to history, are engaging theories and
practices of complexity. It is now possible to engage complex systems like
bricolage with fewer limitations than before. Except *the politics of doing
bricolage* still makes it difficult to proceed, as experienced by Marissa (see
Chapter 7). With the aid of computer and digital technologies, complexity is considered significant, measurable, describable, applicable, and
dynamic in attempts to understand the world. Computer technology has
helped make it possible to deal with complexity within particular limits.
Humanity and the natural world are processes and products of complexity. Systems of feedback looping are important aspects of complexity
and thus performing the bricolage.

Feedback Looping as a Practice of Bricolage

As the authors gaze at approximately 2000 student-generated POETs
with dozens of feedback looping comments on each page, we are faced
with our own entry into complexity! How do we present the practice
of feedback looping in a way that is consistent with the theories and

processes of complexity and with bricolage? How do we represent spontaneity, unexpected turns, redirected paths, bifurcations points, or conditions of equilibrium or near-equilibrium in need of agitation and disturbing truths? After reviewing the texts, we recognize disruptions to the students' 'trains of thought' mainly in the form of questions and theoretical comments. Many times the interventions in the margins or between lines are connected unintentionally to the different areas of the bricolage map. Other times, the comments are theoretical discussions especially when the student bricoleur seems to struggle with unfamiliar terminology, discourse, meanings, and concepts native to bricolage.

The most common starting point for creating a POET tends to be an autobiography of how a bricoleur was attracted to the self-chosen research topic. This is a central starting point for most researchers even in positivistic, empirical and qualitative orientations. In bricolage, however, an autobiography is a constructed text of self and must be examined and critiqued. In our experience, the next areas to which novice and even seasoned bricoleurs (see Kincheloe, 2002) are drawn are those that disrupt the sequential, linear, psychoanalytic history of self. Somehow, the personal is now considered problematic. Deconstructing self and identifying positionality are the most common areas of the map that student bricoleurs visit next. Why this particular pattern of entry into the bricolage?

Upon reflection, we discover that, in many cases, the content of our feedback looping nudges the bricoleurs to question their own autobiographies as problematic. In other words, autobiography is a text of power relationships connected to the vast array of socializing discourses, texts and practices. These socializing devices lie outside the individual at the same time as being inhabited by the individual's autobiography – the intertextuality of life. Our questions and comments direct them to certain areas such as 4 (cultural/social positionalities) and/or 20 (interpretative bricolage). From our feedback, many students reorganize their POET and disturb the linearity of their autobiography. For others, guilt and self-blame prevent them from proceeding in the direction of critical self-analysis. Many are also locked in (unknowingly?) by the dominant discourse of Freudian psychology – the cause-and-effect discourse of childhood, mothers and individual psyche. Further inspection of the feedback looping to the latter two situations reveals both the expertise and the limitations that professors bring to the bricolage process. Since increasing complexity depends on sensitivity to initial conditions, we caution ourselves about how to provide feedback to these students without offending or patronizing them. We also admit, circuitously perhaps, that we have limited background in the area of psychoanalysis but at least some knowledge of the main principles from our educational psychology textbooks.

For the rest of the chapter, examples of feedback looping are provided.

We use them to disrupt, create disequilibrium, contextualize, reflect, and to keep the momentum of complexity dynamic and the integrity of doing bricolage. To help the bricoleur decide where and when these questions and comments might be applied, we list them under the different areas of the bricolage map. A general category has been created to list the feedback looping that does not specifically fit under any area. Needless to say, many of the questions and comments fit under several areas. The examples that follow are extracted from actual works of professors and students. Although the comments and questions are directed at the students' POET and are organized here by the different areas on the bricolage map, in actual use this did not occur. On the over 2000 POETs from which we withdrew the feedback loopings, the comments and questions appeared randomly. For any one word, paragraph or page of the POET, feedback looping was drawn from the different areas of the bricolage map to create spontaneous, far-from-equilibrium conditions in revisiting and rethinking the POET.

1. **General**
A.   How does the bricoleur avoid slippage into formalist discourses to describe and interpret the narratives, data, collected knowledge by self and other researchers? How and why can the bricoleur negotiate the borders between formalist and postformalist discourses that recognize the contradictions between and the limitations of both yet produce new insights, social values, structuring devices, and actions? For example, over time and place, the identity of subject(s) of the research has been constructed by dominant discourse. Their narratives, knowledge and values presented to the bricoleur may indeed be more a 'self-fulfilling' narrative or expected knowledge presented by the subject as truth merely shaped by dominant discourses under which subjects feel they live as normalized, naturalized, universalizing, essentialized and thus see their identity as unchangeable (similar to the discourse and beliefs of 'boys will be boys'). How do bricoleurs reconstitute knowledge about subjects when the dominant discourses of English tend to divide identity into binarisms that privilege one side and marginalize the other (e.g. good mother/bad mother) and reproduce positivistic knowledge? In addition, how does the bricoleur interpret identity as a complex web of historical and socializing discourses ranging from family contexts to societal, political, institutional, and civilizational conditions that govern the ontological (being) and epistemological (knowing) identity of the research subjects? In rethinking conditions, contexts, structures, texts, and discourses about identity, what hegemonic and discursive practices should the bricoleur expose that maintain dignity and agency for the subjects?

2. **Multiple critical social-theoretical discourses**

A. As you, the bricoleur, thread through the POET, what social injustices, inequities, and exclusions are revealed? How does the knowledge constructed by the tools of the bricolage support the basic promise of democracy to include all knowledge and values surrounding the POET?

B. In the first draft of your POET, you decided that this part of your topic on teenage pregnancy is an issue. Look at the discourse and sources of when, how, and by whom this became an issue. By whom? For what reasons? Who has the power or privilege of agency in this area and who does not? Use some of the premises and practices of archaeological genealogy to track and deconstruct how your topic has been constructed as 'an issue'. Other dimensions of the bricolage you might consider in your research on the topic include 2 again and/or 17 from the bricolage map, especially the literature on postcolonialism since you have used quantitative research findings about teenage pregnancy and identified it as a major 'problem' among Aboriginal/First Nations teens. Use the critical social-theoretical discourses from feminist, postcolonial theories also. Keep your original thoughts on this from your first POET draft and show the how and why of the changes in your original thinking on this topic.

3. **Traditional and contemporary research genres/ methodologies and their analytical tools**

A. Once you think there is a definitive answer, think again, revisit. Even mathematical reductions and statistics are a way of structuring, measuring, defining the world and are Eurocentric. So numbers are encoded also with certain knowledge and values. Use the quantitative but examine what knowledge it is producing and for whom. Why do you/we use it so readily as a research tool?

B. This might be a significant place to call on some of the principles and methodology of phenomenology and hermeneutics. The insertion of the lived experience of people who have experienced discrimination in job hiring might illuminate the assumptions embedded in their voices. The purpose of phenomenology is to capture the experience of discrimination without conceptionalization by language. Thus the role of hermeneutics, to bring the experience to language without losing the 'essence' of the experience. Perhaps the combination of the two will strengthen your discussion of discrimination in job hiring. To build the complexity of the experience using the bricolage map, we suggest you move to other areas such as 7 and 8 to use literary intertextuality to expose the hegemonic practices that are intertwined with power relations created by certain social practices that are legitimized within the phenomenological experience.

C. In class we discussed the problem of using any one genre of research design and methodology in these postmodern times. Because each genre produces its own internal logic, this is not a compatible practice in the bricolage. What eventually occurs is the hegemonic legitimization of one genre and thus one logic (monologic). In turn, this reduces the research findings, implications and action to one way, one solution, positivistic cause and effect that might not be the connections to make. Try threading other designs and methodologies through your POET (data) to reveal hidden dimensions of your research that one genre might not expose.

4. **Cultural/social positionalities**
A. What, about you the bricoleur, becomes apparent as you proceed through the multiple texts and discourses of the bricolage? In what ways and by what socializing texts and processes is the bricoleur positioned in the production of knowledge? How does the bricoleur's position in the different discourses/tools of the bricolage influence what she/he chooses to include or exclude in the production of knowledge? How does your position influence the interpretation of findings and actions to take as a result of the findings? In what disciplinary discourses have you been implicated? What discourses do you need to employ to critically reflect on your own auto-biography and recognize how this influences the choices, inter-pretations, inclusions or not, in the production of knowledge? In what ways does the bricoleur ensure that the knowledge produced by engaging the bricolage does not reproduce inequities, exclusions, social injustices when circulated to individuals, society, institutions, media, policies and practices? In other words, responsibilities?
B. Examine your autobiography for locations of race (gender, class, religion, sexuality, etc.). How has race defined your identity or been invisible? What are the markers of race, gender, etc. in your auto-biography?

5. **Disciplinary/interdisciplinary departmentalizations of knowledge**
A. Disciplinary knowledge needs to be contested, especially the dis-cipline of history you are discussing in your POET. While you may think that bricolage is for literary analysis or other texts, what counts as history and whose history counts are important questions to ask – disrupting/challenging the construction of Other in history. Turn to feminist criticism and Afro-American criticisms of Eurocentric con-structions of history. Other areas of the bricolage might help you revisit specific areas of your text.
B. Yes, mathematics and science have tended to work with definitive/right-wing/accurate answers. But so too have all subject disciplines

of modern, Western schooling. Schooling, including university, has been built around the discourses and practices of logical positivism. The field of mathematics, for example, used in your context of public schooling has developed sophisticated measures and structures of what are legitimate ways of knowing, especially those statistical and quantitative in nature. How can you as bricoleur thread areas of the bricolage map through knowledge and structure of traditional disciplinary compartmentalization of knowledge (Kincheloe's disciplinarity in Chapter 3) to disrupt the rationality, logic, and borders of positivism?

6. **Philosophical domains**
A. You are right in asking about the break with logical positivism. There are implications for your decision to incorporate it in your POET as a way to understand and interpret your topic. There are conflicts with the objectivity of logical positivism and the postmodern, post-structural, multilogical notions of what counts as knowledge. And it is not about objective knowledge verses subjective knowledge. Knowledge as constructed by the bricolage is complex – not binary objective/subjective data. In bricolage the two blur together to produce knowledge always in flux, always capable of being viewed in new contexts and processes (Kincheloe's hermeneutics in Chapters 3 and 4).

7. **Modes of power**
A. When you asked about 'why the majority sit back and do nothing', you were raising questions about hegemony. Search the meaning of the word, especially as theorized by Antonio Gramsci. It is a key element in the establishment of power, not necessarily by the majority, but by the ruling classes (especially the bourgeoisie) and to which the masses consent (not necessarily conform, but consent). Why don't people resist discrimination such as name-calling? Why don't others call them to task? You are asking these questions in your POET that need to be excavated and connected to a history of discrimination for your topic under investigation.

8. **Narratological strategies**
A. Well, yes, you have presented us with a major concern of bricolage. Thank you for pointing that out. What narrative strategies do you employ to tell the story of the elders without having to use 'European/Non-First Nations' narrative logic? We suggest you turn to the narrative styles of indigenous/native/Aboriginal/First Nation researchers and authors. Some of the literature on postcolonialist writing and writers from other indigenous groups might be of some help here.

B. Your concern is very valid. There are elements of indigenous narrative that do not appear or are not legitimized by Eurocentric organization of what counts as logical writing especially in an academic thesis. What do you employ and then how do we get this accepted by an institution such as university that constructs knowledge, writing, thesis and what counts as an oral exam based on Euro-American structures and strategies of narrative?

9. **Western grand narratives**

A. Ask about the complexity of child labour laws. How did people fight against these injustices? One response is that these are recent policies produced by unions. After the Industrial Revolution the society no longer needed children to produce goods, for machines would do this. Capitalism is a system that depends on cheap labour (children, women, etc.). So Western capital is gained from countries that do not prohibit child labour. So how do these readings construct childhood, what kind of knowledge does it produce and who benefits by labour laws or not? And how is this connected to your context and other times? Bring these questions into your text.

B. This sounds like the discourse of psychoanalysis (see 9 again). In what ways has this discourse shaped your identity, beliefs, actions? Revisit your POET and name the words, structures, and beliefs that influence your reading of self as psychoanalysis. Briefly research Freudian psychology and find similar discourse and concepts in your POET. Identify how the grand narrative of Freudian psychology invisibly permeates your construction of self through autobiography.

C. Revisit your POET and look at Gardner's multiple intelligences as a discourse that socializes teachers and organizes their thinking and practices around his grand narrative on what counts as intelligence. In what ways is the research you include in your POET complicit or in conflict with the dominant or silenced theories of what and who counts as intelligent? In what ways have you or have you not presented an oppositional reading of Gardner's grand narrative on multiple intelligences? Revisit your POET and challenge your own thinking on this matter.

10. **Contexts of human activity**

A. Yes, you are engaging in the bricolage by noting that the knowledge on classroom discipline is constructed in certain contexts – historical, political, economic, cultural, societal, and intellectual – by certain individuals/groups/powers/texts. Where do these observations lead you? How does this change, or not change, the knowledge/ discourse/practices you first discussed in your POET? Keep the changes in your thinking visible by including your previous thinking on this topic and how it was changed and why by employing threads from other areas of the bricolage map such as 2, 19 and 20.

11. Sources

A. In your POET, for example, I noticed that you picked a very controversial topic such as student discipline. The document circulated by your school board is quickly becoming established as a dominant way of practising school discipline throughout the state. Examine with a critical voice the major policies and programmes that govern what is currently used to direct teachers and the institution of education. Be aware, after examining the document, of symbolic violence and actual violence in everyday practices. Begin to recognize the hegemonic practices to which teachers consent for a variety of reasons. Enter in your POET where and how the document contains symbolic violence.

B. Other students in the class are also working on dismantling or deconstructing the logic of the recent document on school discipline being circulated throughout the state. This might be a good opportunity to meet with them and for each of you to read the document applying the different theories of the bricolage. Ask yourselves what different logics, practices and histories each reading produces. What are the implications for resisting and negotiating what counts as discipline in each of the readings? What does this mean for student agency in formulating disciplinary practices in a school? What logic is the document tied to that produces or does not produce inequities, social injustices, etc.? How can you inform the teachers/parents/schools using the document of its limitations, conflicts with democracy etc., contradictions with public school curricula and totalizing of what counts as discipline?

12. Levels of engagement

A. It is important to identify what are the activities, strategies, needs, procedures, communication, setbacks, intuitive moments and so on that move you from the level of attraction to your topic to that of passion and maybe a bit of insight. Working in the territory of complexity creates several conditions that are part of doing bricolage research. Keep in touch with this movement and do not hesitate to contact your professors and other colleagues to help you move through the complexity. Maybe a discussion as a group of bricoleurs would be a healthy and practical action for us to engage in at the beginning of the process and during the process. What mechanisms can we put in place so that paralysis does not prevent you and other bricoleurs from continuing your engagement with the bricolage?

13. **Archaeological genealogy**
A. How did the discourses, signs, and symbols within and surrounding your POET enter the mainstream and become formalized in society, institutions, policies, literature, film, etc.? By whom? Why? When? Who benefits and who does not?
B. You mentioned how there would not be a large market for a home with modifications to suit the physically different. Pursue this discussion further and tie it to how the dominant capitalist discourse constructs a rationale for not making changes for social justice. Look at the principles of capitalism and ask how they engage (or not) social justice. Track how the dominance of individualism, the rights and responsibilities of the individual are linked to the rise and circulation of capitalism to the exclusion of other economic, political, and social structures. Show the connections between modern capitalism and other areas of your topic under scrutiny employing versions and questions utilized by an archaeological genealogist as theorized by Foucault and others (13 again).

14. **Axiology**
A. Using Figure 5 in Chapter 5, discuss where you locate yourself according to the centre and the margins. In what contexts? Examine where and how your location on the axis shifts according to different contexts, socially, politically, historically, institutionally and so forth. Revisit your autobiography and add the knowledge gained from your exploration of axiology.

15. **Semiotic readings**
A. In your initial POET you mentioned the representations of what constitutes good mothering and the connection to a child's literacy success in school. Take this study further by discussing semiotic readings of the culture of mothering, for example, in the contemporary era, 1950s or other times and places. Look at several signs/signifiers, semiotic relationships between texts that keep reproducing images and representations of what counts as good mothering. Use a variety of sources including advertising, media, TV shows, or photographs. Examine the discourse and texts such as research on literacy and curriculum documents on literacy. Interview mothers, teachers, educational administrators, Ministry of Education personnel and other players involved in creating a culture of what counts as literacy and the connection to what they/texts/policies/research claim is connected to good/bad mothering. Continue a semiotic reading of the binarisms of good/bad mothering and connections to good/poor literacy in school. Layer your findings in a manner that shows the conflicting discourses and practices for locations of mother blaming/bashing/oppression. In your POET keep

the original findings of the literature and research findings that make certain claims and suggest the creation of policies and programmes based on the claims of the texts, players, etc. Deconstruct the binarisms. Look at the political implications, that is, the agency, voice, democratic participation, and roles that mothers play in the constructing of knowledge and practices about mothers and literacy in school. Consider the politics of difference here when talking about who decides about who or what counts as 'good' mothering and the relationship to literacy. Ask if these are sites of domination, negotiation, or resistance. This is only the beginning to engaging the bricolage, but the topic is very complex and you must show that in your POET. Mapping out possible directions from the bricolage and areas to include might help you to get started and to follow your passion through the different levels of engagement (see 12).

16. Levels of privilege/oppression

A. When you consider the effects of discrimination on your selfhood, you are working at the individual level (overtly). Extend this to the discourse and practices that discriminate covertly and in other texts. What exists in societal, institutional and civilizational structures, policies and history that legitimizes the discrimination experienced at the individual level?

B. Look at the discourse in the text you have decided to critique. How does it reproduce the dominant notion of who counts, who is privileged and/or oppressed, or excluded from this text? Why do readers accept the constructs that are discriminatory in your text?

C. Novice bricoleurs tend to discuss the content of their POET at the individual and immediate level (I have a friend who . . ., It happened to me . . ., our school does this . . .). Although this individual level is important in the construction of knowledge, bricolage seeks a more connected understanding of the individual level by embedding it in larger contexts such as the civilizational level. To prompt you to seek the embeddedness of knowledge in a grander world, questions and comments of the feedback looping awaken the bricoleur to search beyond the individual level of culture, use area 16.

17. Encyclopedic structure of bricolage

A. Your POET suggests you are unfamiliar with much of the terminology and concepts of bricolage such as postmodernism, postcolonialism, poststructuralism. There are several encyclopedia-like books available to help you understand literary terms like these, and gain some insight into the field of bricolage. Remember you might read several books on postcolonialism and find conflicting definitions and descriptions. Great. When you recognize the differences within each definition you are well on your way to understanding how bricolage works with this complexity of meanings, how different authors read the terminology and create conflicting discourses and practices even within an area.

18. **Methodological bricolage**
A. Do you sometimes wonder if what you are being told is true? And if you do not accept the dominant and legitimized truths then how, what, why, who do you resist or not? How does one read the research counter-hegemonically? In what contexts can you or can you not?

19. **Theoretical bricolage**
A. How and where can the bricoleur combine the freedoms of existential rights and liberal-humanism with the tapestries of social responsibilities and social justice to provide new insights? Whose/what individual rights count and whose/what social rights count when both are threaded through the point of entry text if a balance of knowledge is important to bricolage research?
B. In the context of the theoretical bricolage, re-examine your POET for discourse and principles that are in fact residues of logical positivism and empirical research (reduction and elimination of variables) that is not bricolage-friendly. For example, you mentioned that proof and conclusions are needed. These are used in the shadow of the dominant research paradigm of modern, scientific rationality and methods. How and why does this conflict (or not) with your thinking as a researcher using bricolage?
C. A host of theories inform the bricoleur on what to include and what kinds of knowledge and value are being produced by each theory. Just to add to your frustration on what theory to choose, recognize that bricolage, true to its definition, takes a little bit of each, whichever theory (tool) does the job best or is available and needed at the time.

20. **Interpretative bricolage**
A. How does the bricoleur utilize the conflicting and complimentary discourses with a field such as hermeneutics, where there as many such discourses within the field as there are between fields of interpretation? There are several discourses within hermeneutics, such as radical, phenomenological, existential, psychological and cold hermeneutics.

21. **Political bricolage**
A. Reconsider here in your POET that Gardner himself claims that intelligence is driven by interest. What are the implications of this main point of his theory for teaching and learning? What are the implications of your acceptance of his theory of multiple intelli-

gences in the present climate of the political clout his theory holds in educational circles, classrooms and documents?

B. Modern Western civilization's organization of knowledge, power, bureaucracy, text, relationships is hierarchical and thus the top of the hierarchy has absolute power often disguised under negotiation, consultation, and cooperation as democratic power. How is this made problematic or not in your context of teaching? What structures, cultures are in conflict or left out of this structure? What different organizational structures are available as oppositional to the hierarchical, conclusion type? Why are other structures not available? What role does capitalism, colonialism, modernization, Westernization of the world, Christianity, patriarchy and other dominant structures play in reproducing the inequities of power relationships?

22. Narrative bricolage

A. Without ending the research/writing as conclusion or closure as in positivistic research/writing, how does the bricoleur finish a text? What conventions can the bricoleur borrow from postmodern/ poststructural/postcolonial fiction and film writers? Read/view these particular books/films to borrow conventions that avoid positivistic structures. Search the Internet and literature/film departments for possible sources.

B. It is interesting how you felt frustrated by writing a POET, then tried to use the feedback in a manner that does not repeat the empirical, patriarchal, objective style of most academic writing. What narrative conventions, styles, sources, genres could you use that might model a way of breaking the dominant type of writing of academia yet fulfil the requirements of academic content?

23. Othering

A. This is a hard one to address. Maybe if you started with asking 'when isn't a writing, even when using bricolage, about the Other?'. Even when writing about self and constructing knowledge, can we ever write without Othering ourselves? Maybe considering positionality (4) and modes of power (7) where you are required in the former to name where you are speaking from (gender, race, class, religion, etc.) and in the latter the relation to power. Bricoleurs should consider, in addition, that the way to write about Other/self is to challenge the centre/dominant. As the expression goes for researchers/ writers who are writing from the margins as colonized (European colonized) people, the Empire (colonized) writes back to challenge the colonizers' constructions of Other. Women writing back to men (the centre), talking back as bell hooks calls it. Women of African descent writing back to white race women.

24. **Identity/essentializing/normalizing**

A. You claim in your POET 'But it's just common sense'. Reconsider this expression, as it tends to be dominant, assumes normality, and as such becomes hegemonic. Knowledge of this kind perpetuates unexamined practices that are exclusionary. Check your statement again. Search the literature on the use of 'common sense' to legitimize taken-for-granted discourses, policies, and practices that, upon the application of the bricolage, expose the legitimizing of inequitable and undemocratic practices.

B. You used 'we' in this statement. Who are you speaking for? You need to name who the 'we' signals.

C. In using the many dimensions and tools of the bricolage, how does the bricoleur avoid/resist generalizing, universalizing, normalizing, naturalizing and essentializing the production of knowledge and values about relationships, groups, gender, race, class, sexuality, spirituality, and the body through language and traditional reductionistic methodologies such as narratives, thematizing and categorization?

D. You write that 'they' don't make these objects (furniture) for us. You are generalizing the 'they', which also removes the responsibility of individuals and society to change the situation.

By no means are these questions and comments comprehensive as examples of feedback looping. What tends to happen as the bricoleurs engage in complexity, the type and the quantity of feedback looping to the POET increases. There are patterns of feedback looping, however, that do emerge since professors and students do have different backgrounds and purposes for providing feedback to loop into the POET. The bricoleurs themselves will be as diverse in their research topics, directions and creations. Starting simple is easy. But employing the bricolage requires a journey into complexity. Feedback looping is the ticket that maintains the complexity and rigour of doing bricolage. In the next chapter, student bricoleurs share their experiences of engaging the bricolage.

Bricolage is many a new thing understood
Kathleen S. Berry

Getting Started

It happened as spontaneously as most moments of the bricolage do. Sadie, the graduate student, and we, the professors, were talking about what would be happening in our next course together, 'Dismantling Educational Discourses'. We rambled and speculated; it was apparent we had not yet organized the course outline and assignments. Sadie interjected: 'Speaking of assignments, the one I did in your last course was on height discrimination. I didn't think I could write enough on the topic but there's even more I could write. I was just starting to get a sense of this bricolage stuff.'

'Yeah, we thought you were just getting into it. Too bad the course ended when it did.' Two days later, we asked Sadie if we could run off copies of her last assignment for the other graduate students in the new course to use as a POET on which to apply the bricolage.

This initial encounter evolved into an entire course embracing the bricolage as a way to open up a text to multiple interpretations and thus the possibility for the production of new knowledge for self and others. Throughout the course, each student and each group application of bricolage to Sadie's POET on height discrimination: (1) unravelled threads of different truths and values; (2) contradicted long-established and taken-for-granted facts and truths; (3) exposed the hegemonic processes that brought us to consent to assumptions about power relations based on height; (4) confronted our own beliefs and values about the politics of difference; (5) situated the knowledge of Sadie's text in historical, social, cultural, political, economic, and intellectual contexts for an archaeological and genealogical analysis; (6) and recovered knowledge, experiences and multiple truths erased by hegemonic decisions over time and place. All this was done in an atmosphere to legitimize bricolage as a way of researching, analysing, interpreting, and producing knowledge and value through multiple readings for social justice and inclusion.

Sadie and her POET made it possible to establish an atmosphere that resonated throughout the rest of the course. The public application of the countless areas of the bricolage to her original text encouraged her graduate peers to explore regions of their own POET. Initially, after exposure to the bricolage map and processes, as illustrated in Chapter 5, most students felt a great deal of resistance, frustration and dread. Perhaps Natalie expressed it best in her weekly submission:

> I have finished reading the ... chapter and I am more confused now than when I left class on Saturday [class on mapping out the bricolage]. The whole chapter was like reading a new language, mostly Greek!! It seems that much of what was being discussed was the idea that our educational [research] approach has been very biased and needs to be questioned. I had the feeling throughout that something is seriously wrong with the way we have been doing things. Many new terms like hermeneutics, semiotics, postformal psychology, psychometrics, epistemology and hyperreality added to my confusion. I believe that it was suggested ... that changing the definition of what constitutes [research] will be met with great resistance by a 'modernist positivistic educational psychology group'. Who are they? Am I a member of that group? I see lots of things to learn before I can understand [bricolage].

Gradually, thanks to Sadie's granting public access to her text, the students soon acquiesced into enthusiasm, rigour, and challenge. The students were able to envision how bricolage relentlessly scrutinizes a text for invisibly encoded, discursive, and hegemonic discourses as well as exclusions of other ways of thinking, being, and acting. Students began to realize how texts (of many sources and variety) work to shape individual and public consciousness, policies and structures. More importantly, they discovered the complexity of how knowledge becomes constructed, circulated, and established as dominant, absolute, totalizing, and legitimate when left unexamined by such instruments as bricolage.

Original Content of Sadie's Paper

In order to understand the changes that occurred because of the application of bricolage, it will help to know the general contents of Sadie's original POET. Her original text consisted of approximately 2500 words and seven references, four of which were taken from the Internet. Her introductory paragraph discussed a general survey of discrimination based on race, ethnicity, class, gender, and sexuality. A quote about height discrimination from an Internet text acted as a segue into the rest of her paper. Surprisingly, she failed throughout her text to criss-cross her discussion (axiology) with these other areas of study which might have revealed some further insights into the complexity of discrimination based on height.

In the rest of the paper, Sadie presented the following discussions:

- the discourse used to discriminate, using words such as runt, shrimp;
- several examples of personal anecdotes (teenager, sports, school);
- standards in housing codes, seatbelts, clothing;
- societal perceptions based on height;
- images of height in popular culture and media (movie stars, wrestling, *Fresh Prince of Bel Air*);
- historical figures (Napoleon, Alexander the Great);
- employment in job markets;
- strategies for resisting height discrimination (isolation, being yourself, confidence, maintaining dignity, societal awareness).

This was Sadie's second sojourn into the bricolage. Her dependence on personal narrative 'data' was obvious and her analysis tended to rely heavily on the discourse of psychoanalysis. This research and interpretational tool works mainly at the individual level while, for example, missing how and why discrimination based on height works at the societal, institutional, and Western civilizational levels. Her examples were also not criss-crossed by an axiological analysis using gender, race, class, and sexuality, as she had mentioned in her opening paragraph. Also absent was archaeological genealogy where connections could be made between historical, political, economic, and socio-cultural contexts in which knowledge about height was produced and reproduced. These few absences would have been detected if Sadie had been aware of the possible insights offered by the landscape of the bricolage. The knowledge produced in her final paper would have been more inclusive, diverse, and comprehensive, with a greater possibility to transform social policies and practices. Her study of the complexity of height discrimination might also have bared the complicity with height discrimination in media, the conflicts and contradictions between theory and practices of discrimination, and a deeper sense of how to resist mainstream thinking and transform practices.

Becoming Bricoleurs

The next rereading of Sadie's text was done on WebCT by her peers. Although they had not been exposed to the bricolage at this point, they were asked to respond to Sadie's initial text. At first, most of their

readings were in the same vein as Sadie's, adding more personal anecdotes:

> *your [Sadie's] comments caused me to think about people that I have known*
> *in leadership roles [where those of] average height were considered strong*
> *leaders and those who were 'shorter' were often described as people with*
> *'little-man syndrome'. (Stephen W.)*

> *I can remember being 11, 12, 13 and wishing I were shorter. I was always*
> *one of the tallest kids in my class, and it wasn't a good thing to tower over*
> *your peers (especially male). It didn't help that the coolest boy in my class,*
> *Noah, was also the shortest. Maybe that small has come to be equated with*
> *childlike, fragile, in need of protection, is oh so similar to what it meant*
> *(means) to be female. (Heather)*

> *It reminded me of a friend who is about five feet tall, who expresses concern*
> *about air bags ... In what percentage (statistics) of the accidents did the*
> *victim's size play a role? (Mary H.)*

Her peers also added examples of representations from different media
consistent with Sadie's examples in her original text:

> *It's amazing how the television and media cover up a person's height! That*
> *Newman and Hanomansing* [well-known TV broadcasters in the area]
> *are just over five feet tall yet on TV positioned to look taller. (Mia)*

Novice and uninformed bricoleurs continued to repeat Sadie's initial
reading in their revisiting of her POET.

What seems important as an outcome of engaging the bricolage is not
as obvious to novice bricoleurs. They still seem locked into positivistic
rationality; that is, that cause-and-effect connections have to be made
with the data, not only in quantitative research but also in qualitative
research. Whether they have used ethnography, phenomenology,
grounded theory, action research or any other genre, the results are
usually entrenched with cause-and-effect interpretations. It is at this
point that we told the 'peanut butter' story (thanks to Paul Parks, University of Western Ontario, *circa* 1978). It demonstrates the problem of
knowledge garnered by cause-and-effect positivism. Furthermore, it
pathologizes our epistemology.

> *A young girl, on holidays with her parents, ordered a peanut butter sand-*
> *wich for her lunch at a [then] Woolworth's restaurant. All during the*
> *ordering and waiting for her sandwich, she kept twirling around on the red*
> *stool. When the sandwich finally arrived, she would take a bite and then*
> *swirl again. After several bites and swirls, she claimed, 'I'm not eating*
> *peanut butter sandwiches ever again. They make you dizzy.'*

Hopefully, novice bricoleurs understand the kind of misconceptions that can be spawned by cause and effect, especially when adopted as social theory and action. Hopefully, they proceed with the conviction that knowledge produced by the bricolage can make a difference in the human condition.

The next readings of Sadie's text were informed by multiple discourses used to read the body. Since the body is the location for readings of height, one of the professors used a handbook that briefly introduced several possible ways to read the body. The book, *The Body for Beginners* by Dani Cavallaro (1999), is a simple introduction to the complexity of multiple discourses and contemporary ways of reading such as post-structuralism, postmodernism, Foucauldian, and a host of other areas included in the bricolage. Books such as these are an effective way to lighten the frustration and fear that students first meet when faced with the complexity of multiple readings and discourses of bricolage. As Dominique L. claims:

My greatest frustration with using bricolage is learning the language and terms. My suggestion to anyone teaching this process to students would be to ensure that the students get a good grounding in the terminology.

The comic book approach of series like these might not suit the academic persona but it certainly made it easier for the students to move even deeper into the complexity of the bricolage. Now they easily recognized that getting started was possible and using bricolage was valid.

'I never thought of that before' was a common comment after each student read chapters of *The Body for Beginners*. Even with just the table of contents, the students realized there were readings of Sadie's text they had not previously known were available or possible to use. General chapter headings included

Why the Body?
The Body and Society
The Body and Philosophy
The Body in the Visual Field
The Body in Cyberculture
Conclusion: Incorporations
. . .
Corpography.

Topics in those chapters included: The Body & Language; Boundaries; Eating Bodies (one they were quite familiar with); Taboos; The Medical Body; A History of the Body; The Gaze; Cyborgs. One student wanted to trade her chapter called Sex/Porn/Eros; she was not sure where it would take her or Sadie! Later she admitted she never thought of the body and its height as a location of culturally constructed norms and objectification of a person.

Even with the condensed version of potential readings of the body, the shift away from, but not excluding, a dependence on psychoanalysis and personal anecdotes seemed almost immediate. The students, now working on WebCT, contributed preliminary notes from the chapters on the body. The feedback to Sadie's text reverberated with a profusion of questions, bifurcations, suggestions, and possible insights to new knowledge about how the body acts as a location for discrimination. Sadie's peers were generous with feedback, in part due to the playful structure of the bricolage. In addition, Sadie received feedback from the professor. While the feedback to her POET was varied, she was left with the freedom to choose what to thread through her text. Sadie's self-organization of the text produced a structure unique to her.

The simplicity of the book for beginners generated surprises – a carnivalesque of ideas – and the entrance into complexity. Whether the students were aware of it or not, the influx of feedback soared in directions that left the simplicity of the beginners' book far behind. Marissa J. contextualized the body in modern times, creating axiological crossings with capitalism and Christianity to compose a mixture of discourses as follows:

> *Although the modern body is read primarily as a material entity in appearance and internally, threading the bricolage through the point of entry text on height discrimination allows for including the spiritual dimension. Discourses that range from Capitalism (body as market value) to Christianity (Western spirituality institutionalized through religion) construct the body as object that acts to separate it from the mind and spirit. Removing spirituality permits hyperrationality and discrimination towards the Other based on difference, in Sadie's case, in body stature. As the bricoleur threads through and recognizes the lack of inclusion or the division of spirituality from the material body as structured by most modern discourses (such as Capitalism and Christianity), the structure of bricolage grants an opportunity for knowledge and value about the body.*

Sadie entered far-from-equilibrium readings, a condition internal to complexity, with all the feedback looping. Linear thought, familiar structures and traditional rationality, blurred by the complexity of the different threads of the bricolage, faded into the background. Mixtures of research genres such as phenomenology and identity politics blended with deconstruction and issues of binarisms, essentialism, and agency. An amalgamation of technologizing and normalizing discourses about the body compounded with a hermeneutic fusion of horizons presented challenges, conflicts, and contradictions to unknown dimensions of Sadie's original POET. Confidence to risk the undetermined and undirected course of the emerging bricolage was also noticeable, especially through a relaxation of formality through the hypertext structure of computer WebCT, feedback looping and threading of ideas. Small wonder that bricolage and computer technologies are handmaidens in rigour and complexity.

The following passage is an example of a feedback loop that jumped between the personal anecdotes of Sadie's seatbelt/airbags discussions and the early attempts to insert threads of bricolage into her original text. One student, Genexa L., attempted to cover a vast range of regions from the bricolage maps of Chapter 5. She introduced numerous possibilities; notably, both quantitative and qualitative research genres, possible sources from which to gather further information, critiques and contextualization of the information, and an exposé of what was missing. Amazingly, this was all in one submission.

What happens to the construction of body as a positivistic reduction of the body to fit agendas of technologizing and standardization; creating norms for capitalist profit? For example, Sadie could investigate the world of car safety and how air bags and seat belts are constructed around size of body and not differences. In doing so, she would need to thread through her text any knowledge from both quantitative and qualitative discourses such as the statistics of people saved or not by air bags and seat belts with correlations of body size including height. She could gather information from insurance companies, medical records and motor vehicle bureaus. She can ask what are the statistical correlations and deviations; gather personal stories and newspapers reports, and search through archival documents to trace the history of car safety and examine locations of height considerations of inclusion and discrimination. Furthermore, it would be crucial to contextualize all these texts and discourses in the historical, political, economic. She would need to apply a critique of all that she found in addition to what she didn't find. Why was some knowledge included and other knowledge excluded? As a bricoleur, she would need to, in hypertext mode, link each piece of textual knowledge to reveal how the discourse of some texts produce particular discursive knowledge about height and how other texts either hegemonically reproduce and legitimize the dominant (and thus normalizing practices) or how they contradict and produce counter-hegemonic knowledge (resistance readings). This search is only the beginning.

The excerpts that follow are composites of students' feedback looping to Sadie. In addition, there are excerpts between students as they exchanged links between group members and from professor feedback to both individual and group correspondences. The examples represent only a few of approximately one hundred pages of entries over a period of a month. The purpose is to illustrate the evolution from the singular readings of Sadie's original POET quoted at the beginning of this chapter to the emergent complexity and rigour once the students engaged the bricolage. Both students and professors moved from novice to auxiliary bricoleurs in a very short period of time.

In this first example, there was a confessional aspect. One of the primary principles of bricolage is that knowledge is constructed by discourses, by certain powers, and in specific contexts. Acceptance of this basic principle arrived spontaneously but dotted with other principles from different regions such as agency and phenomenology. Hannah's feedback looping to Sadie's initial text said:

> The idea that the body is both a biological and socially constructed site is of interest. It is where the notion of the individual self with agency and control over our bodies appears in other texts, policies, and laws that contradict that knowledge. In Sadie's case, how does she resist that knowledge when in fact that is how people perceive her, relate to her, treat her (even with the phenomenological gaze)? What discourses and texts confirm (not prove in the traditional positivistic or quantitative sense) Sadie's experience?

Other students, with hints of a critical studies background, introduced challenges and questions of contextualization to the continued excavation of Sadie's text. Diana I.'s feedback looping echoed with variations and additions to Hannah's comments:

> How does Sadie resist the 'normalizing' discourses that are encoded in the knowledge about the body, notably height? Is shying away from social interaction being resistant but fulfilling the intents of the dominant discourse by failing to change the status quo, the dominant representation about height? This repeats the question of what counts as knowledge and whose knowledge counts that is complicit with status quo or different from the historical/cultural/economic/political contexts in which knowledge about the body is constructed. And by whom? The knowledge and value about the body also have patterns and processes of construction. Track and examine those to get at how, in the present, the body is still a site for discrimination. Only then can we provide knowledge about the body that transforms individual, societal, institutional and civilizational policies and practices. In the future, inequities and discrimination against a person and groups based on the height of their body will not be possible or discursively coded in discourses and texts.

Various professors' participation in feedback looping added to the rigour and complexity. In addition to lectures and seminars on theoretical background and terminology that inform the operation of the bricolage, they were responsible for fuelling an interest and enthusiasm to propel the process forward. At times, the professors were as spontaneous, surprised and non-linear as the students in directing them through the process. On other occasions, they oscillated between the individual needs of each student and the importance of guiding the students through the complex frameworks of the bricolage. Perhaps the most crucial functions the professors performed were the insertions, questions, disruptions, and challenges to the students' text that compelled them to reflect, negotiate, and renegotiate assumed truths and even challenge their own thinking. Chapter 6 presented patterns of feedback looping and questions to students' POET. Included here are some specific examples of professors' feedback looping to Sadie's text on height discrimination.

Yes our identity is tied to the body so how does a person and society take agency in changing exclusions, inequities based on knowledge and value of the body?

Why is it important to do different readings of the body? What readings are possible using bricolage that will give different readings of the body and change how individuals, society, texts and different contexts think and act towards the Others' body in ways that are democratic, socially just and inclusive of difference? How would the texts and discourses of race, gender, class, sexuality, and other fields of study provide different readings of the body?

When is it really important in daily life to distinguish body features? What if there was a discourse that removed tall/short binarisms and also avoided essentialism? Would saying Sadie is 4′11″, Melissa is 5′10″ and Kathy is 5′7″ change the discourse and thus the way we live in or relate to the body?

What discourses/texts about the body produce normalizing and exclusionary practices? What's the history of the discourses and practices (Foucault's archeology of knowledge) about the body produced over time and space? How did they produce current representations and relationships about the body? How are they connected (genealogy) to the dominate discourses and texts about the body over time and space? What has changed, shifted or stayed the same in the way individuals, society, institutions and Western civilization represent and relate to the body?

Locate/situate the knowledge/texts already produced and what you are researching about the body in individual, community, historical, cultural, geographical, national, political, economic, communication technologies, and other contexts. Discuss how the context produced and circulated certain knowledge about the body and left out/erased other knowledge. Why? By whom?

What are the conflicting and contradictory discourses and knowledge that the bricoleur must bring to the point of entry text in order to challenge any totalizing narratives or taken-for-granted absolute truth about the body? At what points (bifurcation and axiological) and how does the bricoleur decide to thread the conflicting and contradictory discourses through the point of entry text? How many ways and times must a bricoleur revisit and re-thread before the text becomes meaningless?

The entire content of this chapter to this point happened within a six-week period of approximately five hours a week of reading, writing and communicating. Of the twenty graduate students in the course, nine were formerly enrolled in a research course on bricolage. The remaining students were new to both the theory and practice of bricolage, four of whom were new to graduate studies. For the next six weeks each student operated within one of four groups to use the bricolage for his/her own text and supply feedback to the texts of the other members in the group. At the end of the six weeks, each student submitted his/her original POET plus the feedback loopings from each group member along with, after several applications of the bricolage, the final text.

Being Bricoleurs/Doing Bricolage

Once students were *introduced* to the theoretical premises of bricolage (Chapter 1–4), *mapped out* a potential journey through bricolage (Chapter 5), and *framed* questions that bricoleurs ask (Chapter 6), they were ready to actually begin applying bricolage to their own texts. They started the socializing process of being bricoleurs by doing (enacting) bricolage. In the case of Sadie's text on height discrimination, we moved from her personal text and her attempts at multiple readings to the public scrutiny of her text by peers. Most of her peers, uninformed about the bricolage and by very few, if any, of its potential domains, utilized reader-response and psychoanalytic discourse. This seemed to indicate the dominance of the discourse of educational psychology as an analytical research tool in colleges of education. Understandably so for these students: Freudian type psychology has a high degree of legitimacy in many circles – especially in education and research. It reproduces the Cartesian cause-and-effect explanation of human activity legitimized by decades of what counts as knowledge and research. Mainstream psychology as a research and interpretation tool also works in harmony with formalist, logical, empirical positivism – hegemonic partners in maintaining power.

At other times, students might be informed by other dominant research tools such as statistics, ethnography or case-study research. Many times, a research tool is employed singularly, giving a linear, monological method and analysis, thus creating its own internal logic. In turn, this knowledge slides into public discourse, structures, and practices that reproduce dominant knowledge and powers. The bricolage recognizes the limitations of monological research and interpretation. Once students realized the limitations for reading Sadie's text, engaging in the complexity, rigour, and multidisciplinarity of the bricolage became compelling. For other professors, teachers, students, and cultural workers, beginning in this manner might not be necessary or possible. In this and several other courses we taught, however, this is a familiar process for socializing students into the culture of the bricolage.

From this point on, several events occurred that propelled the students further into engaging the bricolage. First, each of the twenty students brought in six copies of an essay, a report, a draft thesis proposal, a draft paper of interest or relevance, or an assignment he/she had written previously. These texts acted as each student's POET. Second, a copy was given to each group member and one to the professors (professors received a copy from every student). Third, each group of five members then decided who was going to apply what areas of the bricolage to each other's copy. Each member of the group selected two different areas from one of the possible areas of the bricolage map found in Chapter 5. Thus, ten different possible areas of the bricolage map (delineated in Chapter 5) were applied to one text. Some chose areas related to the central question or area of inquiry for a thesis; while others felt adventurous enough to create a new map using a pot-pourri of areas from the vast range of possibilities. Some individuals felt the need to utilize what was essential to reveal hegemonic and discursive messages. Some dared to attempt an archaeological genealogy based sketchily on the work of Michel Foucault (Agnello, 2002).

The next part of the process rigorously utilized the current technology of WebCT and the Internet in addition to the theory and practices of the bricolage presented in Chapters 1–6. After reading each group member's original POET, individual members constantly wrote back and forth (feedback looping) to each other on WebCT. Some of the key points that emerged:

- asked questions borrowed from Chapter 6;
- provided theoretical inserts based on the areas they chose;
- evoked 'informed' critical reflection;
- pointed to taken-for-granted knowledge, assumptions of knowledge, opinion, and value;
- challenged the thinking of each other and themselves;
- distinguished different discourses that produce certain policies and practices;
- pushed for connections (genealogy) and contextualizations (historical, economic, social, political, intellectual, institutional, Western civilization);
- directed the author to other sources such as institutional documents and media texts.

For the professors, tracking the unfolding texts using the bricolage process was as rigorous as it was for the students. In addition to feedback looping, they posed questions and inserted theoretical comments. They also extended the students' knowledge of the bricolage by proposing other areas to thread through the POET. Further feedback recommended possible ways to examine hidden dimensions. Contemporary areas of study such as poststructuralism, postmodernism, and postcolonialism were promoted, as were axiological criss-crossings of gender, race, class, sexuality, and so forth. Many times, the students were directed to the various areas of the bricolage map delineated in Chapter 5. No one area was used extensively. A bricoleur does not have to proceed in linear, chronological or procedural fashion or use any one area in depth. In fact, it is closer to the spirit of the five dimensions of the bricolage (theoretical, interpretative, etc.) and to the structure of complexity, rigour, and multidisciplinary studies when both professor and student avoid slippage into monological research and interpretation. It worked better when the professors acknowledged the diversity of feedback looping that the students themselves generated.

It is difficult in the constraints of the written form to recreate what evolved next in the bricolage process. As the student bricoleurs adopted the configurations of WebCT, their feedback looping accessed threads of the bricolage in a manner difficult to replicate here. The capabilities of computer technology to link, thread, and hypertext quickly and non-linearly correspond with the butterfly structure of complexity. To transfer these capabilities to a different medium like a book format compromises the complexity and rigour yielded by the bricolage process. Professors and students needed to be aware of these obstacles.

The following threads of the bricolage were taken from the interactions of student bricoleurs' communicating back and forth on WebCT. For a period of five weeks, the interactions continued with a freestyle threading and feedback looping through each other's text. The professors, also performing threading and feedback looping, were party to the POET of each student and to the interactions of all four groups. Between and within all these intercommunication routes, the bricolage was activated. We begin with some of the threadings by one group into a member's POET about the termination of vocational education in a Canadian province.

Ruby had completed one previous course on the theory and practice of the bricolage. She also had a strong literary and critical studies background so she was assigned, in spirit, a leadership role. To begin, she addressed all her group members – Dominique (one course in bricolage studies), Melissa and Emma (both new to bricolage), and Nelson (new to bricolage and graduate studies) – with a general statement on using bricolage:

> How does the bricolage force me [us], as an educator, to think about the equity in the curriculum offered to my students? How does the bricolage hold me [us] accountable in ways that no external or quantitative measurement could?

In this brief quip alone, Ruby raised some very deep questions that reflected her own level of engagement with the bricolage (remember she was also using Heathcote's levels of engagement chart outlined in Chapter 5). Her reflective questioning reverberated throughout her group. Some group members used it to question their own engagement with the bricolage. In her various feedback loopings to Nelson's text about the termination of vocational education, Ruby drew on several areas of the bricolage, including a host of questions and challenges to his text:

> *I am looking at your paper from the phenomenological and the political areas of the encyclopaedia of terms. Can you think of a very specific incident that makes you experience this* [termination]*? Also when you begin your historical examination of the various legislation that instituted this area* [voc ed] *look at how it is or isn't connected* [genealogy] *to capitalism. Then give personal anecdotes of* [name of school] *and community action, arguments that were listened to but by closed* [she used 'deaf' which is a misused trope/cliché] *ears. And how countered by those ears? Examine the policies and processes that had community colleges take over control with federal $$$. How* [did] *this change the need for career counselling programs in schools? You talk about this as hard-luck for students. Critique this discourse as just a way of labelling and placing non-academic, classed students in certain labour-directed programs. Is this … another perspective for your point of entry text?*

For other threadings to Nelson's original POET, Emma was responsible for feedback looping from the bricolage areas of power, class, and gender. She informed Nelson:

> *I read your paper and made notes on positions of power, class and gender. Discuss the power of academic over voc ed. What role did the previous Premier of the province mandate for voc ed? What about the power of small* [rural] *communities over urban areas to keep or get rid of voc ed?*

Dominique was assigned to thread questions and discourse from semiotics through Nelson's text. She had never heard of this area of the bricolage before, so she offered to pursue it. Wisely she also cautioned Nelson to read his text semiotically but mingle this area with his selected area of institutional power:

> *In what ways do the signs and symbols get buried to produce a system of signs and symbols that legitimizes an institutional action such as getting rid of voc ed?*

Nelson chose institutional power and constructions of heroes from the encyclopedia of critical terms. Sometimes the areas of the bricolage seem remote from one another. It is possible that the twain shall meet in bricolage – a moment of surprise. On this occasion, one professor was very doubtful that including constructions of heroes would contribute any worthwhile knowledge to help Nelson understand how and why the termination of vocational education occurred. Perhaps in the process of doing bricolage, Nelson will rule out constructions of heroes when he assembles his final text from all the scraps of knowledge he collects. However, at some point in his travels through the bricolage, he may find a reason to reroute through constructions of heroes. Meanwhile, Nelson revisited and applied a discussion on institutional power to his own text.

Institutions are a system based on hierarchy. There are links but can they challenge or distribute power?

Melissa threaded discourse and questions borrowed from archaeological genealogy to Nelson's POET. She brilliantly added the element of contextualization that demanded an increase in rigour to track, trace, examine, deconstruct, and critique his text. It seemed we heard sighs of exhaustion through cyberspace when we realized there was still a lot more to do.

The following ramblings are taken from one feedback looping entry of four pages. Space limitations do not allow for the full text to be included. We have tried here to capture the essence of how the threading and multiple feedback looping of bricolage required a structure of complexity and a process of rigour. First Melissa briefly defined archaeological genealogy for all of her group:

My understanding of this research genre is that I look at the point of entry text and peel back the layers, that is, I attempt to contextualize it historically, politically, societally and make connections by tracing what influenced what is going on.

Melissa continued to employ the framework of archaeological genealogy (see Chapter 5) to steer Nelson back to his text:

One of the steps in this process [archaeological genealogy] is to look at how the text or discourse moves into formal, institutional and political processes. You began your paper with the statement 'the history of vocational education has strong significant roots in this [state/province]'. You might explore the following questions; why did vocational training move from apprenticeships into the formal institutions of schools? What were the political reasons for this at the time? How did the legislation/policies help this transition into the schools? [Melissa wrote half a page more in line with these questions.]

Further interrogation of his text invited Nelson to include a contextualization of the knowledge about vocational education:

You mentioned that the Provincial Vocational Act of 1918 started the introduction of voc ed in schools. Why at this time? What was going on to prompt the enactment of this legislation? Who was pressuring the legislation? Industry? Postwar demand for manufacturing? [Melissa had Nelson threading these questions and many more back into his text.]

Melissa threaded epistemological considerations back into Nelson's text:

You mentioned that 'technology based courses have replaced voc ed curriculum'. Why did the schools move from one type of knowledge to another? Can't the two knowledges work together? Aren't the trades becoming more technological-computer based diagnostics in automotive repair? Why pick one knowledge over the other? Why not both? [Melissa's knowledge was informed by the postmodern binarisms of both/and equal distribution of power instead of modernism's either/or unequal distribution of power.]

Melissa's feedback to Nelson's point of entry text occurred concurrently with group members threading other areas of the bricolage into his text. A map of these threadings would be an image comparable to the butterfly effect of increasing complexity. Other feedback not only created complex readings and reflections on the POET for Nelson but also brought about the entry of diverse knowledge from various sources into the initial reading of vocational education in the province.

The assortment of epistemological questions and other feedback loops arrived at different times, from nebulous regions of WebCT cyberspace, and converged in the POET. Threads liberated from any area of the multifaceted maps of the bricolage were not collected in any familiar manner. No group member's feedback looping was procedural or linear, planned or empirically logical. Feedback materialized randomly, spontaneously, and was fragmented – in the manner of chaos and complexity. Each group member lived safely and comfortably in the far-from-equilibrium conditions of the mounting complexity. No restrictions or formalized rules were placed on the apprentice bricoleurs. The noise of complexity was stored in the computer's cyberweb, standing by if needed for later interpretation and multiple readings. Noise was new information for the bricoleur. It was not immediately evident where it 'fitted' in the text. Ruelle (1993) states that 'a [text] is complex if it embodies information that is hard to get at, has no sharp meaning and depends on self-organization' (p. 136). Patti, a student bricoleur, concurs with Ruelle:

Bricolage is frustrating in the sense that it is a highly complex process. It is not concrete/linear and does not have an endpoint/closure. The terminology is complex/unique and it takes a while to understand and incorporate the terminology into your thought process [but] *I enjoyed using one paper to introduce the group to bricolage. I really appreciated the feedback to my own thinking.*

Doing bricolage requires stamina and a great sense of playfulness similar to that of ludic postmodernism. Melissa was unrelenting in her feedback to Nelson's POET. As she looped archaeological genealogy back into Nelson's text, in conjunction with the parallel threads of the rest of her group, an epistemological epiphany took place, an event that is welcomed and common when doing bricolage research. In one of the previous weekly WebCT discussions, Ruby had looped back questions about conflicting discourses into several of her group's POETs, including Nelson's and Melissa's. Somehow, Ruby's questions implicitly remained quietly submerged in Melissa's consciousness for a period of time. During the feedback to Nelson's text, Ruby's questions about conflicting discourses converged with Melissa's feedback on archaeological genealogy, Nelson's area of institutional power, and Emma's discussions on class and gender. What Joe Kincheloe described in Chapter 3 as a symbiotic hermeneutics emerged in this context, as the students focused on the nature of these discursive relationships. At the junction of all this complexity was a thread of insight – conflicting discourses. Whether she was aware of it or not, Melissa had worked the complexity of the bricolage into Nelson's original POET. Several areas of the bricolage materialized with Nelson's text as the axis. A few of those threads are presented in the following different excerpts of Melissa's feedback looping including that of the conflicting discourses:

You mentioned that the demand for skilled trades people is currently rising and is expected to last into the next decade. You are saying one thing and the newspaper is saying another. It said that of the 550 IBEW members in the city of ——— , 350 are unemployed. Maybe not all trades are experiencing a shortage. It would seem that these electrical workers can't find jobs. You mention later in the paper that a project in Woodstock was cancelled because they couldn't find industrial electricians. What about ... how this is a version of contradiction but not exactly conflicting discourses because maybe the ideologies or political agendas or capitalist base was the same? [Melissa recognized conflicting discourses between the workers and media and later the discourse of the monopoly company.]

You trace the lack of skilled workers back to students' lack of 'vocational awareness' because they are not exposed to voc ed. What about our society in general? What is societal context? Institutional? Etc? What evidence is there in society that trades are devalued?

Look at the influence of the [monopoly] company in the push to reintroduce voc ed.

You mentioned the decline of voc ed in the 1980s when computer technology invaded high schools. This is a very strong word with connotations. Sets up a good/bad thing as a binarism. Rethink?

Think about the power struggles. Was there any resistance? By whom? Why?

The gender issue. Although girls can take voc ed. are teachers still mainly men?

The multiple threads of the bricolage accessed knowledge and read the student's text in ways that monological research might or could not do. The feedback looping within and between the student's texts only skimmed the surface features of each area of the bricolage but drew out a complexity of questions and possibilities for new interpretations. As Derrida claims, the bricoleur is:

> somebody who doesn't care about the purity or the stability of the system s/he uses, but rather uses what's there to get a particular job done ... Bricolage doesn't worry about the coherence of the words or ideas it uses. For example, you are a bricoleur if you talk about penis envy or the oedipus complex and you don't know anything about psychoanalysis; you use the terms without having to acknowledge the whole system of thought that produced these terms and ideas ... you don't care if psychology is true or not ... as long as the terms and ideas are useful to you. ... Bricolage is mythopoetic, not rational. The idea of bricolage produces a new way to talk about, and think about, systems without falling into the trap of building a new system ... It provides a way to think without establishing a new center, a subject, a privileged reference, an origin. ... [T]otalization is impossible. (Klages 2001)

The student bricoleurs came of age. No one thread became dominant. No one seemed to suggest that one type of reading was best or *the* truth. Yes, totalization was impossible. Just as one thread became foregrounded and started seizing the text, the bricoleurs of each group challenged their peers with questions and counter-discourses. The bricoleurs could not rest with any one position or interpretation. Using multiple areas and discourses of the bricolage as they wrote, the bricoleurs attempted to circumvent any unilateral methodology and strived to include multi-disciplinary elements and multilogical understandings. The passage from positivistic, linear thought to the complexity and rigour of the bricolage pushed the student bricoleurs and professors into realms that crossed modern borders of what counts as research and knowledge.

Limits and Lineage of the Bricolage

One of the major factors for the employment or not of the bricolage as a way to research, including data collection and interpretation, was the degree of legitimizing people and practices in the academy. The course from which most of the previous examples and anecdotes were taken was one of two recently offered by the faculty on the subject of the bricolage. Colleagues within and from other fields across the university were familiar with inter/multidisciplinary research. Intellectual sources were limited but an increase in materials like journals and books was apparent. Needless to say, the Internet and hypertext programs were major sources for the students. This is the age of research in cyberspace, and students took advantage of that fact, especially in a region that is very rural.

The reasons for continuing or not continuing the bricolage were varied. There were many areas of the bricolage that were not included in the first rounds of feedback looping. The few areas used, however, roused dimensions of the original POET that surprised the student bricoleurs. From the first application to Sadie's text to the individual final submissions at the end of the course, students progressed through as many possible fields of study as time, space, and resources permitted. Some students moved on to other courses and engaged the bricolage. A lot of students did not. Others, like Marissa, used it sparingly in their theses. At other levels, the bricolage was a menace to the neutralized objectivity and efficiency of positivistic, statistical research. Government, private, and public corporations rely on the knowledge produced by these latter methods and analyses. They rely on the rapidity and reduction of the complexity of the world to numbers and categories of standardization. Control on a large scale is an outcome – control that produces, circulates, and maintains knowledge that legitimizes the standardization and reduction, the assimilation and homogenization of humanity. And it happens in ways so discursive, so invisible as in the multi-encoded truths and values that the student bricoleurs had taken for granted in their original POET.

Other important factors to include while trying to avoid a slippage into positivistic, scientific rationality were not presented in our discussion of doing the bricolage. Questions, discourses, and concerns about essentializing, normalizing, generalizing and positionality were not considered in this class to any great degree. Essentializing, for example, was noted briefly. Mia started essentializing and creating binarisms with 'we' and 'they' in her feedback to Sadie's text on height discrimination. Aware of the problems both these areas create, she noted that she was engaging in the very practice that bricoleurs claim is reductionistic. When 'we' was used by Mia, who was the 'we' she was referring to? From what positionality was she speaking? On whose behalf was she speaking? Emma echoed Mia by essentializing, yet not recognizing how she did this. She talked about 'our ways of thinking about the body', but neglected to identify on whose behalf she was speaking. In addition, she did not designate who the 'we' was in 'our' way of thinking about the body. Dominique casually noted the issue of essentializing in research: *'Should we assume most vertically-challenged people have the same experience?'* Natalie used 'average' height but then recognized she was 'normalizing' the body with this discourse. She also asked: *'who decided what was average anyway and has that definition always been the same over the years?'* Other moments of positivistic elements were present but not elaborated at length. At least the student bricoleurs were aware of the potential for slippage into positivistic research.

Positionality was another consideration that was lacking in the students' initiation into the bricolage. It is crucial that bricoleurs locate themselves in the discourses of the bricolage. What a bricoleur selects or does not select and how he/she interprets the text has been influenced by the multiple socializing contexts and discourses through which he/she has passed. Thus, positionality is one area that needs to be included in all readings, writings, and research that employs bricolage. No matter which areas of the bricolage map the bricoleur selects from, she/he must constantly thread personal, critical autobiography through the POET. When the bricoleur fails to do so, positivistic rationality remains encoded in the reading, writing, and interpretation of text. Without the inclusion of critical autobiography, established systems of knowledge, truth, and value, created by the bricoleur, circulate and maintain the status quo.

Form was another consideration that presented difficulty for the novice bricoleurs. The students' vagueness about what the possible areas of the bricolage are and how to thread them through their POET demanded a great deal of creativity on their part. In what form to present the final text remained a hurdle and still does. It was also problematic for the professors. Accustomed to structuralist narrative and essay writing over countless years of schooling in positivistic rationality, combined with institutional pressure to conform to conventional forms, both students and professors, like feminist writers, were caught in the trap of reproducing the 'master's voice'. Some students with a literary background used postcolonial, postmodern and poststructural literature. Others used film structures, such as *Pulp Fiction*, *Memento*, *Run Lola Run*, and other poststructural forms to steer away from long-established forms of empirical formats. Some students, like Mary, experimented with CD-ROM. Others tried hypertext. Most reverted to traditional formats but at least included the multiple threads and discourses of the bricolage. Mia, like many others, used the traditional heading and sub-heading design of essay and report writing. What was very evident in the final text was the level of commitment that these student bricoleurs achieved. The complexity and rigour of the bricolage remained no matter what the final form.

Without romanticizing the process of the bricolage, the rigour fascinated and, in some cases, consumed the professors and the students. As professors, a massive stretch in expertise was required. No longer could either professor stay within their disciplinary boundaries. The range of knowledge needed was garnered from the maps of the bricolage with many possibilities still unlisted or abandoned. In some ways this was a hindrance. In other ways, the lack of expertise placed professors and students on complementary paths of pedagogy. While the professors could suggest possible areas and discourses to thread through the POETs, the students were also exploring the landscape of the bricolage. In addition, group work exploded the boundaries of the original text and its monological construction of knowledge. Individual texts went through major transformations. Individuals were also transformed, their eyes opened to new possibilities for researching as much as for new insights about their chosen topics. Hopefully, the bricoleurs will transform the policies and practices that relate to everyday life; policies and practices that fulfil the complexity of human relationships. The impact of the knowledge accumulated from performing the bricolage should also move individuals, society, institutions and Western civilization toward discourses, policies and practices of equality, inclusiveness, and social justice.

The Politics of Doing Bricolage

Marissa, excited by doing bricolage, wanted to apply it to all her writing for other courses and in preparation for her thesis proposal. Her draft proposal consisted of several papers written for other courses in her masters' programme, all on the same topic. Over a period of a year and a half, she applied a different area of the bricolage to each paper. In her research class where she was introduced to bricolage, she began with a personal narrative (POET) of extreme personal importance to her and a family member. Over the course of the year and a half in different courses, to the original POET she added:

- axiology (14 on the bricolage map);
- three different research approaches including statistical data, phenomenology, case study and interviewing (3);
- an archaeological genealogy (13) by searching the provincial archives for curriculum;

- documents and policies (11) related to the topic, and connected it to the dominant discourses at different historical periods;
- a sequence of events and pamphlets (17) as she met with medical doctors, school psychologists and other experts (9);
- an analysis of several of her papers for modes of power, mainly discursive and hegemonic (7);
- resistant readings (15) of the expert's discourse and diagnosis regarding the person who the topic was about, even to the point of doing a semiotic reading of the professional's office;
- a postmodern analysis (2), and found how all the texts and practices were anchored in the institutional and societal levels (16) of modern constructions of the topic;
- a literary analysis of the topic based on background from her undergraduate degree in English literature studies (5);
- a thorough discussion of her positioning in all the discourses and practices surrounding the topic (4).

From the above list, it is evident that doing bricolage is possible. Marissa threaded through at least 12 different areas of the bricolage and returned to some of them several times. Each visit and revisit produced some changes and modifications to the original POET. The complexity increased at least 12-fold. She ended her course work for her master's with at least 12 different readings of her topic. An amalgamation of her 12 different papers was to be the next step in preparation for her thesis proposal. What happened next was discouraging but a reality which many students and professors will most likely face.

Faculty members not versed or in agreement with the premises and practices of bricolage cannot provide students like Marissa with knowledge or support for this type of research. Without the traditional guidelines and expectations of empirical research, no one felt comfortable proceeding with the proposal. It was suggested that she select one type of research methodology such as narrative or autobiography. And policies about *what counts as research* had not yet found a home in the academic institution. Although university is the institution for leading-edge research and the production of new knowledge, Marissa was not working in the normal research culture. Kuhn (1962) acknowledges that research is a social and political construct defined by the institution and carried out by 'experts'. Paradigm shifting from logical positivism and the binarism of quantitative/qualitative research places in jeopardy and often isolates those who are working in a different structure of scientific revolutions. Bricoleurs like Marissa seem to be caught in this web.

Endless Returns to the Map

When does it end? How do you know when you're finished? These are very common questions at the conclusion of a course using bricolage. We laughed in one class when the students shared with Patti the sense of frustration and paralysis that bricoleurs experience at the beginning of a course. And now we were expressing another kind of frustration about bricolage. When one of the professors read some of the students' comments about doing bricolage, everybody was giving the phenomenological wink or nod. We had shared experiences, similar in some ways but very different in other ways. On a final note, the students shared the process, the purpose, and the outcome of doing bricolage, in theory and in practice. Patti started with the rigour and changes that occurred for her:

> *Bricolage is a process that allows a person to expand/deepen their under-standing of the multiple meanings of their text (point of entry). The process seeks to uncover hidden meanings, conflicting discourses and the broader social implications of the text. This is accomplished (although never com-pleted!) using critical discourses and threading your text through these dis-courses. The process continues but is never exhausted. If a bricoleur was to approach the same topic/point of entry text again, it would be with a deeper/broader understanding.*

Melissa continued the thread of complexity:

> *I would say that this whole year of study has been a sort of 'bricolage' but I didn't even know what the term meant until I took a course on Discourse. The professor said that the bricolage came from the French meaning 'building something using the tools you have at hand'. So what does that mean for me as a teacher? We were asked to pick a text as a point of entry and then explore the complexity, chaos and hypertext that is the structure of the point of entry text. I have come to understand that dismantling the original text from various perspectives or research genres does not mean destroying the text but looking at ways to include different readings and reflect on what has been left out and why.*

Hannah E. noticed the change in how she reads texts now that she was informed by the bricolage:

> *I now understand bricolage to be a never-ending process of questioning what are supposed to be 'truths.' We bring our own point of view, experiences, beliefs, values into bricolage. We go from this point and push ourselves to question from the view of ideology, ritual or cultural criticism and extend our knowledge of various research paradigms. Problems I have experienced are: I had no idea what bricolage meant; looking at the encyclopaedia of*

terms scared me. I was unsure of how to start the dismantling process. It has been an enlightening process and I know when I look at forms of the text, I no longer take them at face value.

Bricolage as a way of researching was a way of confronting the injustices in systems and what to change. Annie and Melissa respectively felt the same:

To me bricolage allows me/forces me to look at the text differently. It encourages me to critically examine the text but also what is not included in the text. It is a framework to examine my text and provides a new way to examine issues.

It connects with social justice in the sense that it uncovers inequities, oppressions that arise from dominant ideologies (reflected in our point of entry text) and allows the writer to rethink their approach to the issue/ subject with an enlightened perspective.

Almost a year later, Jane S. shared with a colleague:

I really enjoyed it [doing bricolage] *but most of it was over my head until we used the bricolage map. I wasn't sure what or why we needed to do bricolage but it made me think about my own thinking.*

Needless to say, if we continued applications of bricolage to any one POET the possibilities are limitless.

References

Agnello, M. (2002). Synthesizing archaeology and genealogy: Foucauldian methodologies for textual and power analysis. *Taboo: Journal of Culture and Education*, **6**, 1, pp. 61–78.

Allard, S. (2002). Digital libraries and organizations for international collaboration and knowledge creation. *The Electronic Library*, **20**, pp. 369–81.

Allen, M. (2000). Voice of Reason. *http://www.curtin.edu.au/learn/unit/10846/arrow/vorall.htm* (accessed January 2001).

Apffel-Marglin, F. (1995). Development or decolonization in the Andes? *Interculture: International Journal of Intercultural and Transdisciplinary Research*, **28**, 1, pp. 3–17.

Benhabib, S. (1996). *Democracy and Difference: Contesting the Boundaries of the Political*. Princeton, NJ: Princeton University Press.

Bereiter, C. (2002). *Education and Mind in the Knowledge Age*. Mahwah, NJ: Lawrence Erlbaum.

Berry, K. (2001). Standards of complexity in a postmodern democracy. In J. Kincheloe and D. Weil (eds) *Standards and Schooling in the United States: An Encyclopedia*. Santa Barbara, CA: ABC-Clio.

Berry, K. (2004). Radical critical thinking: Parts I and II. In D. Weil and J. Kincheloe (eds) *Critical Thinking and Learning: An Encyclopedia for Parents and Teachers*. New York: Greenwood.

Blackler, F. (1995). Knowledge, knowledge work, and organizations: An overview and interpretation. *Organization Studies*, **16**, 6.

Blommaert, J. (1997). Workshopping: Notes on professional vision in discourse. *http://africana.rug.ac.be/texts/research-publications/publications_on-line/workshopping.htm* (accessed April 2004).

Bohm, D. and Peat, F. (1987). *Science, Order, and Creativity*, New York: Bantam Books.

Bookchin, M. (1995). *The Philosophy of Social Ecology: Essays on Dialectical Naturalism*, 2nd edition. Montreal: Black Rose Books.

Bridges, D. (1997). Philosophy and educational research: A reconsideration of epistemological boundaries. *Cambridge Journal of Education*, **27**, 2.

Bruner, J. (1996). *The Culture of Education*. Cambridge, MA: Harvard University Press.

Burbules, N. and Beck, R. (1999). Critical thinking and critical pedagogy: Relations, differences, and limits. In T. Popkewitz and L. Fendler (eds) *Critical Theories in Education*. New York: Routledge.

Capra, F. (1996). *The Web of Life: A New Scientific Understanding of Living Systems*. New York: Anchor Books.

Capra, F., Steindl-Rast, D. and Matus, T. (1991). *Belonging to the Universe: New Thinking about God and Nature*. New York: Penguin.

Carter, R. (2004). Visual literacy: Critical thinking with the visual image. In D. Weil and J. Kincheloe (eds) *Critical Thinking and Learning: An Encyclopedia*. New York: Greenwood.

Carter, R. and Villaverde, L. (2001). Art – new standards for art education: Disassembling the canon. In J. Kincheloe and D. Weil (eds) *Standards and Schooling in the US: An Encyclopedia*. Santa Barbara, CA: ABC-Clio.

Cary, R. (2004). Art and aesthetics. In D. Weil and J. Kincheloe (eds) *Critical Thinking and Learning: An Encyclopedia for Parents and Teachers*. New York: Greenwood.

Cavallaro, D. (1998). *The Body for Beginners*. New York: Writers and Readers.

Ceccarelli, L. (1998). Polysemy: Multiple meanings in rhetorical criticism. *The Quarterly Journal of Speech*, **84**, 4, pp. 395–415.

Chandler, D. (1998). Processes of mediation. *http://www.aber.ac.uk/~dgc/process.html* (accessed January 2001).

Coveney. P. and Highfield, R. (1995). *Frontiers of Complexity: The Search for Order in a Chaotic World*. New York: Fawcett Columbine.

Cronin, P. (1997). Learning and assessment of instruction. http://www.cogsci.ed.ac.uk/~paulus/work/vranded/litconsa.txt (accessed January 2001).

Dahlbom, B. (1998). Going to the future. *http://www.viktoria.infomatik.gu.se/~max/bo/papers.html* (accessed January 2001).

Dei, G. (1995). Indigenous knowledge as an empowerment tool. In N. Singh and V. Titi (eds) *Empowerment: Toward Sustainable Development*. Toronto: Fernwood Press.

Denzin, N. and Lincoln, Y. (1994). *Handbook of Qualitative Research*. Thousand Oaks, CA: Sage.

Denzin, N. and Lincoln, Y. (2000). *Handbook of Qualitative Research*, 2nd edition. Thousand Oakes, CA: Sage.

DeVault, M. (1996). Talking back to sociology: Distinctive contributions of feminist methodologies. *Annual Review of Sociology*, **22**, pp. 29–50.

Dewey, J. (1916) *Democracy and Education*. New York: Macmillan.

Dhingra, K. (2004). Critical thinking in science. In D. Weil and J. Kincheloe (eds) *Critical Thinking and Learning: An Encyclopedia for Parents and Teachers*. New York: Greenwood.

Dicks, B. and Mason, B. (1998). Hypermedia and ethnography: Reflections on the construction of a research approach. *Sociological Research Online*, **3**, 3.

Fenwick, T. (2000). Experiential learning in adult education: A comparative framework. *http://www.ualberta.ca/~tfenwick/ext/aeq.htm* (accessed January 2001).

Fernandez-Balboa, J. (2004). Emancipatory critical thinking. In D. Weil and J.

Kincheloe (eds) *Critical Thinking and Learning: An Encyclopedia for Parents and Teachers.* New York: Greenwood.

Fischer, F. (1998). Beyond empiricism: Policy inquiry in postpositivist perspective. *Policy Studies Journal,* **26**, 1, pp. 129–46.

Foster, R. (1997). Addressing epistemologic and practical issues in multimethod research: A procedure for conceptual triangulation. *Advances in Nursing Education,* **202**, 2.

Foucault, M. (1980) *Power/Knowledge: Selected Interviews and Other Writings,* ed. C. Gordon. New York: Pantheon.

Frankenberg, R. (ed.) (1997). *Displacing Whiteness: Essays in Social and Cultural Criticism.* Durham, NC: Duke University Press.

Freire, P. (1970). *Pedagogy of the Oppressed.* New York: Herder and Herder.

Friedman, S. (1998). (Inter)disciplinarity and the question of the women's studies PhD. *Feminist Studies,* **24**, 2.

Gabriel, J. (2004). Critical thinking in the English classroom. In D. Weil and J. Kincheloe (eds) *Critical Thinking and Learning: An Encyclopedia for Parents and Teachers.* New York: Greenwood.

Gadamer, H. (1989). *Truth and Method.* New York: Continuum Books.

Gee, J., Hull, G. and Lankshear, C. (1996). *The New Work Order: Behind the Language of the New Capitalism.* Boulder, CO: Westview.

Geeland, D. and Taylor, P. (2000). Writing our lived experience: Beyond the (pale) hermeneutic. *Electronic Journal of Science Education,* **5**. *http://unr.edu/homepage/crowther/ejse/geelanetal.html* (accessed April 2004)

Geyer, F. (1994). The challenge of sociocybernetics. Paper presented at the 13th World Congress on Sociology, Bielefeld, Germany.

Giroux, H. (1997). *Pedagogy and the Politics of Hope: Theory, Culture, and Schooling.* Boulder, CO: Westview.

Gleick, J. (1992). *Genius: The Life and Science of Richard Feynman.* New York: Pantheon Books.

Goodson, I. (1999). The educational researcher as public intellectual. *British Educational Research Journal,* **25**, 3, pp. 277–97.

Griffin, D. (1997). *Parapsychology, Philosophy, and Spirituality: A Postmodern Exploration.* Albany: State University of New York Press.

Grondin, J. (1994). *Introduction to Philosophical Hermeneutics.* New Haven, CT: Yale University Press.

Haggerson, N. (2000). *Expanding Curriculum Research and Understanding: A Mythopoetic Perspective.* New York: Peter Lang Publishing.

Hall, S. (1997). *Representation: Cultural Representations and Signifying Practices.* London: Sage.

Heathcote, D. (1984). Personal communication. Newcastle upon Tyne, UK.

Hinchey, P. (2004). Diversity and critical thinking. In D. Weil and J. Kincheloe (eds) *Critical Thinking and Learning: An Encyclopedia for Parents and Teachers.* New York: Greenwood.

Hoban, G. and Erickson, G. (1998). Frameworks for sustaining professional learning. Paper presented at the Australasian Science Education Research Association, Darwin, Australia.

Horn, R. (2000) *Teacher Talk: A Postformal Inquiry into Educational Change.* New York: Peter Lang.

Horn, R. (2001). A postformal conversation about standardization and accountability in Texas. In J. Kincheloe and D. Weil (eds) *Standards and Schooling in the US: An Encyclopedia*. Santa Barbara, CA: ABC-Clio.

Horn, R. (2004). Scholar-practitioner leaders: The empowerment of teachers and students. In D. Weil and J. Kincheloe (eds) *Critical Thinking and Learning: An Encyclopedia for Parents and Teachers*. New York: Greenwood.

Jardine, D. (1998). *To Dwell with a Boundless Heart: Essays in Curriculum Theory, Hermeneutics, and the Ecological Imagination*. New York: Peter Lang.

Karunaratne, V. (1997). Buddhism, science, and dialectics. *http://humanism.org/opinions/articles.html* (accessed January 2001).

Kellner, D. (1995). *Media Culture: Cultural Studies, Identity and Politics between the Modern and Postmodern*. New York: Routledge.

Kincheloe, J. (2001a). *Getting beyond the Facts: Teaching Social Studies/Social Sciences in the Twenty-first Century*. New York: Peter Lang.

Kincheloe, J. (2001b). Describing the bricolage: conceptualizing a new rigour in qualitative research. *Qualitative Inquiry*, **7**, 6, 679–92.

Kincheloe, J. (2002). *The Sign of the Burger: McDonald's and the Culture of Power*. Philadelphia: Temple University Press.

Kincheloe, J. (2004). Into the great wide open: Introducing critical thinking. In D. Weil and J. Kincheloe (eds) *Critical Thinking and Learning: An Encyclopedia for Parents and Teachers*. New York: Greenwood.

Kincheloe, J. and Steinberg, S. (1993). A tentative description of post-formal thinking: The critical confrontation with cognitive theory. *Harvard Educational Review*, **63**, 3, pp. 296–320.

Kincheloe, J. and Steinberg, S. (1997). *Changing Multiculturalism*. Buckingham: Open University Press.

Kincheloe, J., Steinberg, S. and Hinchey, P. (1999a). *The Postformal Reader: Cognition and Education*. New York: Falmer Press.

Kincheloe, J., Steinberg, S. and Tippins, D. (1999b). *The Stigma of Genius: Einstein, Consciousness, and Education*. New York: Peter Lang.

Kincheloe, J., Steinberg, S. and Villaverde, L. (eds) (1999c). *Rethinking Intelligence: Confronting Psychological Assumptions about Teaching and Learning*. New York: Routledge.

Klages, M. (2001). Structure, sign, and play in the discourse of the human sciences – a reading guide. http://www.colorado.edu/English/ENGL2012Klages/1997derridaB.html (accessed April 2004).

Kogler, H. (1996). *The Power of Dialogue: Critical Hermeneutics after Gadamer and Foucault*. Cambridge, MA: MIT Press.

Korn, C. (2004). Young children, critical thinking and education in the arts. In D. Weil and J. Kincheloe (eds) *Critical Thinking and Learning: An Encyclopedia for Parents and Teachers*. New York: Greenwood.

Kovel, J. (1998). Dialect as praxis. *Science and Society*, **62**, 3, pp. 474–80.

Kuhn, T. (1962). *The Structure of Scientific Revolutions*. Chicago: University of Chicago Press.

Lather, P. (1991). *Getting Smart: Feminist Research and Pedagogy with/in the Postmodern*. New York: Routledge.

Lather, P. (1993). Fertile obsession: Validity after poststructuralism. *Sociological Quarterly*, **34**, pp. 673–93.

Lee, A. (1999). Researching MIS. In W. Currie and R. Galliers (eds) *Rethinking Management Information Systems*. Oxford: Oxford University Press.

Lepani, B. (1998). Information literacy: The challenge of the digital age. *http://www.acal.edu.au/publications/papers/occasional/lepani.shtml* (accessed April 2004).

Lester, S. (2001). Learning for the twenty-first century. In J. Kincheloe and D. Weil (eds) *Standards and Schooling in the US: An Encyclopedia*. Santa Barbara, CA: ABC-Clio.

Lemke, J. (1999). Important theories for research topics. http://academic.brooklyn.cuny.edu/education/jlemke/theories.htm (accessed April 2004).

Lévi-Strauss, C. (1966). *The Savage Mind*. Chicago: University of Chicago Press.

Lincoln, Y. (2001). An emerging new *bricoleur*: Promises and possibilities – a reaction to Joe Kincheloe's 'Describing the bricoleur'. *Qualitative Inquiry*, **7**, 6, pp. 693–6.

Lomax, P. and Parker, Z. (1996). Representing a dialectical form of knowledge within a new epistemology for teaching and teacher education. Paper presented at the American Educational Research Association, New York.

Lutz, K., Jones, K. and Kendall, J. (1997). Expanding the praxis debate: Contributions to clinical inquiry. *Advances in Nursing Science*, **20**, 2.

McCarthy, M. (1997). Pluralism, invariance, and conflict. *The Review of Metaphysics*, **51**, 1.

McLaren, P. (2000). *Che Guevara, Paulo Freire, and the Pedagogy of Revolution*. Lanham, MD: Rowman and Littlefield.

McLaren, P. (2001). Bricklayers and bricoleurs: A Marxist addendum. *Qualitative Inquiry*, **7**, 6, pp. 700–5.

McLaren, P., Hammer, R., Reilly, S. and Sholle, D. (1995). *Rethinking Media Literacy: A Critical Pedagogy of Representation*. New York: Peter Lang.

McLeod, J. (2000). Qualitative research as bricolage. Paper presented at the Society for Psychotherapy Research Annual Conference, Chicago.

Madison, G. (1988). *The Hermeneutics of Postmodernity: Figures and Themes*. Bloomington: Indiana University Press.

Malewski, E. (2001). Queer sexuality – the trouble with knowing: Standards of complexity and sexual orientations. In J. Kincheloe and D. Weil (eds) *Standards and Schooling in the US: An Encyclopedia*. Santa Barbara, CA: ABC-Clio.

Marcum, J. (1998). Excursions beyond information: Learning and knowledge as a new purpose of academic libraries. *http://www.library.csi.cuny.edu/chief/excursions.html* (accessed January 2001).

Marijuan, P. (1994). Information revisited. Paper presented to the First Conference on the Foundations of Information Science, Madrid, Spain.

Maturana, H. and Varela, F. (1987). *The Tree of Knowledge*. Boston: Shambhala.

Maurial, M. (1999). Indigenous knowledge and schooling: A continuum between conflict and dialogue. In L. Semali and J. Kincheloe (eds) *What Is Indigenous Knowledge? Voices from the Academy*. New York: Falmer.

May, T. (1993). *Between Genealogy and Epistemology: Psychology, Politics, and Knowledge in the Thought of Michel Foucault*. University Park, PA: Penn State Press.

Mayers, M. (2001) Interpretation – Hermeneutics' invitation to meaning-making: The ecology of a complexity of standards, educational research, policy, and praxis. In J. Kincheloe and D. Weil (eds) *Standards and Schooling in the US: An Encyclopedia*. Santa Barbara, CA: ABC-Clio.

Mayers, M. and Field, J. (2004). Critical hermeneutics in the classroom. In D. Weil and J. Kincheloe (eds) *Critical Thinking and Learning: An Encyclopedia for Parents and Teachers*. New York: Greenwood.

Moran, J. (2002). *Interdisciplinarity*. New York: Routledge.

Morawski, J. (1997). The science behind feminist research methods. *Journal of Social Issues*, **53**, 4, pp. 667–82.

Mosha, R. (2000). *The Heartbeat of Indigenous Africa: A Study of the Chagga Educational System*. New York: Garland.

Mueller-Vollmer, K. (ed.) (1988). *The Hermeneutics Reader: Texts of the German Tradition from the Enlightenment to the Present*. New York: Continuum.

Murphie, A. (1998). Hyping the text, cyberfictions and hypertext: What is happening to text? *Culture and Technology Lectures*, 15 May.

O'Sullivan, E. (1999). *Transformative Learning: Educational Vision for the 21st Century*. London: Zed.

Owen, D. and Doerr, M. (1999). *None of the Above: The Truth behind the SATs*. Lanham, MD: Rowman and Littlefield.

Palmer, C. (1996). Information work at the boundaries of science: Linking library services to research practices. *Library Trends*, **44**, 2, pp. 165–92.

Paulson, R. (1995). Mapping knowledge perspectives in studies of educational change. In P. Cookson, Jr. and B. Schneider (eds) *Transforming Schools*. New York: Garland.

Peyton, J. (1996). The Einstein curriculum. *http://www.puppetools.com/einstein.htm* (accessed January 2001).

Pickering, J. (1999). The self is a semiotic process. *Journal of Consciousness Studies*, **6**, 4, pp. 31–47.

Pinar, W. (2001) The researcher as bricoleur: The teacher as public intellectual. *Qualitative Inquiry*, **7**, 6, pp. 696–700.

Polanyi, M. (1958). *Personal Knowledge: Towards a Post-critical Philosophy*. Chicago: University of Chicago Press.

Prigogine, I. and Stengers, I. (1984) *Order Out Of Chaos: Man's New Dialogue with Nature*. New York: Bantam Books.

Pryse, M. (1998). Critical interdisciplinarity, women's studies, and cross-cultural insight. *NWSA Journal*, **10**, 1, pp. 1–11.

Rabinow, P. (ed.) (1984). *The Foucault Reader*. New York: Pantheon Books.

Rapko, J. (1998). Review of *The Power of Dialogue: Critical Hermeneutics after Gadamer and Foucault*. *Criticism*, **40**, 1, pp. 133–8.

Reason, P. and Bradbury, H. (2000). Introduction: Inquiry and participation in search of a world worthy of human aspiration. In P. Reason and H. Bradbury (eds) *Handbook of Action Research: Participative Inquiry and Practice*. Thousand Oaks, CA: Sage.

Resnick, M. and Wilensky, U. (1999). Diving into complexity: Developing probabilistic decentralized thinking through role-playing activities. *Journal of Learning Sciences*, **7**, 2.

Richardson, F. and Woolfolk, R. (1994). Social theory and values: A hermeneutic perspective. *Theory and Psychology*, **4**, 2, pp. 199–226.

Richardson, L. (2000). Writing: A method of inquiry. In N. Denzin and Y. Lincoln (eds) *The Handbook of Qualitative Research*, 2nd edition. Thousand Oaks, CA: Sage.

Ritzer, G. (1996). *The McDonaldization of Society*, rev. edn. Thousand Oaks, CA: Pine Forge Press.

Roberts, P. (1998). Rereading Lyotard: Knowledge, commodification and higher education. *Electronic Journal of Sociology*, **3**.

Rose, K. and Kincheloe, J. (2003). *Art, Culture, and Education: Artful Teaching in a Fractured Landscape*. New York: Peter Lang.

Rosen, S. (1987). *Hermeneutics as Politics*. New York: Oxford University Press.

Ruelle, D. (1993). *Chance and Chaos*. Toronto: Penguin.

Said, E. (1979). *Orientalism*. New York: Vintage.

Scheurich, J. (1997). *Research Methods in the Postmodern*. Philadelphia: Falmer.

Schon, D. (1995). The new scholarship requires a new epistemology. *Change*, **27**, 6.

Schumaker, P. (1990). *Critical Pluralism: Evaluating Democratic Performance in the Resolution of Community Issues*. Manhattan, KS: University Press of Kansas.

Selfe, C. and Selfe, R. (1994). The politics of the interface: Power and its exercise in electronic contact zones. *http://www.hu.mtu.edu/~cyselfe/texts/politics.html* (accessed April 2004)

Semali, L. and Kincheloe, J. (1999). *What Is Indigenous Knowledge? Voices from the Academy*. New York: Falmer.

Shaker, P. and Kridel, C. (1989). The return to experience: A reconceptualist call. *Journal of Teacher Education*, **40**, 1, pp. 2–8.

Shapin, S. (1995). Here and everywhere: Sociology of scientific knowledge. *Annual Review of Sociology*, **21**, pp. 289–321.

Simpson, D. and Jackson, M. (2001). John Dewey and educational evaluation. In J. Kincheloe and D. Weil (eds) *Standards and Schooling in the US: An Encyclopedia*. Santa Barbara, CA: ABC-Clio.

Smith, D. (1999). *Pedagon: Interdisciplinary Essays in the Human Sciences, Pedagogy, and Culture*. New York: Peter Lang.

Smith, L. (1999). *Decolonizing Methodologies: Research and Indigenous Peoples*. New York: Zed.

Soto, L. (ed.) (2000). *The Politics of Early Childhood Education*. New York: Peter Lang.

Steinberg, S. (ed.) (2001). *Multi/intercultural Conversations*. New York: Peter Lang.

Sumara, D. and Davis, B. (1997). Cognition, complexity, and teacher education. *Harvard Educational Review*, **67**, 1, pp. 75–104.

Tarnas, R. (1991). *The Passion of the Western Mind*. New York: Random House.

Thayer-Bacon, B. (2000). *Transforming Critical Thinking: Thinking Constructively*. New York: Teachers College Press.

Thomas, G. (1998). The myth of rational research. *British Educational Research Journal*, **24**, 2.

Thwaites, T., Davis, L. and Mules, W. (1994). *Tools for Cultural Studies: An Introduction*. South Melbourne: Macmillan.

Vattimo, G. (1994). *Beyond Interpretation: The Meaning of Hermeneutics for Philosophy*. Stanford, CA: Stanford University Press.

Varenne, H. (1996). The social facting of education: Durkheim's legacy. *Journal of Curriculum Studies*, **27**, pp. 373–89.

Varela, F. (1999). *Ethical Know-how: Action, Wisdom, and Cognition*. Stanford, CA: Stanford University Press.

Villaverde, L. (2003). Developing curriculum and critical pedagogy. In D. Weil and J. Kincheloe (eds) *Critical Thinking and Learning: An Encyclopedia for Parents and Teachers*. New York: Greenwood.

Ward, S. (1995). The revenge of the humanities: Reality, rhetoric, and the politics of postmodernism. *Sociological Perspectives*, **38**, 2, pp. 109–28.

Weil, D. (2001). Functionalism – From functionalism to neofunctionalism and neoliberalism: Developing a dialecticial understanding of the standards debate through historical awareness. In J. Kincheloe and D. Weil (eds) *Standards and Schooling in the US: An Encyclopedia*. Santa Barbara, CA: ABC-Clio.

Weil, D. and Kincheloe, J. (Eds.) (2004). *Critical Thinking and Learning: An Encyclopedia for Parents and Teachers*. New York: Greenwood.

Weinstein, M. (1995). Critical thinking? Expanding the paradigm. *http://www.chss.montclair.edu/inquiry/fall95/weinste.html* (accessed April 2004).

Wexler, P. (2000). *The Mystical Society: Revitalization in Culture, Theory, and Education*. Boulder, CO: Westview.

Williams, S. (1999). Truth, speech, and ethics: A feminist revision of free speech theory. *Genders*, **30**. *http://www.genders.org* (accessed April 2004).

Willinsky, J. (2001). Raising the standards for democratic education: Research and evaluation as public knowledge. In J. Kincheloe and D. Weil (eds) *Standards and Schooling in the US: An Encyclopedia*. Santa Barbara, CA: ABC-Clio.

Woodhouse, M. (1996). *Paradigm Wars: Worldviews for a New Age*. Berkeley, CA: Frog.

Woods, A. and Grant, T. (1998). Reason in revolt: Marxism and modern science. *http://easyweb.easynet.co.uk~zac/chapter7.htm* (accessed January 2001).

Young, I. (2000). *Inclusion and Democracy*. Oxford: Oxford University Press.

Young, T. and Yarbrough J. (1993). Reinventing sociology: Mission and methods for postmodern sociologists. *Transforming Sociology Series*, 154. Red Feather Institute.

Zammito, J. (1996). Historicism, metahistory, and historical practice: The historicization of the historical subject. *http://home.cc.umanitoba.ca/~sprague/zammito.htm* (accessed January 2001).

Index

THE MORAL FOUNDATIONS OF EDUCATIONAL RESEARCH
Knowledge, Inquiry and Values

Pat Sikes, Jon Nixon and Wilfred Carr (eds)

The Moral Foundations of Educational Research considers what is distinctive about educational research in comparison with other research in the social sciences. As the contributors all agree that education is always an essentially moral enterprise, discussion about methodology starts not with the widely endorsed claim that educational research should be 'useful' and 'relevant', but with the attempt to justify and elaborate that claim with reference to its moral foundations. The book suggests that educational research requires a fuller and more rounded understanding that takes account of the moral values of those who conduct it.

Contents
Introduction – Educational research and its histories – Towards a social history of educational research – Living research: thoughts on educational research as moral practice – The virtues and vices of an educational researcher – Against objectivism: the reality of the social fiction – Research as thoughtful practice – On goodness and utility in educational research – Method and morality: practical politics and the science of human affairs – Index.

192pp   0 335 21046 5 (Paperback)   0 335 21100 3 (Hardback)

A HANDBOOK FOR TEACHER RESEARCH
From Design to Implementation

Colin Lankshear and Michele Knobel

This book provides a comprehensive and detailed approach to teacher research as systematic, methodical and informed practice. It identifies five requirements for all kinds of research, and provides clear and accessible guidelines for teachers to use in conducting their own classroom-based studies.

Features:

- A clear definition of teacher research which insists on more than 'stories' and anecdotal 'retrospectives'
- Easy-to-use and widely applicable tools and techniques for collecting and analysing data in qualitative research
- Acknowledges the relevance of quantitative and document-based as well as qualitative forms of inquiry in teacher research
- Accessible and informative discussions of key issues in teacher research, such as interpretation, ethics, and validity.

A Handbook for Teacher Research provides everything the teacher researcher needs in order to conduct good quality practitioner research. It is ideal for upper level undergraduate Education programmes and for postgraduate research, as well as for teacher researchers who conceive and drive their own independent studies.

Contents

320pp   0 335 21064 3 (Paperback)   0 335 21065 1 (Hardback)

DISSEMINATING QUALITATIVE RESEARCH IN EDUCATIONAL SETTINGS

Christina Hughes (ed)

The processes and practices of the dissemination of research findings are exceptionally neglected fields in research methods. Yet disseminating and using our findings are significant reasons why we undertake research. Organized in three parts, this text provides an accessible, critically informed and up-to-date overview of key aspects of dissemination:

- Provides a critical review of contemporary policy and dissemination models in education.
- Enables researchers to develop 'informed practice' in respect of disseminating research in a range of educational settings.

In addition, the book contains a series of case studies produced by internationally respected researchers in a range of educational fields. Drawing on their extensive experiences of dissemination, these case studies illuminate how dissemination works in qualitative research projects as well as showing the dilemmas that face qualitative researchers who strive to disseminate their work.

Contents
Acknowledgements – Introduction – Part one: From dissemination to impact historical and contemporary issues – Models of dissemination – Part two: Dissemination and identity tales for the school gates – The creation and dissemination of feminist research in education: facts or fictions? – Analysis or anecdote?: defending qualitative data before a sceptical audience – Intricacies of dissemination in ethnographic research – Mis/representations issues of control and closure in an academic career – Dissemination, or critique and transformation? – Developing informed practice for disseminating qualitative research – References – Index.

160pp   0 335 210422 (Paperback)   0 335 210430 (Hardback)